"This book should make a significant contribution to all school leaders who desire to improve their school resource management. It is one of the few books I will keep handy and read more than once. I'm confident that those who read this book will find it valuable and insightful."

—Dr. Cheryl Crates, Community Unit School District 300, Carpentersville, Illinois; adjunct professor, Northern Illinois University

"As a school principal, superintendent, and business manager for the past thirty years, I believe Drs. Schilling and Tomal present a practical and refreshing aspect to school resource management for the experienced and novice administrator."

—Dr. Raymond J. LaPorte, interim business manager, School District 157, Frankfort, Illinois

"An outstanding research-based book for all school leaders and graduate students. . . . The most thorough resource for financial, facility, and human resource management."

—L. Arthur Safer, executive director, Division of Research and Doctoral Programs, Concordia University Chicago

"This book is a 'must have' for anyone desiring current information on school resource management."

—Dr. Robert Wilhite, chair, Education Leadership, Concordia University Chicago

Resource Management for School Administrators

Optimizing Fiscal, Facility, and Human Resources

CRAIG A. SCHILLING
AND DANIEL R. TOMAL

ROWMAN & LITTLEFIELD EDUCATION
A Division of
ROWMAN & LITTLEFIELD PUBLISHERS, INC.
Lanham • New York • Toronto • Plymouth, UK

Published by Rowman & Littlefield Education
A division of Rowman & Littlefield Publishers, Inc.
A wholly owned subsidiary of The Rowman & Littlefield Publishing Group, Inc.
4501 Forbes Boulevard, Suite 200, Lanham, Maryland 20706
www.rowman.com

10 Thornbury Road, Plymouth PL6 7PP, United Kingdom

British Library Cataloguing in Publication Information Available

Library of Congress Cataloging-in-Publication Data

Schilling, Craig A., 1950-
Resource management for school administrators : optimizing fiscal, facility, and human resources / Craig A. Schilling and Daniel R. Tomal.
pages cm
Includes bibliographical references and index.
ISBN 978-1-4758-0251-1 (cloth : alk. paper) — ISBN 978-1-4758-0252-8 (pbk. : alk. paper) — ISBN 978-1-4758-0253-5 (electronic) 1. School budgets—United States. 2. Education—United States—Finance. 3. School management and organization—United States. I. Tomal, Daniel R. II. Title.
LB2830.2.S35 2013
371.2'06—dc23

2012040039

The paper used in this publication meets the minimum requirements of American National Standard for Information Sciences—Permanence of Paper for Printed Library Materials, ANSI/NISO Z39.48-1992.

Printed in the United States of America

Contents

Foreword

Education more than ever needs good fiscal management because of low funding coupled with the need and pressure for improved student performance. Doing more with less requires a deep understanding of both the issue and example of how to make that happen. This book helps people do that with practical and proven solutions.

Schilling and Tomal have written a very timely book in the middle of the most turbulent fiscal times our nation has experienced in recent decades. At the same time the pressure to improve student performance in quantifiable terms has reached an apex and is supported by both political parties. This means that shrinking revenues and improved student performance has mandated that school districts have the means to tie budgets to student achievement. The book describes school finance in terms the average graduate student can understand while providing a historical and real-setting background to all issues.

As a professor of school finance for over thirty years, this is the first book I have seen that has a whole chapter dedicated to facilities and another to human resources; both of which are usually not within a basic school-finance text. In most of the districts I was employed in as the school business official during this same thirty-year period, both of those areas were my responsibility. Having these topics included in the same text covers all the key points of financial management for aspiring school administrators.

This book should make a significant contribution to all school leaders who desire to improve their school-resource management. It is one of the few books I will keep handy and read more than once. I'm confident that those who read this book will find it valuable and insightful.

Dr. Cheryl Crates, CFO
Community Unit School District 300, Carpentersville, Illinois
Adjunct Professor Northern Illinois University

Preface

The ability to operate a school requires effective skills in fiscal, facility, and human resource management. The strategies described in this book have been developed based upon years of study, research, consulting, and school administration experience. The book includes many of the strategies that have been found successful in operating at both the school-district and school-building level and is especially centered on providing information on the connection between finance and student achievement. While primarily directed toward public schools, the strategies in this book can also be effective for private elementary and secondary schools, as well as charter schools. The information and strategies are practical and useful techniques that can be used by any school administrator or graduate finance student who desires to optimize fiscal, facility, and human resources.

The first chapter provides a foundation on fiscal-management principles and a historical perspective. The concepts of *equity*, *equality*, and *adequacy* of public-school funding are presented. Several federal legal rulings that have impacted school funding are given along with current national perspectives on educational funding. The chapter also includes future challenges to funding public education with several statistics on demographic and enrollment trends.

The second chapter covers planning school-district budgets and the various types of school budgeting such as *systems*, *traditional*, *community-based*, *priority-based*, and *site-based* approaches. Details and examples are given on how to actually develop a school-district budget.

Several formulas for funding are explained along with *equalization methods*, *flat-grant funding*, *full-state*, and *local-effort equalization* formulas. The chapter concludes with a detailed description of basic accounting structures for budgeting, revenue collection, and expenditures.

Chapter 3 provides comprehensive information on accounting, budgeting, and reporting. It covers the topics of fund accounting, budgeting revenues and expenditures, mechanics of budgeting and encumbrance accounting, accountability and student activity funds, fundraising activities, good internal control systems, and audits and financial statements.

Chapter 4 contains extensive information on managing resources to achieve higher performance and productivity. Linkage between student achievement and funding is explained; managing educational resources, strategies for allocating resources for higher productivity and efficiency, and understanding the impact of educational choice on public-school finance are some of the topics covered in this chapter. There is also a comprehensive case on aligning student outcomes with educational resources.

Chapter 5 provides practical strategies for human resources management. Examples are provided in projecting student enrollment, recruiting and selecting applicants, employment laws and evaluating employees, administering compensation programs, and collective bargaining. Practical examples and forms are also provided in this chapter. Also, there is a challenging concluding case study that can be helpful in understanding and applying the principles and strategies in the chapter.

Chapter 6 covers facilities-resource management. Topics include school facilities in the United States, facility design and student achievement, school-facility planning, and environmental issues. There is a challenging case study on facility management at the end.

The last chapter covers auxiliary services: food, safety, security, and transportation. Federal and state building regulations and codes, facilities management, funding, contracting, transportation, safety and security, and special-needs facilities are other areas covered in this chapter. Several practical strategies and examples of managing facilities and auxiliary programs are provided along with a concluding case study.

FEATURES OF THE BOOK

Nothing can be worse than reading a book that is boring, dry, and impractical for educators. This book is unique in that it provides many engaging examples that can be used by all educators. One feature of the book is the correlation of the objectives of each chapter with professional organizational standards of the National Council for Accreditation of Teacher Education (NCATE), the specialized professional association (SPA) of the Educational Leadership Constituent Council (ELCC), the Interstate School Leaders Licensure Consortium (ISLLC), and National Standards for Quality Online Teaching (NACOL), and Southern Regional Education Board (SREB).

Another valuable feature of the book is the incorporation of many diverse strategies related to school finance, leadership, motivation, recruiting and selecting candidates, and disciplining, compensating and bargaining, and terminating employees. They are provided in a straightforward and practical manner. The topics in this book are useful for any administrator who desires to optimize fiscal, facility, and human resources.

Other features of this book include:

- practical examples of operating and balance statements
- examples of basic school accounting structures, budgeting revenues, student activity funds, fundraising, internal control systems and audits, and financial statements
- up-to-date guidelines, EEOC laws, and legal considerations
- practical strategies in giving employees feedback and taking action for improvement
- administering compensation programs
- strategies in collective bargaining
- examples of planning and managing facilities resources
- facility planning and food, safety, security, and transportation management
- auxiliary services, forecasting, and handling transportations, safety, and security.

The strategies for optimizing fiscal, facility, and human resources presented in this book have been based upon years of experience as a school administrator, and consulting with school districts. While there are many books written on school finance, it is unique to find a book that covers all three critical areas of finance, facility, and human resources. This book saves you from the need to purchase several books that cover these areas.

Lastly, this book also contains a rich source of educational and reference materials so that educators can apply the concepts for school resource management. Some of these materials include:

- case illustrations and figures in applying leadership and finance strategies
- examples of motivation strategies that have improved academic performance
- a sample of field-based educational issues
- actual examples of assessments and real-life case studies

ORGANIZATION OF THE BOOK

This book has been organized in a straightforward manner so educators can understand these three critical school-resource management areas of fiscal, facility, and human resources and how to optimize these areas for the school organization. Each chapter builds upon the other. However, each chapter is also distinct in itself because it covers a specific topic that relates to the three topics. Lastly, each chapter includes basic theories and examples of applying these theories, and case studies and exercises and discussion.

Acknowledgments

Appreciation is extended to the many people who have assisted and worked with the authors. Special appreciation is given to the authors' students, colleagues, former business associates in the corporate world, Susan Webb for typing part of the manuscript, and Laurel Schilling for her editorial review and suggestions. The authors would also like to recognize and extend appreciation to the many school districts where the authors have provided consulting, such as the Chicago Public Schools, Bellwood School District 88, Cicero School District 99, Lake Central School Corporation, Proviso Township High Schools, West Chicago District 33, School District 131, Michigan City Township High Schools, Findlay Schools, Glenbrook High School District 225, West Northfield District 31, Lindop School District 92, Schiller Park District 81, Norridge School District 80, Rich Township High School District 227, Marquardt School District 15, Concordia University Chicago, and Lutheran Church Missouri Synod schools. Lastly, the authors would like to extend gratitude to the many people who endorsed this book and provided insight for this project.

1

Financial Management Principles and Historical Perspectives

OBJECTIVES

At the conclusion of this chapter you will be able to:

1. Understand the concepts of adequacy, equity, and equality as they relate to school finance (ELCC 3.1, ISLLC 3).
2. Describe the impact of the courts on shaping education finance policy (ELCC 6.2, 6.3, ISLLC 6).
3. Reflect on the historical trends that have shaped the financing of education in the United States (ELCC 6.3, ISLLC 6).
4. Review the current issues and challenges for funding education (ELCC 6.3, ISLLC 6).
5. Understand the demographics and enrollment trends affecting education (ELCC 6.3, ISLLC 6).

ADEQUACY, EQUITY, AND EQUALITY

Equity, *adequacy*, and *equality* have been the mainstays of the debate regarding the funding of public schools for over fifty years (Cubberley 1906; Slater and Scott 2011). Educators, politicians, and the federal and state courts have attempted to invoke these principles as a means to solving the problems associated with providing equal access to quality public-school education for all students. Many of these attempts, however, have failed. In recent history the focus has been on attempting to tie student performance to funding. *No Child Left Behind* (NCLB) and *Race to the Top* are good examples of federal mandates designed to tie funding to student performance. States likewise have revamped their funding formulas in an attempt to more fairly distribute resources. The question is: has this worked? Are there are alternatives to the system we have now? Can site and district level administrators make a difference?

Is the American public-education system fundamentally inequitable? Should the quality of a student's educational opportunity be a function of where his or her parents live? What roles do local, state, and federal governments have in ensuring equal opportunity? Has the focus shifted from merely financial equity to outcome-based equity? What historical trends have influenced how schools are funded today? These are important questions that educators need to ponder to improve our educational system.

Adequacy

Any discussion of education finance ultimately involves the concepts of *adequacy*, *equity*, and *equality*. These terms mean different things to different people. Before examining the historical and current state of education financing, it is important to understand these terms and how they have been operationally defined.

Determining *adequacy* involves several factors. Those factors are efficiency, outcomes desired, and the ability of the government to provide the appropriate funding level required. The first factor, efficiency, is relatively easy to define but often difficult to quantify. Figure 1.1 illustrates the possible relationships of the cost of education to student achievement. Note there are four possible outcomes: high achievement/high cost, high achievement/low cost, low achievement/high cost, and low cost/low achievement. If a school has low cost of operation and low achievement, it can be classified as ineffective. A school that has a high cost and low achievement can be described as wasteful. This is probably the worst school situation. The school that has high cost and high achievement may be producing good student outcomes, but is inefficient in using fiscal resources. The ideal situation is a school that has low cost and produces high achievement (the optimum school).

Establishing an optimum-achievement/low-cost model is not as easy as it seems. School systems that would reflect this model are often not representa-

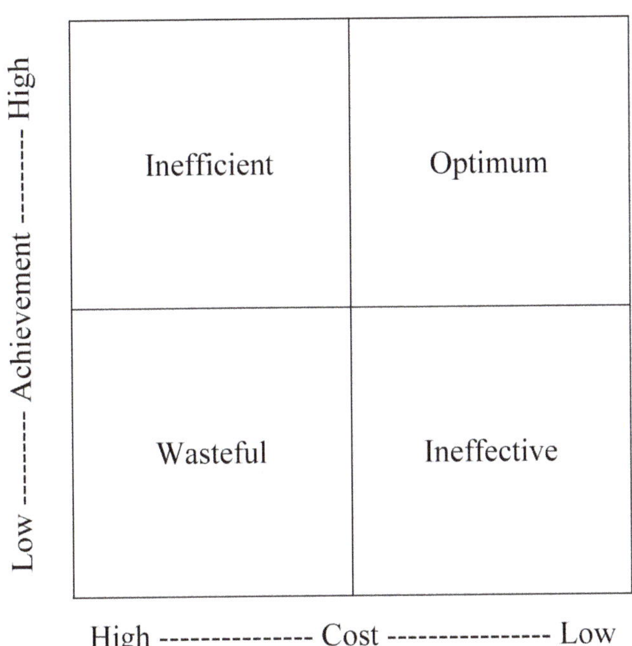

FIGURE 1.1
School Fiscal Achievement Model

tive of the general school community. They are blessed with a homogenous population that puts a high value on education. They offer a basic curriculum that provides students with a good chance of academic success and performance. Schools with significant populations of special needs students—low income, special education, and English as a second language, for example, would be hard pressed to fit in this definition. They often need to provide additional resources to their students. By the very nature of the students they must educate, their costs are higher than average.

State and federal governments have tried to address this issue in part by establishing both general and categorical funding categories, or in some cases student-weighting systems, which reflect the special needs/costs associated with some students. Variations in cost also occur due to a district's size and geographical location. Succinctly, most educators might subscribe to the words of legendary UCLA coach John Wooden that the "mark of a true champion is to always perform near your own level of competency." For the education community, the question is: what resources are adequate to make that a possibility for every child?

Student outcomes are the second factor in determining adequacy. Outcomes can be as simple as a score on an achievement or performance measure or as complicated as a set of standards that take into account academic success, life skills, and extra/cocurricular opportunities. Simply put, what are our expectations? What academic opportunities and skills do people want students to have and at what level of performance? What co/extracurricular opportunities do people want students to have? What is the educational delivery model for ensuring that these outcomes are obtained? Not all states, for example, require preschool or full-day kindergarten. Are these programs essential to achieving success and the desired outcomes for all students? All states have some type of minimum requirements for high school graduation and some type of performance testing. Is this simple combination good enough to define what an adequate education is? What about rural and urban school districts.

Rural districts are often challenged with offering the same academic opportunities as suburban/urban districts because of size or proximity. The bottom line is how do educators want to define adequate? Is it exemplary or merely passing? One of the criticisms of *No Child Left Behind* was the fact that states set different standards as to what they consider to be passing for students.

Equity

Equity is a term that seems to have gone out of favor over time. *Adequacy* and *equality* are sometimes used to define equity. Generally, equity refers to the parity of educational opportunity. How educators define educational opportunity can take many paths and is impacted by the outcomes and values we have as a nation.

Horizontal equity is the equal treatment of equals. In educational terms, horizontal equity implies that the educational opportunities afforded two individuals should be the same. Using this concept, two gifted students should receive the same opportunity as would two similarly situated special-needs students. Likewise, the funding to support those educational opportunities of equals would be the same.

Vertical equity is the equal treatment of unequals. Unfortunately, not all students are equal. Attempting to treat all students fairly often results in different levels of and access to different educational resources. Vertical equity is finding that level of services that is appropriate for each subgroup. In doing so, it is almost certain that the funding for each of these subgroups will vary based on the complexity and extent of educational resources needed.

Performance equity is assuring that each individual attains a minimum level of performance. Under *No Child Left Behind* all states were required to implement high-stakes testing for all students along with measures of success (No Child Left Behind 2012). Unfortunately, states were allowed to establish their own passing criteria. While in one state a passing score of 70 percent might indicate competency, in another state the passing criteria might only be 50 percent. If we define or use performance equity as our measure then funding levels would be established to ensure students receive the appropriate instruction and educational resources to perform at a predetermined level on an appropriate assessment that measures the outcomes desired.

Opportunity equity is providing equal access to educational resources so that individuals may reach their fullest potential. For most of our history, generations have operated under the axiom that "with hard work and education you can do anything." Unfortunately, what this meant for the educational system was that many subgroups were not given the tools to be successful. In fact it was not until the twentieth century that laws were passed to provide these groups with equal access to educational resources. The recognition that some subgroups need additional protection and funding has expanded the opportunities for these students.

Social equity is not something that schools have control of but directly affects their ability to educate children. Schools will always be inequitable as long as there is socioeconomic segregation. When funding is based on where you live it determines the quality of your education and opportunities for equity will be difficult, if not impossible, to achieve. To date, there has been no systemic resolution of how to provide equal opportunity for students across different socioeconomic classes.

Equality

Equality has been used in education as a basis for defining educational opportunity. In no place has the role of the federal government been more apparent than in the area of equality. Differences in educational opportunity and equality have persisted in the United States since its inception. Since the early 1950s equality has taken center stage with regard to a number of protected classes.

Racial equality: The first challenge to the concept of the educating to blacks occurred with the Supreme Court of the United States in *Plessy v. Ferguson* (1896). In the South it was common that blacks and whites attended separate schools. The average expenditures for white schools exceeded that of black schools and resulted in inferior schools for blacks. Facilities for most black schools were inferior to those of whites as were teachers' pay. In 1954 the Supreme Court unanimously ruled in *Brown v. Board of Education* of Topeka that racial segregation in public schools was unconstitutional, overturning the doctrine of "separate but equal."

Despite the decision, segregation nonetheless continued even after the Brown decision. In Brown, the justices noted, "Education is perhaps the most important function of state and local governments." The justices went on to note that "separate but equal" has no place. "Separate educational facilities are inherently unequal" (*Brown v. Board of Education* 1954). What occurred after the Brown decision was almost twenty-five years of litigation as to how best to best implement it. By the mid-1960s additional federal funds were available to schools as well as corresponding guidelines that required desegregation. The federal government began taking a much harder line with the passage of the *Civil Rights Act of 1964.*

In the 1970s the Supreme Court ruled that the courts had the power to use busing as a means of achieving desegregation in schools. Three years later the court dealt with the concept of *de facto* and *de jure* segregation in a case in Detroit. In *Milliken v. Bradley* (1974) the courts ruled that suburban districts could not be held responsible for the segregation issues existing in the city of Detroit. By the mid-1970s the court began to recognize that its role was limited in what changes it could affect with regard to desegregating schools.

The implications for school finance were:

1. The integration of public schools in the United States requiring interventions to overcome segregation such as busing, improved facilities, hiring additional teachers, and school-district consolidation.
2. Changes in financial resource allocation at the local, state, and federal level.

Gender equality: The landmark legislation with regard to gender equity was Title IX of the 1972 Federal Education Amendments. Title IX prohibited discrimination on the basis of gender in educational institutions that received federal aid. As a result, opportunities for female students in public education expanded as well as the opportunity to be fairly compensated. The implications for school finance were that:

1. Facilities as well as coaching staffs had to be expanded to accommodate women's sports.
2. Women employees in areas such as custodial services within public schools had to be paid what their male counterparts were receiving.
3. Coaching stipends and other pay had equalized based on objective criteria such as length of season, time worked, and level of responsibility.

Students with disabilities equality: Although *The Elementary and Secondary Act*, signed by President Johnson in 1965, gave hope to parents of children with disabilities for expanded access to public-school education, it was not until the passage of the *Education for All Handicapped Children Act* (EHA) and the *Individuals with Disabilities Act* (IDEA) were passed that this came to fruition. EHA established the right to a public education for all children regardless of their disability, while IDEA requires that individualized or special education services be provided to children with qualifying disability.

The implications for school finance are:

1. Special-education funding was included in those line items for which funding may be cut as required in the *Budget Control Act of 2011*.
2. There were approximately 6.5 million students ages three through twenty-one receiving benefits under IDEA, Part II in the fall of 2010 (Data Accountability Center 2010).

Undocumented children: In *Phyler v. Doe* (1982), the Supreme Court ruled in a five to four decision that local school districts could not withhold educational services from illegal aliens under the equal protection clause of the Fourteenth Amendment. Generally, equal protection requires that the plaintiff establish that they have been treated differently with respect to a

Table 1.1. Children Who Speak a Language Other Than English at Home by Region: 2009

In thousands (11,227 represents 11,227,000), except percent. For children 5 to 17 years old. Based on the American Community Survey; see text Section 1, and Appendix III. For composition of regions, see map inside front cover.

Characteristic	*US*	*Northeast*	*Midwest*	*South*	*West*
Children who speak another language at home	11,227	1,888	1,359	3,661	4,318
Percent of children 5 to 17 years old	21.1	20.9	11.8	18.4	33.6
Speak Spanish	8,067	1,023	816	2,889	3,339
Speak Spanish "very well"	6,131	808	611	2,117	2,535
Speak Spanish less than "very well"	1,936	215	205	713	803
Speak other Indo-European languages	1,487	516	286	385	299
Speak English "very well"	1,206	411	228	320	247
Speak English less than "very well"	281	105	58	66	52
Speak Asian and Pacific Island languages	1,242	248	159	286	549
Speak English "very well"	914	186	111	215	403
Speak English less than "very well"	327	62	48	71	146
Speak other languages	431	101	99	100	131
Speak English "very well"	342	79	75	83	104
Speak English less than "very well"	90	23	23	17	27
Have difficulty speaking English [1]	2,634	405	334	867	1,028
Language spoken at home in linguistically isolated households [2]	2,960	468	333	989	1,170
Speak only English	170	35	21	58	57
Speak Spanish	2,134	254	207	777	896
Speak other Indo-European languages	226	79	39	61	46
Speak Asian and Pacific Island languages	352	82	42	78	150
Speak other languages	78	18	25	15	21

[1] Children aged 5 to 17 who speak English less than "very well."

[2] A household in which no person aged 14 or over speaks English at least "very well."

Source: US Census Bureau, 2009 American Community Survey, B16003, "Age by Language Spoken at Home for the Population 5 years and Over in Linguistically Isolated Households" and C16004, "Age by Language Spoken at Home by Ability to Speak English for the Population 5 Years and Over," factfinder .census.gov/ (accessed January 2011).

fundamental right or as a suspect group. While education is neither a right under the constitution nor are undocumented aliens a suspect class, nonetheless the court ruled that the state had not established a substantial interest in denying educational benefits. In fact, the court reasoned that these children were in the United States through no fault of their own. The court concluded that they were entitled to the same K–12 education that the state provided to children who are citizens or legal residents. The court noted that education is a child's only means to becoming a "self-reliant and self-sufficient participant in society."

The implications for school finance are:

1. The Washington-based PEW Hispanic Center estimates approximately 6.8 percent of the children attending public K–12 schools have undocumented parents. The states with the highest numbers of unauthorized immigrant populations are California, Texas, Florida, New York, and New Jersey (Passel and Cohn 2009).
2. The Federation for American Immigration Reform (FAIR) states:

> Based on an estimate of slightly more than 3.5 million children of illegal aliens in public schools, the total cost of K-12 education to state and local governments is about $40.9 billion annually. Our estimate is conservative also because our state studies have identified the fact that average educational expenditures tend to be higher in metropolitan areas, which are more heavily impacted by illegal migration. (Martin and Ruark 2010)

NATIONAL PERSPECTIVES ON FINANCING EDUCATION

There is no mention of the right to an education in the US Constitution or its amendments. From a historical perspective, the evolution of public schools has centered on a number of underlying premises. Those premises are:

1. What is the role of public education in a democracy?
2. What steps should the government take to insure equal access to a public education?
3. What is the government's role in funding education at the local, state, and federal levels?
4. What is an adequate education?

5. How do we measure educational quality and what are our expectations relative to student achievement? (United States Department of Education, 1967)

The national government's first involvement in financing public education was through the use of land grants. Land grants such as the *Northwest Ordinance of 1787*, the *Ordinance of 1802*, and the *Morrill Acts of 1862* and *1890* recognized the need for public education by setting aside public lands for common schools and higher education. Although the federal government assisted in the establishment of public schools through the use of land grants, it nonetheless did not provide operating funds for the year-to-year operations of public schools. The federal government did not consider public-school education as its responsibility, as neither education nor references to a system of public schools is contained anywhere in the US Constitution.

The *National Defense Act of 1958*, the *Elementary and Secondary Education Act of 1965*, the *Vocational Education Act of 1963*, and the *International Education Act of 1966* all addressed the nation's concern that not only was the United States falling behind in math, science, and foreign language but that education opportunities for low-income students was woefully inadequate. Theses series of laws marked a change and expansion of the federal government's role in public education and its funding.

In addition to being a litigious period, the 60s and 70s were also a period where the federal government instituted a number of programs that have had a major impact on the funding of schools. The most far-reaching legislation was the *Elementary and Secondary Education Act* (ESEA), which was passed in 1965 as part of the "War on Poverty." ESEA's basic purpose was to establish accountability, standards, and equal access to education. The major provisions of ESEA were:

- Title I—Improving the Academic Achievement of the Disadvantaged
- Title II—Preparing, Training, and Recruiting High Quality Teachers and Principals
- Title III—Language Instruction for Limited English Proficient and Immigrant Students
- Title IV—Twenty-First-Century Schools
- Title V—Promoting Informed Parental Choice and Innovative Programs

- Title VI—Flexibility and Accountability
- Title VII—Indian, Native Hawaiian, and Alaska Native Education
- Title VIII—Impact Aid Program
- Title XI—General Provisions
- Title X—Repeals, Redesignations, and Amendments to Other Statutes

Title I was intended to address grade-level proficiency for economically disadvantaged students by supplementing regular public-school expenditures. Title I grants are primarily distributed through state education agencies although "concentration" grants are available for districts with high percentages of eligible students. Title II grants provide funds for school library resources and other instructional materials, including textbooks. Title IV provides funds for educational research. Title V provides funds to establish a single reporting agency for each state.

Corporate and government leaders saw ESEA as a means for establishing national standards for satisfactory school performance. The tension between top-down school policy at the federal level and local funding and control of schools has its beginnings in ESEA. During this same time period, other federal programs were initiated such as *Head Start* (1964) and *Emergency School Aid Act* (ESAA) (1972). Head Start funds targeted improving school readiness for low-income children. ESAA provided funds to assist school districts in integrating their schools.

IDEA was passed in Congress in 1975. It expanded the access to public education for special-needs children. At the time, Congress pledged that it would provide 40 percent of the funds needed to provide services for these children. By the 1999/2000 school year it was estimated that the total federal funding for IDEA accounted for only 10.2 percent of total IDEA expenditures (Chambers et al. 2004). Of the various funding grants under IDEA, Part B is by far the largest. Part B provides grants to states for funding services for children with disabilities in school. Under IDEA, school-age children from three to twenty-one are to receive a free and appropriate education as well as be protected by certain procedural safeguards. In 1997, the formula for Part B grants was altered to try to provide more funds for children who have not been identified as exceptional but need early intervention.

Congress established the Department of Education in 1980 as a cabinet-level agency to promote student achievement, promoting excellence and equal opportunity. Three years later, *A Nation at Risk* was published by the National Commission on Excellence in Education. Kantrowitz (1993) noted that the total federal budget for education had actually declined 1 percent in 1989–1990 since the report was issued and that states and school systems were struggling to address the needs identified in the report. The commission made the following recommendations with regard to leadership and fiscal support:

1. Principals and superintendents must play a crucial leadership role in developing school and community support for the reforms we propose, and school boards must provide them with the professional development and other support required to carry out their leadership role effectively. The commission stresses the distinction between leadership skills involving persuasion, setting goals, and developing community consensus behind them, and managerial and supervisory skills. Although the latter are necessary, we believe that school boards must consciously develop leadership skills at the school and district levels if the reforms we propose are to be achieved.
2. State and local officials, including school board members, governors, and legislators, have *the primary responsibility* for financing and governing the schools, and should incorporate the reforms we propose in their educational policies and fiscal planning.
3. The federal government, in cooperation with states and localities, should help meet the needs of key groups of students such as the gifted and talented, the socioeconomically disadvantaged, minority and language minority students, and the handicapped. In combination these groups include both national resources and the nation's youth who are most at risk.
4. In addition, we believe the federal government's role includes several functions of national consequence that states and localities alone are unlikely to be able to meet: protecting constitutional and civil rights for students and school personnel; collecting data, statistics, and information about education generally; supporting curriculum improvement and research on teaching, learning, and the management of schools; supporting teacher training in areas of critical shortage or key national needs; and providing student financial assistance and research and graduate training. We believe the assistance of the federal government should be provided with a minimum of administrative burned and intrusiveness.

5. The federal government has *the primary responsibility* to identify the national interest in education. It should also help fund and support efforts to protect and promote that interest. It must provide the national leadership to ensure that the nation's public and private resources are marshaled to address the issues discussed in this report.
6. This commission calls upon educators, parents, and public officials at all levels to assist in bringing about the educational reform proposed in this report. We also call upon citizens to provide the financial support necessary to accomplish these purposes. Excellence costs. But in the long run mediocrity costs far more.

In 2001, the Elementary and Secondary Education Act was reauthorized under the acronym *No Child Left Behind Act* (NCLB). The four pillars of NCLB were:

- Strong accountability for results: close the achievement gap and make sure all students, including those who are disadvantaged, achieve academic proficiency.
- More freedom for states and communities: school districts have unprecedented flexibility in how they use federal education funds. For example, it is possible for most school districts to transfer up to 50 percent of the federal formula grant funds without separate approval.
- Proven education methods: puts emphasis on determining which educational programs and practices have been proven effective through rigorous scientific research.
- More choices for parents: in schools that do not meet state standards for at least two consecutive years, parents may transfer their children to a better-performing public school, including a public charter school, within their district. (NCLB 2012)

NCLB expanded the role of the federal government in education by instituting accountability standards for student progress. Those accountability measures included the annual testing of students, academic progress, teacher qualifications, reading grants, and funding changes. Concerns regarding NCLB focused on both the requirement for schools to make adequate yearly progress (AYP) and funding. By 2011, several states saw failure rates over 50 percent (McNeil 2011). Funding has also been an issue as the number of failing schools rose. Cash-strapped districts and states struggled with allocating additional funds to address those areas in which they were failing to make AYP. One of the deficiencies in NCLB is that there is a strong incentive to keep standards low due to the penalties and high cost of funding high standards. In February 2011 President Obama approved giving NCLB waivers to ten states.

In 2009 the *American Recovery and Reinvestment Act of 2009* (ARRA) was signed into law. ARRA provided $4.35 billion for the Race to the Top fund. Race to the Top funds can be used for implementing plans in any of four core education reform areas:

- Adopting standards and assessments that prepare students to succeed in college and the workplace and to compete in the global economy;
- Building data systems that measure student growth and success, and inform teachers and principals about how they can improve instruction;
- Recruiting, developing, rewarding, and retaining effective teachers and principals, especially where they are needed most; and
- Turning around our lowest-achieving schools. (ARRA 2009)

Race to the Top is a competitive grant process that rewards states for their success in raising student achievement and best reforms. Unfortunately, some districts have found out that the math for Race to the Top recipients just doesn't add up. In New York, the state received $700 million in funds. One district superintendent remarked:

> "No one did the math," said Ken Mitchell, South Orangetown's superintendent. "Race to the Top was fast-tracked, and there was no discussion about the costs. South Orangetown got a $23,366 piece of the State's Race to the Top pie and spent it in two days during the summer on administrator training," Mitchell said. "But the district expects to spend almost $2 million over four years to meet the program's demands." (Winerip 2012)

STATE PERSPECTIVES ON FINANCING EDUCATION

By 1791, fourteen states had their own constitution and several states included provisions for education. Prior to that time education was largely a local phenomenon and centered on literacy and religious training. The Massachusetts' *Ye Olde Deluder Satan Act of 1642* was enacted to provide literacy training primarily to support the reading and understanding of scripture. The act provided a teacher for settlements with over fifty households and a grammar school for those with over one hundred households. Local townships were authorized to levy taxes to support these services.

Thomas Jefferson introduced the first real proposal for public education in the Virginia legislature in 1779. Jefferson's *Bill for the More General Diffusion of Knowledge* called for the creation of publicly supported schools. Meritoctratic in nature, the bill called for a small number of gifted students to advance from publicly supported elementary schools through a publicly supported state college. Jefferson's bill did not pass the Virginia legislature initially.

The system of public education as we know it began in the nineteenth century. Horace Mann argued for education of all children in "common schools." He saw public schools as a way to equalize educational opportunity and believed that the wealth of individuals could be increased through educational opportunity. Mann established Massachusetts' first State Board of Education and became its first secretary. John Joseph Hughes, the first archbishop of New York, argued unsuccessfully in the 1840s that Catholic schools in that state should receive public funds. His campaign, although unsuccessful, did help set in motion the secularization of public schools. Catherine Beecher advocated for women's education and Booker T. Washington, founder and head of Tuskegee Institute, advocated vocation education for African Americans.

The first compulsory law for student attendance was passed in 1852 by the state of Massachusetts. All states had passed laws requiring children to attend at least elementary school by 1918. At the same time, many individuals objected to public education. In 1925, the Supreme Court ruled that states could not require children to attend a public school, and that parents had a right to send their children to private schools (*Pierce v. Society of Sisters* [1925]).

In the late 1800s a number of challenges to the funding of public education began to appear. In *Stuart v. School District No. 1 of Village of Kalamazoo* (1874), the taxpayers in Kalamazoo, Michigan, challenged the state's legal basis for supporting public high schools through levying local property taxes.

At the start of the twentieth century, W. E. B. Dubois said what African Americans needed was a "real education" to teach them how "to know, to think and to aspire." The Smith-Hughes Act of 1917 helped create vocational programs in high schools. Elmwood Cubberley, considered by many as the "pioneer" of modern school finance, brought industrial management theory to school leadership as well as a scholarly interest in how to distribute state revenues to compensate differences in local property wealth. A controversial figure, Cubberley believed that efficiency and the educational bureaucracy could address many problems. He did not, however, ascribe to the concept of equality in a democratic society (Cubberley 1906).

Following Cubberley were a number of academics in the burgeoning field of school finance. Probably the most notable were George D. Strayer and Robert Murray Haig. In 1923, Strayer and Haig developed the concepts that today are referred to as *foundation* programs. Foundation programs are used by approximately forty states today. The main premise of foundation programs is that they provide a minimal level of funding for each student. (See chapter 2 for a full discussion of the Strayer and Haig approach.)

In the 1930s there was a general taxpayer revolt of sorts in the states against the property tax. Nearly a third of the states adopted individual and corporate income taxes after the great Depression. (*Wikipedia* 2012) As noted by the Tax Foundation (2005) "Expenditure demands on the one side and stress upon the existing tax system on the other induced a striking change in state finances from 1933 to 1940. State governments grew in absolute size. States adopted new general sales, personal income, alcohol, tobacco and other taxes to supplement and eventually supplant the state property tax." This corresponded to an emerging consensus that education was the responsibility of the state government. It was at this time that the notion of using attendance days in determining state aid would create a more uniform school year.

Flat grants and nonequalizing state allocations for school districts were the norm. Consideration of proportional aid to districts was just emerging as a concept. By 1940 there were over 117,000 school districts in the United States. Due to school districts' consolidation efforts, that number dropped to just over fifteen thousand in 1990. In 1940 local property taxes accounted for 68 percent of the revenue to fund public education. By 1990, that number dropped to 48 percent with the states picking up most the remainder of the funding (Snell 2009).

Post–World War II—Early School Finance Theory

The period from 1940 to 1960 is generally regarded as the era of the Strayer-Haig "foundation." Under Strayer-Haig foundation programs,

Table 1.2. Number of Schools by Enrollment

(Enrollment in thousands (49,054 represents 49,054,000). For school year ending in 2009. Data reported by schools, rather than school districts. Based on the Common Core of Data Survey; see source for details.)

Enrollment Size of School	*Number of Schools*					*Enrollment*[1]			
	Total	*Elementary*[2]	*Secondary*[3]	*Combined*[4]	*Other*[5]	*Total*	*Secondary*[3]	*Combined*[4]	*Other*[5]
Total	**98,706**	**67,148**	**24,348**	**5,623**	**1,587**	**49,054**	**16,055**	**1,520**	**32**
PERCENT									
Total	**100.00**	**100.00**	**100.00**	**100.00**	**100.00**	**100.00**	**100.00**	**100.00**	**100.00**
Under 100 students	10.51	5.88	17.76	38.56	44.26	0.94	1.11	5.33	8.45
100 to 199 students	9.53	8.30	11.42	17.27	14.75	2.76	2.38	8.12	12.18
200 to 299 students	11.42	12.46	8.62	10.00	16.94	5.56	3.04	7.91	23.68
300 to 399 students	13.76	16.20	7.89	7.76	13.11	9.31	3.88	8.79	26.30
400 to 499 students	13.86	16.87	6.60	6.72	8.20	12.00	4.19	9.73	20.36
500 to 599 students	11.30	13.67	5.78	5.06	1.64	11.95	4.51	9.04	5.20
600 to 699 students	8.33	9.78	5.14	3.60	1.09	10.40	4.73	7.59	3.84
700 to 799 students	5.74	6.53	4.09	2.79	–	8.27	4.35	6.77	–
800 to 999 students	6.42	6.50	6.98	3.08	–	11.00	8.87	8.82	–
1,000 to 1,499 students	5.39	3.43	11.66	3.20	–	12.49	20.40	12.43	–
1,500 to 1,999 students	2.03	0.31	7.33	1.01	–	6.78	18.05	5.58	–
2,000 to 2,999 students	1.41	0.06	5.57	0.51	–	6.45	18.72	4.00	–
3,000 or more students	0.31	0.01	1.17	0.43	–	2.11	5.77	5.90	–
Average enrollment1	517	470	704	308	177	517	704	308	177

– Represents zero.

[1]Excludes data for schools not reporting enrollment.

[2]Includes schools beginning with grade 6 or below and with no grade higher than 8.

[3]Includes schools with no grade lower than 7.

[4]Includes schools beginning with grade 6 or below and ending with grade 9 or above.

[5]Includes special education, alternative, and other schools not classified by grade span.

Source: US National Center for Education Statistics, *Digest of Education Statistics*, annual. See also www.nces.ed.gov/programs/digest/.

wealthy districts would receive no state funds while other districts would receive state funds necessary to provide the foundation program. Each district would be required to levy local taxes that were required in the wealthiest districts to provide the foundation program. The difference between the foundation program amount and the amount generated by the required local tax levy was what each school district would receive from the state. This was the start of the modern general state-aid formulas. During the 1950s a number of refinements were made to the Strayer-Haig foundation model. Most notably was the notion that funds should be distributed based on enrollment and/or average daily attendance.

The first state law providing the right for government employees to collectively bargain was enacted in Wisconsin in 1959. In 1964 Albert Shanker was elected president of the United Federation of Teachers (UFT). Only three years later he led a strike of the New York public-school system. Shanker became the first president of the American Federation of Teachers in 1974 and remained in the post until his death. The rise of public-education unions has had a significant impact on school finance. With salaries and benefits representing 70 to 80 percent of most school-district budgets, collective bargaining impacts not only the wages and working conditions of public-school teachers and support personnel but also funding.

The Social Revolution—The Search for Equity

The 1960s and 70s marked the beginning of a long period of litigation surrounding how schools were state funded. Most notable were the following cases:

McGinnis v. Shapiro (1969) was an Illinois case in which the plaintiffs alleged that the state system of public-school finance violated their guarantees under the Fourteenth Amendment. Furthermore, they alleged that the current method of funding Illinois schools created wide variation in expenditure per student. The US District Court ruled against the plaintiffs on the following grounds:

- There was no requirement under the Fourteenth Amendment that expenditures be based solely on "educational need."
- The amount spent on each student was not the only or exclusive means of determining educational quality.

- There were no judicial standards by which the court could determine whether or not the Equal Protection Clause had been violated or satisfied.

The dismissal of the suit was based on a lack of the court finding any form or invidious discrimination. The court said that "an inevitable consequence of decentralization" is the inequitable distribution of funds between school districts. McGinnis-type cases represent the first wave of largely unsuccessful court challenges to state financing systems.

Serrano v. Priest (1971) is probably one of the best known challenges to a state's system of financing schools. Serrano marked a new era in school finance cases that were largely successful by challenging in state courts that property-tax-based state systems discriminated against classes of children solely as a function of where they lived. In *Serrano v. Priest* the court held that the existing system of funding California public schools was unconstitutional. The court stated that:

> We have determined that this funding scheme invidiously discriminates against the poor because it makes the quality of a child's [public] education a function of the wealth of his parents and his neighbors. Recognizing, as we must the right to an education in our public schools is a fundamental interest which cannot be conditioned on wealth, we can discern no compelling state purpose necessitating the present method of financing constitutional challenges and must fall before the equal protection clause. (*Serrano v. Priest* 1971)

In 1970, California ranked thirteenth in per-pupil expenditures. The disparity between districts was significant, with the wealthiest district spending 6.2 times more than the poorest one. The tax effort, however, was twice as high in the poorer district. The importance of Serrano as a landmark case was that it marked the first major victory for education reform advocates in the courts. It also ushered in an era of additional challenges to state finance systems along similar lines.

San Antonio Independent School District v. Rodriguez (1973) was decided by a margin of five to four by the Supreme Court. The case challenged the constitutionality of the Texas system to finance public education. Specifically, the court was asked to decide (1) "whether the Texas system of financing public education operates to the disadvantage of some suspect class or impinges upon the fundamental right explicitly or implicitly protected by the Constitution, thereby requiring strict judicial scrutiny," and (2) "whether [the Texas system] furthers some legitimate, articulated state purpose and therefore does not constitute an invidious discrimination in violation of the Equal Protection Clause of the Fourteenth Amendment."

Funds for financing public schools were generated from both state and local sources. The state's Minimum Foundation Program provided approximately half of the revenues for Texas public schools. The Minimum Foundation Program was designed to provide a minimum instructional level for each district in the state. The state contributed approximately 80 percent of the program while local districts were responsible for 20 percent. Local revenues were generated and varied by both the tax rate and the value of taxable property in a district, resulting in large disparities in per-pupil spending levels between districts.

In addressing the second issue, the court decided that the "Texas system [did] not operate to the peculiar disadvantage of any suspect class." In reaching this conclusion, Justice Powell noted:

> The absence of any evidence that the financing system discriminates against any definable category of "poor" people or that it results in the absolute deprivation of education—the disadvantaged class in not susceptible of identification in traditional terms. (*San Antonio Independent School District v. Rodriguez* 1973)

The facts in *Rodriquez* indicated that except for the poorest and richest district, 90 percent of the districts sampled by the expert witnesses for the respondent showed that the relationship between median family income and district spending was inverted—that is, in districts with the higher median family incomes, per-pupil spending was lower than in districts with lower median family incomes.

With regard to whether or not the Texas financing system encroached on the exercise of a "fundamental right" to education, the court observed that education is not afforded protection under the Federal Constitution. The court's basis for reaching that decision was that a right to education is not explicitly or implicitly guaranteed by the constitution.

The court recognized that managing a statewide public-school system was complex, and that various states might devise different, although equally valid, methods of providing a quality education to their students within their own budgetary constraints (Schilling 1989). These decisions, the court felt, were best left to state and local officials.

But for lack of one vote, the outcome could have been much different. Justices Douglas, Brennan, White, and Marshall concluded that because parents and children in poor districts could not supplement minimum state funds to the same degree as more affluent districts, they were being discriminated against. The basis of their dissenting opinion was that parents in wealthier districts could raise more property taxes than those in poorer districts with the same tax rate.

In *Robinson v. Cahill*, the New Jersey Supreme Court upheld a lower court decision that New Jersey's system of financing its public schools was unconstitutional. In 1970, Jersey City sued the state on behalf of an eleven-year-old African American student, Kenneth Robinson, who was living in a housing project. The suit alleged that New Jersey's reliance on local property taxes created a situation in which poor school districts could never spend as much as rich school districts—even if they taxed themselves at a higher rate. The State Supreme Court ruled that New Jersey's current method of funding public schools did not meet the constitutional guarantee of a "thorough and efficient" educational system. As a postscript, it took two and one-half years for the state to pass an income tax to support changes in education funding.

Late Twentieth Century—The Search for Adequacy

The 1980s and 1990s were also a period of litigation surrounding how schools were funded. In 1985, sixty-six property-poor rural districts in Kentucky asserting that the current method of financing public schools was unconstitutional filed a suit. In *Rose v. Council for Better Education* (1989) the Kentucky Supreme Court ordered the state to provide an adequate education for each child in the state.

> Lest there be any doubt, the result of our decision is that Kentucky's entire system of common schools is unconstitutional. There is no allegation that only part of the common school system is invalid, and we find no such circumstance. This decision applies to the entire sweep of the system—all its parts and parcels. This decision applies to the statutes creating, implementing and financing the system and to all regulations, etc., pertaining thereto. This decision covers the

> creation of local school districts, school boards, and the Kentucky Department of Education to the Minimum Foundation Program and Power Equalization Program. It covers school construction and maintenance, teacher certification—the whole gamut of the common school system in Kentucky. (*Rose v. Council for Better Education* at 215 1989)

The court listed seven learning goals in their decision—many which have served as the basis for other similar cases. Those learning goals are:

1. Sufficient oral and written communication skills to enable students to function in a complex and rapidly changing civilization;
2. Sufficient knowledge of economic, social, and political systems to enable the student to make informed choices;
3. Sufficient understanding of governmental processes to enable the student to understand the issues that affect his or her community, state, and nation;
4. Sufficient self-knowledge and knowledge of his or her mental and physical wellness;
5. Sufficient grounding in the arts to enable each student to appreciate his or her cultural and historical heritage;
6. Sufficient training or preparation for advanced training in either academic or vocational fields so as to enable each child to choose and pursue life work intelligently; and
7. Sufficient levels of academic or vocational skills to enable public-school students to compete favorably with their counterparts in surrounding states, in academics or in the job market. (*Rose v. Council for Better Education* 1989)

Rose v. Council for Better Education started a third wave of national school-finance litigation based on adequacy claims and education clauses in state constitutions. Two other cases were important in the development of adequacy challenges to state constitutions—*Edgewood v. Kirby* (1989) and *Helena Elementary School District No. One v. State of Montana* (236 Mont. 44, 769 P 2d. 684).

In 1984 the *Mexican American Legal Defense and Educational Fund* filed suit against the Texas commissioner of education. Sixty-seven school districts along with the Edgewood Independent School District and individual children and parents asserted that the Texas system for educating public-school children violated the state's constitution. The Texas Supreme Court noted that:

> There are glaring disparities in the abilities of the various school districts to raise revenues from property taxes because taxable property wealth varies greatly from district to district. The wealthiest district has over $14,000,000 of property wealth per student, while the poorest has approximately $20,000; this disparity reflects a 700 to 1 ratio. The 300,000 students in the lowest-wealth schools have less than 3% of the state's property wealth to support their education while the 300,000 students in the highest-wealth schools have over 25% of the state's property wealth; thus the 300,000 students in the wealthiest districts have more than eight times the property value to support their education as the 300,000 students in the poorest districts. The average property wealth in the 100 wealthiest districts is more than twenty times greater than the average property wealth in the 100 poorest districts. Edgewood I.S.D. has $38,854 in property wealth per student; Alamo Heights I.S.D. in the same county, has $570,109 in property wealth per student. (Texas State Historical Association 2012)

The court further noted the "property-poor districts are trapped in a cycle of poverty from which there is no opportunity to free themselves." While the defendants argued that the word "efficient" be defined as "simple and inexpensive," the court chose to interpret "efficient" as "effective or productive of results and connotes the use of resources so as to produce results with little waste . . . [that] the constitution framers and ratifiers did not intend a system with such vast disparities as now exist." Consequently, the court found the state's financing system was neither financially efficient nor efficient in dispersing knowledge and thereby declared it unconstitutional. Interestingly, it took until 1993 for the Teas state legislature to pass a plan that was acceptable to the court.

In *Helena Elementary School District No. 1 v. State* (769 p.2d 684, 1989), the plaintiffs brought suit charging that the Montana system of financing public schools prevented students from equal educational opportunity under the state's constitution. Montana's education clause provides that "It is the goal of the people to establish a system of education which will develop the full educational potential of each person. Equality of educational opportunity is guaranteed to each person of the State." It also provides that "the State recognizes the distinct and unique cultural heritage of the American Indians and is committed in its educational goals to the preservation of their cultural integrity." In declaring the current system unconstitutional, the Montana Supreme Court noted "that the spending disparities among the State's school districts translate into a denial of quality of educational opportunity."

FUTURE CHALLENGES TO FUNDING PUBLIC EDUCATION

While there have always been concerns regarding the costs of education and the performance of students, the 2008 US recession seemed to bring a number of issues to the forefront in a way no one could have imagined. This has manifested itself in changes in teacher tenure, bargaining regulations, pensions, state budgets, and teacher evaluation. These initiatives will have a profound effect on school financing in the future. Not only will they affect the fiscal ability of the states to pay for education but also impact local school-district budgets. A secondary issue is a new wave of court challenges to state systems of finance. Some of the challenges are employing new strategies on old themes while others are breaking new ground.

As of 2011 at least thirty states were spending less on funding education than they were in 2008—in some states the funding was over 20 percent lower (Baker 2012). In fact, the New Jersey Supreme Court ruled in 2011 that the current levels of funding in the state violated the New Jersey School Funding Reform Act of 2008. The court ordered the reinstatement of $500 million in state funding for the state's poorest school districts. At least for New Jersey, failing to fully fund reforms passed in 2008 was unconstitutional (Bloomberg et. al 2011).

In May 2011, the *American-Statesman* reported that the "Largest school finance lawsuit in Texas takes shape." More than sixty school districts representing more than 60 percent of the state's students are involved in the lawsuit. The current lawsuit represents the eighth filed since 1968. At issue is the lack of progress made in implementing a permanent funding solution as required by the 2005 Texas Supreme Court decision declaring the current system unconstitutional (Alexander 2011). A secondary issue is a new wave of court challenges to state systems of finance. Some of the challenges are employing new strategies on old themes while others are breaking new ground. Slater and Scott (2011, p. 52) report that "California is on the verge of a fourth wave of school finance litigation that challenges the state to provide adequate financing for all students to meet state curriculum standards."

IDEA Reauthorization

Renewal of NCLB has been under consideration since 2007. Ten states were given waivers to the current NCLB law in February 2012. According to President Obama, he believes that NCLB "is driving the wrong behaviors, from teaching to the test to federally determined, one-size-fits-all interventions" (Hu 2012). NCLB has its advocates as well as detractors. On one hand it has focused educators on improving education for disaggregated groups such as low-income and bilingual students. On the other hand, it is probably the biggest unfunded mandate outside of special education ever to be passed and enacted by the federal government.

Pensions and State Debt

California and Illinois share the notoriety of being the two states with the most underfunded public-school pension systems. According to California Watchdog, the state has approximately a half billion dollars in pension debt and CalPERS and CalSTRS will run out of money by 2026-2027 (Grimes 2010). The Pew Center on the States indicates that only 54 percent of Illinois' pension obligations are funded as of the 2008 fiscal year—the worst of all the states (Pew Charitable Trusts 2010). Illinois borrowed $3.5 billion dollars to fund its pension obligations (Lambert 2010). Illinois borrowed the money to increase the availability of funds for day-to-day operations (CNNMoney.com 2010).

Rhode Island lawmakers made that state the first to approve comprehensive pension reform. Called the Rhode Island Retirement Security Act, the Rhode Island legislation would suspend cost-of-living adjustments for those collecting state pensions and raise the retirement age for most employees. The legislation would establish a hybrid system for state teachers, mixing a traditional pension with a retirement account similar to a 401k. The fact that the legislation affects current as well as future retirees makes it an unusually aggressive measure targeted at reducing the state's pension liability.

State Shortfalls and the Economy

Indiana changed the way it funds schools just prior to the start of the 2008 recession, resulting in immediate shortfalls to the state's school districts.

According to the Center for Evaluation and Education Policy at Indiana University, since the change in funding the success rate for passing school referendums has only been 40.7 percent. This is about 20 percent less than the success rate for states like Illinois and Minnesota. In 2009 the state indicated it would cut $300 million from education funds due to shortfalls in state revenue. Also, Oregon's legislature funded $5.75 billion for schools in 2009 for the fiscal years 2010 and 2011. Unfortunately, the amount needed to adequately fund schools according to the Quality Education Commission for the two years was $8.35 billion (Oregon Secretary of State 2012).

Pennsylvania's proposed 2012–2013 budget only provided new funds to basically cover the state's pension payments. As a result of shortfalls in Pennsylvania, the city schools cut spending by about 25 percent over the past two years (Murphy 2012). Illinois' 2011–2012 budget prorated general state aid, and the prospect for 2013 is that it will be prorated again. The Institute for Illinois' Fiscal Sustainability at the Civic Foundation has estimated that without further interventions Illinois' unpaid bills will reach $34.8 billion by the end of fiscal year 2027—the main contributors to the dilemma are Medicaid, health care, and pensions. The effect on educational funding would be dire.

These are but examples of the types of fiscal challenges states are facing. Other states are facing similar challenges. Combine this with the pension-debt crisis and the economic downturn of 2008 and you have a recipe for disaster. In fact, a number of states have had to come to the rescue of local districts that have become fiscally unsound.

Enrollment and Demographics

The future of education and its funding will be impacted by both future demographics and enrollment trends. As shown in Table 1.3, the K–12 enrollment in the United States is expected to increase through 2020.

There are two major demographics realities that will affect schools and how they are funded. The first is the shift in population from the Northeast and Midwest to the South and West. The shift is captured in Table 1.4.

The second is the changing face of the American public-school student. According to the US Census Bureau statistics 5.2 percent or 2.8 million children ages five to seventeen had a disability in 2010. The percentage of public-school children living in districts with at least a 20 percent poverty level was 45 percent in 2010, and another 34.3 percent living in districts with between

Table 1.3. School Enrollment: 1980 to 2020

In thousands (58,306 represents 58,306,000) as of Fall

	All levels			Pre-K–Grade 8		Grades 9–12		College[3]	
Year	*Total*	*Public*	*Private*	*Public*	*Private*[1,2]	*Public*	*Private*[1]	*Public*	*Private*
1980	58,305	50,335	7,971	27,647	3,992	13,231	1,339	9,457	2,640
1985	57,226	48,901	8,325	27,034	4,195	12,388	1,362	9,479	2,768
1990	60,683	52,061	8,622	29,876	4,512	11,341	1,136	10,845	2,974
1991	62,087	53,357	8,730	30,506	4,518	11,541	1,163	11,318	3,049
1992	62,987	54,208	8,779	31,088	4,528	11,735	1,148	11,385	3,102
1993	63,438	54,654	8,784	31,504	4,536	11,961	1,132	11,189	3,116
1994	64,385	55,245	9,139	31,896	4,856	12,215	1,138	11,134	3,145
1995	65,020	55,933	9,087	32,338	4,756	12,502	1,163	11,092	3,169
1996	65,911	56,732	9,180	32,762	4,755	12,849	1,178	11,121	3,247
1997	66,574	57,323	9,251	33,071	4,759	13,056	1,185	11,196	3,306
1998	67,033	57,676	9,357	33,344	4,776	13,195	1,212	11,138	3,369
1999	67,667	58,167	9,500	33,486	4,789	13,371	1,229	11,309	3,482
2000	68,685	58,956	9,729	33,686	4,906	13,517	1,264	11,753	3,560
2001	69,920	59,905	10,014	33,936	5,023	13,736	1,296	12,233	3,695
2002	71,015	60,935	10,080	34,114	4,915	14,069	1,306	12,752	3,860
2003	71,551	61,399	10,152	34,201	4,788	14,339	1,311	12,859	4,053
2004	72,154	61,776	10,379	34,178	4,756	14,618	1,331	12,980	4,292
2005	72,674	62,135	10,539	34,204	4,724	14,909	1,349	13,022	4,466
2006	73,066	62,496	10,570	34,235	4,631	15,081	1,360	13,180	4,579
2007	73,451	62,783	10,668	34,205	4,546	15,087	1,364	13,491	4,757
2008	74,075	63,237	10,838	34,285	4,335	14,980	1,373	13,972	5,131
2009, proj.[4]	75,198	64,092	11,106	34,440	4,151	14,842	1,337	14,811	5,617
2010, proj..	75,286	64,231	11,054	34,637	4,092	14,668	1,306	14,926	5,657
2011, proj.	75,435	64,420	11,014	34,892	4,057	14,530	1,266	14,998	5,691
2012, proj.	75,633	64,665	10,968	35,129	4,034	14,512	1,229	15,023	5,704
2013, proj.	76,082	65,093	10,988	35,368	4,025	14,545	1,194	15,180	5,769
2014, proj.	76,775	65,713	11,063	35,579	4,027	14,689	1,160	15,445	5,875
2015, proj.	77,488	66,342	11,146	35,829	4,042	14,830	1,134	15,682	5,970
2016, proj.	78,182	66,947	11,234	36,161	4,073	14,877	1,103	15,909	6,059
2017, proj.	78,869	67,545	11,324	36,491	4,110	14,939	1,077	16,115	6,137
2018, proj.	79,556	68,133	11,422	36,803	4,146	15,000	1,060	16,330	6,217
2019, proj.	80,260	68,736	11,523	37,1212	4,181	15,083	1,052	16,532	6,290
2020, proj.	80,955	69,342	11,612	37,444	4,216	15,222	1,056	16,676	6,340

[1]Since the biennial Private School Universe Survey (PSS) is collected in the fall of odd-numbered years, even-numbered years are estimated based on data from the PSS.

[2]Includes private nursery and prekindergarten enrollment in schools that offer kindergarten or higher grades.

[3]Data beginning 1996 based on new classification system. See footnote 1, Table 278.

[4]Pre-K through 12 are projections; college data are actual.

Source: US National Center for Education Statistics, *Digest of Education Statistics*, annual, and *Projections of Education Statistics*, annual. See also www.nces.ed.gov/annuals>.

Table 1.4. Population Change for the United States, Regions, States, and Puerto Rico: 2000 to 2010

(For information on confidentiality protection, nonsampling error, and definitions, see www.census.gov/prod/cen2010/doc/p194-171.pdf)

	Population		*Change*	
Area	*2000*	*2010*	*Number*	*Percent*
United States	281,421,906	308,745,538	27,323,632	9.7
REGION				
Northeast	53,594,378	55,317,240	1,722,682	3.2
Midwest	64,392,776	66,927,001	2,534,225	3.9
South	100,236,820	114,555,744	14,318,924	14.3
West	63,197,932	71,945,553	8,747,621	13.8

a 10 and 20 percent poverty level. Table 1.5 shows that while public-school enrollment is expected to increase 2.5 percent, per-pupil expenditures will increase 5.4 percent through 2016. The obvious question is: "Is this enough?"

SUMMARY

Public education in the United States has evolved from a system of privately run religious schools to a system that involves local, state, and federal governments. According to Brimley, Verstegen, and Garfield (2012, p. xx), a majority of Americans now support some federal government involvement in education. While funding for education is still a state function, the federal government's role has expanded greatly. As states struggle financially, they have relied more and more on federal education dollars. The problem is that federal funds are not "free." They are provided contingent on a myriad of rules, regulations, and standards. NCLB and Race to the Top are just two examples of the federal government driving state educational goals and consequently how schools spend money.

The financing of education has gone through a number of iterations. These changes were due to new definitions of equity, equality, and adequacy as well as the inclusion of more and more children obtaining access to quality public education. While school-finance academics were perfecting foundation-level programs, society was challenging the notion of equality. The equal access of blacks and undocumented children to the system redefined public-education enrollment. The inclusion of females in sports and other activities under Title IX also called for new facilities and staff. Today, we have school-finance

Table 1.5. School Enrollment, Faculty, Graduates, and Finances—Projections: 2010 to 2016

[As of fall, except as indicated (54,770 represents 54,770,000)]

Item	*Unit*	*2010*	*2011*	*2012*	*2013*	*2014*	*2015*	*2016*
ELEMENTARY AND SECONDARY SCHOOLS								
School enrollment, total	1,000	54,770	54,704	54,746	54,905	55,133	55,455	55,836
Prekindergarten–Grade 8	1,000	38,592	38,729	38,949	39,163	39,394	39,606	39,872
Grades 9–12	1,000	16,179	15,975	15,797	15,742	15,739	15,849	15,964
Public	1,000	49,282	49,306	49,422	49,642	49,915	50,268	50,659
Prekindergarten–Grade 8	1,000	34,440	34,637	34,892	35,129	35,368	35,579	35,829
Grades 9–12	1,000	14,842	14,668	14,530	14,512	14,545	14,689	14,830
Private	1,000	5,488	5,398	5,324	5,263	5,219	5,187	5,176
Prekindergarten–Grade 8	1,000	4,151	4,092	4,057	4,034	4,025	4,027	4,042
Grades 9–12	1,000	1,337	1,306	1,266	1,229	1,194	1,160	1,134
Classroom teachers, total FTE[1]	1,000	3,644	3,668	3,679	3,696	3,725	3,752	3,782
Public	1,000	3,207	3,240	3,253	3,274	3,306	3,334	3,364
Private	1,000	437	428	426	422	419	19	418
High-school graduates, total[2]	1,000	3,321	3,22	3,220	3,197	3,154	3,132	3,165
Public	1,000	3,013	2,982	2,926	2,912	2,875	2,867	2,904
Public schools:[2]								
Average daily attendance (ADA)	1,000	46,041	46,063	46,172	46,377	46,631	46,962	47,328
Current dollars:[3]								
Current school expenditure	Bil. Dol.	517	526	536	550	570	(N/A)	(N/A)
Per pupil in fall enrollment	Dollar	10,482	10,670	10,855	11,081	11,410	(N/A)	(N/A)
Constant (2008–2009) dollars:[3,4]								
Current school expenditure	Bil. Dol.	511	514	515	518	525	541	557
Per pupil in fall enrollment	Dollar	10,377	10,425	10,428	10,434	10,524	10,760	10,987

N/A = Not available.

[1]Full-time equivalent.

[2]For school year ending in June the following year.

[3]Limited financial projections are shown due to the uncertain behavior of inflation over the long term.

[4]Based on the Consumer Price Index (CPI) for all urban consumers, US Bureau of Labor Statistics. CPI adjusted to a school year basis by NCES.

Source: US National Center for Education Statistics, *Projections of Education Statistics to 2020*. See also www.nces.ed.gov/surveys/AnnualReports/.

formulas that attempt not only to provide equal access but additional funding for protected classes such as low-income and special-education students.

What is the future for education funding in the United States? That depends on whom you ask. There are many competing interests. State budgets are under stress like never before due to increased Medicaid and public-pension demands. Education funding, once the "holy grail" in most state budgets, is being reduced as are other programs. The solution to education funding will involve resolution to a number of problems. Succinctly, those would include:

1. Improvements in state budgets and unfunded liabilities
2. New and improved definitions of adequacy that address the variations in funding that still exists in many states
3. Recognition that the funding of school districts by relying on local property taxes is inherently unfair and promotes "haves and have-nots"
4. Resolution of the national debate on the definition of student achievement, outcomes, and standards
5. Addressing the national debt
6. Recruiting and retaining high-quality teachers while addressing the emerging issues surrounding collective bargaining

CASE STUDY

"The Governor's Speech"

This is a time of great economic turmoil and one in which education has never been more important. The State of Illinois must address both the issues of increasing funding and providing a more equitable playing field for students in all districts—urban areas, suburbs, and downstate. Not to address these issues will result in Illinois falling behind other states and will make our students disadvantaged in the world arena.

As a state, we only provide 36.8 percent of the revenue needed to fund our schools. Local revenue represents approximately 73.2 percent, excluding federal grants. This is unacceptable.

My proposal is really very simple—increase revenue and increase education funding. Currently, the state spends about $10.3 billion on education. My proposal will increase education funding by $1.4 billion and, at the same time, provide much-needed property tax relief in these trying times. Specifically, I am proposing:

- Increasing the State Aid Foundation level to $5,500 from its current level of $4,700 (cost $1.4 billion)
- Reduce the property tax by 25 percent state wide (cost $2.3 billion)

This would result in a shift of almost 100 percent with the state providing 64.1 percent and local revenue only accounting for 35.9 percent.

The obvious question is how would I do this?

1. Raise the individual income tax from 3 percent to 4 percent—revenue $2.7 billion
2. Raise the income tax on corporations from 4.8 percent to 6.4 percent—$332 million
3. Tax all public pensions now exempt—$500 million
4. Institute a tax on consumer services—$500 million

This totals about $4 billion, of which all but $300 million would go to education funding.

If we do not do this we will be forced to consider funding cuts which none of us want.

EXERCISES AND DISCUSSION QUESTIONS

1. Referring to the "Governor's Speech" and budget:
    a. How would taxpayers in your school district react to the governor's speech?
    b. Is requiring the state to provide over 60 percent of the funding the right decision? Do you agree with the governor's decision to reduce property taxes? What would be the pros and cons of relying more on the state for funding?
    c. Almost all the governor's increase is in general state aid to school districts. Is that fair? Should more money be allocated to categorical aid for special education, free lunch, transportation, and other programs?
    d. How would the budget be viewed from the perspective of a school administrator?
2. From a historical perspective, what do you think has had the most significant impact on public education?

3. Do you agree with the author's definition of equity, equality, and adequacy? Why or why not?
4. Has the federal government gone too far in setting standards for education? From your perspective, what do you think the proper role of the federal government is in funding education? What "strings" do you think should be attached to federal money?
5. What are the current issues such as public pensions, taxation, deficits, and/or the economy impacting school funding in your state and/or district?
6. How will changes in the demographics of children attending public schools in the future affect education financing?

REFERENCES

Alexander, K. (2011, Dec 22). Largest school finance lawsuit in Texas takes shape. Statesman.com: *American-Statesman.* http://www.statesman.com/news/texas-politics/largest-school-finance-lawsuit-in-texas-takes-shape-2049530.html

American Recovery and Reinvestment Act. (2009). www.Recovery.gov.

Baker, B. D. (2012). Revisiting that age-old Question: Does money matter in education? The Albert Shanker Institute. http://www.shankerinstitute.org/images/doesmoneymatter_final.pdf

Bloomberg, D., Dopp T., and Glovin, D. (2011, May 24). New Jersey supreme court orders Christie to restore some school funding cuts. http://www.bloomberg.com/news/2011-05-24/christie-s-fight-to-remove-school-funds-overruled-by-new-jersey-high-court.html

Brimley Jr., V., Verstegen, D., and Garfield, R. (2012). *Financing education in a climate of change.* Boston: Pearson Education.

Brown v. Board of Education, 347 US 483 (1954).

Buse v. Smith, 223 Wis.2d 799 (Wis., 1976).

Chambers, J., Parrish, G., Thomas, B. and Harr, J. (Updated 2004). What are we spending on special education services in the United States, 1999–2000. *Report 1: Special Education Expenditure Project, American Institute for Research.* csef.air.org/publications/seep/national/AdvRpt1.PDF.

CNN Money.com "Illinois: Our very own Greece?" July 14, 2010. http://money.cnn.com/2010/07/13/news/economy/illinois_debt/index.htm?hpt=T2

Cubberley, E. P. (1906). *School funds and their apportionment.* New York: AMS Press.

Data Accountability Center. (2010). *Individuals with Disabilities Act (IDEA) data.* https://www.ideadata.org/arc_toc12.asp#partbCC.

Edgewood v. Kirby, 777 S.W. 2d 391 (Texas, 1989).

Grimes, K. (2010). Pension "pain train" coming. *Cal Watchdog.* July 8. www.calwatchdog.com/2010/07/08/new-pension-"pain-train"-coming/.

Helena Elementary School District No. One v. State of Montana, 236 Mont. 44, 769 P2d. 684. (1989).

Hu, W. (2012). Ten states are given waivers from education law. *New York Times.* February 9. www.nytimes.com/2012/02/10/education/10-states-given-waivers-from-no-child-left-behind-law.html.

Kantrowitz, B. (1993). A nation still at risk. *Newsweek* 121 (16): 46.

Lambert, L. (2010). US state pension funds have $1 trillion gap: Pew. *Reuters.* February 10. www.reuters.com/article/2010/02/18/us-states-pensions-idUSTRE61H13X20100218.

Martin, J., and Ruark, E. (2010, July; revised 2011, February). The fiscal burden of illegal immigration on United States taxpayers. *Federation for American Immigration Reform.* www.fairus.org/site/DocServer/USCostStudy_2010.pdf.

McGinnis v. Shapiro 293 F.Supp 327 (1969).

McNeil, M. (2011). Are 82 percent of schools "failing" under NCLB, as Duncan warned? *Education Week.* August 3.

Milliken v. Bradley, 418 U.S. 717 (1974).

Murphy, J. (2012). Corbett's budget plan would give more money to schools, but most would go to pensions. *Pennlive.com.* February 8. www.pennlive.com/midstate/index.ssf/2012/02/corbetts_budget_plan_would_giv.html.

Naone, E. (2011). Rhode Island lawmakers approve pension overhaul. *Reuters.* November 18. www.reuters.com/article/2011/11/18/us-usa-rhodeisland-pensions-idUSTRE7AH0E020111118.

No Child Left Behind. (2012). www.Ed.gov/esea.us.departmentofeducation.

Oregon Secretary of State (2012). Public Education in Oregon. bluebook.state.or.us/education/educationaintro.htm.

Passel, J., and Cohn, D. (2009). *A Portrait of unauthorized immigrants in the United States.* Washington, DC: Pew Research Center.

Pew Charitable Trusts. (2010). *The trillion dollar gap: Underfunded state retirement systems and the road to reform.* February 18. www.pewcenteronthestates.org/report_detail.aspx?id=56695.

Phyler v. Doe, 457 U.S. 202 (1982).

Pierce v. Society of Sisters, 268 U.S. 510 (1925).

Plessy v. Ferguson, 163 U.S. 537 (1896).

Robinson v. Cahill, 119 N.J. Super 40, 289 A2d. 569 (NJ, 1973).

Rose v. Council for Better Education, 790 S.W.2nd 186, 60 Ed. Law Rep. 1289 (KY, 1989).

San Antonio Independent School District v. Rodriques, 411 U.S. 1 (1973).

Schilling, C. (1989). *An analysis of the impact of Supreme Court decisions on the autonomy of public school districts during the Burger Court 1969–86.* DeKalb: Northern Illinois University Press.

Serrano v. Priest, 5 Cal.3d at 603, 487 P.2d at 1254 (1971).

Slater, C., and Scott, J. (2011). California on the verge of a fourth wave of school finance reform. *American Association of School Administrators (AASA) Journal of Scholarship & Practice* 8 (2): 51–60.

Snell, R. (2009). *State finance in the Great Depression.* National Conference of State Legislatures.. www.ncsl.org/issues-research/budget/state-finance-in-the-great-depression.aspx.

Stuart v. School District No. 1 of Village of Kalamazoo (1874).

Tax Foundation, The. (2005). *Facts and figures on government finance.* 38th ed. *Book of the States*, IV, 113. Washington, DC. www.taxfoundation.org/publications/show/147.html.

Texas State Historical Association. (2012). *The handbook of Texas online.* tshaonline.org.

United States Department of Education. (1983). *A nation at risk: the imperative for educational reform: A report to the Nation and the Secretary of Education.* Washington, DC: National Commission on Excellence in Education.

United States Office of Education. (1967). *Profile of ESEA, the Elementary and Secondary Education Act of 1965, title I, II, III, IV, V* (OE Series, United States. Office of Education, 20088-A). Washington, DC: US Government Printing Office.

Watchdog. (2010). Illinois faces second pension battle. August 5. watchdog.org/6104/illinois-faces-second-pension-battle/.

Wikipedia: The Free Encyclopedia. State income tax. en.wikipedia.org/w/index.php?title=State_income_tax&oldid=473622806.

Winerip, M. (2012). In Race to the Top, the dirty work is left to those on the bottom. *New York Times.* January 22. www.nytimes.com/2012/01/23/education/in-obamas-race-to-the-top-work-and-expense-lie-with-states.html?_r=1&pagewanted=all.

2

Resource Allocation and Financial Planning

OBJECTIVES

At the conclusion of this chapter you will be able to:

1. Understand the keys to good financial planning (ELCC 3.3, ISLLC 3).
2. Understand the purpose of a school district budget (ELCC 3.3 ISLLC 3).
3. Discuss the various approaches to developing a budget and allocating resources (ELCC 3.3, 4.3, ISLLC 3).
4. Identify the primary sources of revenue at the local, state, and federal levels (ELCC 3.3, ISLLC 3).
5. Identify the major distribution methods for general state aid ELCC 3.3, ISLLC 3).
6. Understand the differences between proportional, progressive, and regressive taxes (ELCC 6.1, 3.3, ISLLC 3, 6).

PLANNING SCHOOL-DISTRICT BUDGETS

Most state budgeting systems for public schools are designed based upon the Department of Education's *Handbook II, Revised*. Generally, there are four sources of revenues: local, flow-through, state, and federal. Expenditures are categorized by function as well as object. The use of these categories allow for a program-accounting approach to budgeting. Individual states have modified the accounting system to meet their own objectives and reporting requirements. Variations in account structure also exist between various school districts and states depending on program offerings and organizational size.

Many school administrators are well versed in instructional methodology and organizational theory. However, it is often a constant struggle to effectively manage the budget and finances of the school (Cooper 2011). A budget is a blueprint. It is a means of communicating to the public, parents, and staff what a district values. To some, budgeting may seem too complicated. Others may lack education or simply lack time. The adoption of the school budget is usually completed after a long and arduous process that results in the appropriation of public funds for a school district. Using a standard accounting structure allows school districts and states to gather important data on a systemic basis. This allows for the analysis of district data throughout a state. In-school budgets in most states, along with other financial data, are now available on the web. This makes it even more important that school districts do a good job of estimating their revenues and expenditures each fiscal year.

William Hartman, author of *School District Budgeting* (1999), defines education budgeting as a "working tool" for the successful operation of states and local school districts, and as a "significant opportunity to plan the mission, improve their operations, and achieve their education objectives." As such, the budgeting process provides districts the opportunity to "make better financial and program decisions, improve operations, and enhance relations with citizens and other stakeholders" (National Advisory Council on State and Local Budgeting, 1995, 2). A budget is both an estimate of resources and an outline of a district's education program. Table 2.1 illustrates public elementary- and secondary-school revenues and expenditures by school district size on a national basis.

Fiscal planning is a year-long process. Fiscal responsibility involves all levels of district governance and supervision: school boards, district administration, and school administration. There are basically two levels of compliance: legal and fiscal stewardship. Legal compliance is the adherence to state and federal rules and regulations regarding the procurement and use of resources. Fiscal stewardship is insuring that funds are used in an effective and efficient manner to support student achievement. Toward that end, it means that the organization has developed a vision how funds are to be used and parameters that avoid deficits, program cuts and unethical behavior.

Short-Term and Long-Term Fiscal Plan

Short-term fiscal plans project the district's fiscal from one to three years. Short-term plans may be required by some states to alleviate budget deficits. *Long-term fiscal plans* usually project a district's fiscal position for five years or longer. Remember that accuracy diminishes over time so the longer the projection the less likely it is to be accurate. Compounding one teacher salary at $50,000 with 3 percent increases would result in an impact of $154,545 over the life of a three-year plan. The effect of that same scenario over ten years would be $573,194. Therefore, significant changes in the fiscal health of a school system can be impacted dramatically by both the magnitude of the change and the duration of the plan.

Some states, such as Ohio, require school districts to complete five-year financial projections. In Ohio's case, these projections are posted on the state Board of Education's website (Ohio Department of Education 2012).

Approaches to Financial Planning

There are many approaches an administrator or district can take with regard to developing a school district budget. A typical traditional planning cycle would include developing the budget calendar, guidelines, and assumptions; financial projections; and resource-allocation model. It would include the involvement of key stakeholders such as staff, the board, parents, students, and taxpayers. The purpose of financial planning is to create a template for a school system to follow that ensures not only that the resources are available to fund its vision and goals but also ensures the financial stability of the organization.

The first step for most school districts is to establish a budget calendar that outlines the major due dates in the budget process. Typically, a budget calendar will include meeting dates, legally required deadlines, and allocation timelines. The budget calendar can also include benchmarks for completing instruction, facility, and building-related inputs. A sample budget calendar is shown in Table 2.2.

Once a budget calendar is created, the next step is for the district to develop a set of financial projections that typically span three to five fiscal years. Some states require multiyear projections as either a part of their budget process or based on a "trigger." A "trigger" is normally something that would indicate the district is headed toward financial problems. As such, the state board of

Table 2.1. Public Elementary- and Secondary-School Finances by Enrollment-Size Group: 2008 to 2009

[In millions of dollars (590,948 represents $590,948,000,000). Data are based on the Annual Government Finance Survey. For details, see source.

		School Systems with Enrollments of –						
Item	*All School Systems*	*50,000 or More*	*25,000 to 49,999*	*15,000 to 24,999*	*7,500 to 14,999*	*5,000 to 7,499*	*3,000 to 4,999*	*Under 3,000*
TOTAL								
General revenue	590,948	124,377	73,579	53,837	84,808	52,690	70,586	131,070
From federal sources	55,900	13,217	7,360	5,136	7,815	4,019	5,476	12,977
Through state	51,997	12,473	6,873	4,908	7,172	3,758	5,143	11,671
Child nutrition programs	10,687	2,567	1,576	1,111	1,521	827	1,108	1,979
Direct	3,903	744	387	228	643	261	333	1,307
From state sources[1]	276,154	55,190	36.080	27.980	41,018	23,262	30,977	61,648
General formula assistance	187,040	33,747	25,454	19,677	28,671	16,101	21,031	42,360
Compensatory programs	6,224	1,340	1,045	680	1,034	491	568	1,066
Special education	16,471	3,951	1,705	1,281	2,090	1,381	2,000	4,063
From local sources	258,894	55,970	30,239	20,721	35,976	25,410	34,134	56,445
Taxes	175,902	29,474	21,069	14,744	25,922	18,710	25,027	40,958
Contributions from parent government	45,826	19,519	4,868	2,817	5,073	3,595	4,762	5,192
From other local governments	5,924	501	696	398	626	527	837	2,339
Current charges	14,666	2,474	1,700	1,282	2,129	1,311	1,798	3,972
School lunch	6,968	1,052	815	663	1,107	707	92	1,672
Other	16,575	4,002	1,905	1,480	2,226	1,267	1,710	3,984
General expenditure	604,856	129,807	76,570	55,800	86,336	53,811	70,578	131,953
Current spending	517,708	109,271	64,047	47,150	74,088	46,358	61,489	115,304
By function: Instruction	311,891	68,224	38,283	28,422	44,746	28,170	37,112	66,935
Support services	178,694	35,357	22,315	16,142	25,509	15,933	21,328	42,109
Other current spending	27,124	5,689	3,449	2,586	3,833	2,255	3,050	6,260
By object: Total salaries and wages	310,334	65,516	39,818	29,189	45,011	27,825	36,658	66,317
Total employee benefits	109,188	23,834	12,305	9,838	16,051	10,397	13,138	23,626
Other	98,186	19,921	11,925	8,123	13,026	8,136	11,693	25,362

Capital outlay	68,045	16,147	9,959	6,919	9,543	5,613	6,943	12,921
Interest on debt	17,141	4,090	2,468	1,693	2,476	1,594	1,914	2,904
Payments to other governments	1,963	298	96	38	229	247	231	824
Debt outstanding	399,118	91,379	55,310	40,941	58,440	36,694	46,664	70,140
Long-term	390,652	90,050	54,584	39,896	57,347	35,815	45,563	67,398
Short-term	8,466	1,329	726	595	1,092	879	1,101	2,743
Long-term debt issues	42,396	9,485	5,606	4,121	6,521	3,685	5,132	7,846
Long-term debt retired	28,521	5,919	3,298	2,498	4,260	2,775	3,817	5,955
PER PUPIL								
Fall enrollment (1,000)	48,239	10,055	6,611	4,880	7,272	4,256	5,625	9,541
General revenue	12,250	12,369	11,139	11,033	11,663	12,381	12,548	13,738
From federal sources	1,159	1,314	1,098	1,053	1,075	944	973	1,360
From state sources[1]	5,725	5,489	5,458	5,734	5,641	5,466	5,507	6,462
General formula assistance	3,877	3,356	3,850	4,032	3,943	3,783	3,739	4,440
Special education	341	393	258	263	287	324	355	426
From local sources[1]	5,367	5,566	4,574	4,247	4,947	5,971	6,068	5,916
Taxes	3,646	2,931	3,187	3,022	3,565	4,396	4,449	4,293
Contributions from parent government	950	1,941	736	577	698	845	847	544
Current charges	304	246	257	263	293	308	320	416
School lunch	144	105	123	136	152	166	169	175
General expenditure[1]	12,305	12,650	11,369	11,251	11,671	12,391	12,311	13,571
Current spending	10,499	10,608	9,475	9,479	9,987	10,639	10,696	11,826
By function: Instruction	6,369	6,669	5,698	5,766	6,071	6,487	6,490	6,928
Support services	3,704	3,516	3,376	3,308	3,508	3,744	3,791	4,414
By object:Total salaries and wages	6,433	6,516	6,023	5,982	6,190	6,538	6,517	6,951
Total employee benefits	2,263	2,370	1,861	2,016	2,207	2,443	2,335	2,476
Capital outlay	1,411	1,606	1,506	1,418	1,312	1,319	1,234	1,354
Interest on debt	355	407	373	347	31	375	340	304
Debt outstanding	8,274	9,088	8,367	8,298	8,037	8,622	8,295	7,352
Long-term	8,098	8,956	8,257	8,176	7,886	8,415	8,100	7,064

[1]Includes other sources not shown separately.

Source: US Census Bureau, Public Education Finances, 2009, May 2011, www.census.gov/govs/school.

Table 2.2. Sample Budget Calendar

When	*What*	*Who*
September	Facilities Planning	Staff
	Facilities	Facilities Committee
October	Update Facilities Status & Costs	Board of Education
November	Tentative Tax Levy	Board of Education
	Enrollment Projections	Staff
	Tentative Enrollment Projections	Finance Committee
December	Approve Tax Levy	Board of Education
	Review Building Projects	Facilities Committee
January	Preliminary Financial Projections Student Fee Proposal	Executive Cabinet
February	Preliminary Financial Projections Student Fee Proposal	Finance Committee
	Staffing Preliminary Financial Projections Student Fee Recommendations	Board of Education
	Approve Staffing	Board of Education
	Technology Plan	
	Review Bid Results	Facilities Committee
March	Financial Projections Building Operating Budgets Approve Facilities Bids Approve Capital Outlay Approve Tech Plan	Board of Education
April	Review Tentative Budget	Finance Committee
May	Approve Tentative Budget	Board of Education
June	Hold Public Hearing on Budget Adopt Budget	Board of Education

education may require additional information and/or projections to verify whether or not it needs to intervene. This may also include a requirement to submit some type of budget reduction plan to demonstrate how a district will address any budget shortfalls.

Creating a financial projection also involves generating and agreeing on a set of guidelines or assumptions. These guidelines are usually generated administratively and then presented to the board for approval. Assumptions might include such items as projected salary and benefit increases, enrollment changes, staffing needs, class-size guidelines, significant events affecting the budget, energy cost increases, revenue increases, and so forth. An example of a basic set of guidelines and significant events is illustrated in Table 2.3.

Table 2.3. Guidelines and Significant Events of a Budget

- Enrollment will increase approximately 2 percent per year.
- Economy—investment income is estimated to drop by $300,000.
- Tax Cap Cost of Living Increases—for 2011 is 1.5 percent.
- Tax Cap Cost of Living Increases—for 2012 is 3 percent.
- Property-tax revenue from new construction will drop significantly over the next two years.
- 2010–2011 is the last year for teachers to take advantage of the grandfathering of retirement benefits. This will result in about $750,000 in retirement expenses in 2009–2010. This is $250,000 lower than originally projected.
- Support staff retirement costs will increase 51 percent over the next two years, resulting in about $600,000 in additional expenses per year. This is due to the devaluation of investments in the retirement fund.
- As a result of the state's fiscal crisis there may be a delay or proration of payments at year's end.
- The district will pay the special education cooperative $2,000,000 for renovations and expanded special education cooperative facilities.
- The facilities projects outlined in the 2010 referendum will be completed in 2012–2013.
- The next opportunity to address significant facilities issues will be in 2011.
- New Naval housing units are not projected to be completed in time to have any significant impact until 2014–2015.
- Any funds received from the federal economic stimulus package will be used for one-time expenses so as to not commit the district to future reoccurring costs with no revenue source.

The next step in the financial-planning process is determining how funds and/or staff will be allocated and who is responsible for making that happen. This step is dependent on having reliable enrollment data. Enrollment projections are usually completed in the fall. Once these have been completed, resource allocations including staff can begin. Resource allocation is discussed later in the chapter but the basic approaches are site-based, zero-based, line-item, priority-based, and program-based budgeting. Allocation systems may also include some type of weighting for students with special needs.

Once all the data are collected, the district then develops one more draft of the budget to share with the board. This process may last several weeks, several months, or, as is the case in California, an entire year (California requires multiple amended budgets throughout the fiscal year). After review, public comment and/or hearing, the budget is adopted. States vary on this process. This could be as simple as the board of education approving the budget after some type of opportunity for the public to comment on it, or could be as involved as actually having the community vote and approve it.

Most states have rules that require a budget to be amended if it changes significantly. This traditional approach to financial planning and budget development assumes the final decision point is the actual budget itself not the process. In other words, administrators go through the process not knowing if the budget will be approved in the end or not. This approach of going through numerous revisions always causes consternation by both staff and parents—the "nothing is final until it is final" approach is difficult on all parties. Additionally, this process often encourages micro-management.

One of the keys to successful budget development and financial planning is the trust level between building and district administrators and the board of education. This is often reflected in the type of resource-allocation system a school administrator chooses. For example, in a district with a low degree of trust, the board members may want to review every line item in a budget. In a high-trust district, the board members may be content to simply allocate resources and let the administrators determine how they should be spent.

One alternative to this traditional approach to financial planning and budget development would be to use a *systems approach model* (Schilling 1998). That model would include the following components:

1. Identifying fiscal policy and instructional goals.
2. Developing a decision making calendar.
3. Enrollment/facilities allocation/approval.
4. Revenue projections/guidelines.
5. Site-based resource allocation and approval.
6. Compilation of the budget.
7. First draft/budget summary.
8. Revision and adoption.

The advantages of a *systems approach* are:

1. Fosters order, not control of the system by district administrators.
2. Promotes inclusion, not exclusion.
3. Promotes reliance on teams of professionals.
4. Promotes reliance on partnerships between the school business manager and other professionals.
5. Promotes high standards.

A *systems approach* allows all stakeholders to discuss, review, and make informed decisions in a timely manner based on previously agreed-to criteria. It relies on connecting various components of the planning process in a logical manner. The goal of a *systems approach* is to have thoroughly discussed all of the major components making up the budget before the first draft is even crafted. Consequently, compiling the budget is simply a result of the process, not a means to an end.

The first step in a *systems approach* is to identify the vision, fiscal policy, and other instructional goals the district wishes to achieve.

1. Fiscal Vision
   - Average class size of twenty-three (regular level).
   - Full range of course offerings and electives.
   - Sufficient extracurricular and athletic opportunities.
   - Maintain and expand support services.
   - Maintain and expand superlative signature programs.
2. Fiscal Policy
   - Unrestricted reserves in the operating funds shall be maintained at a level equal to 5 percent of the next year's projected operating budget.
   - The budget shall first provide for staff and operating expenses to meet projected changes in student enrollment and mandated programs.
   - The budget shall reflect the board's desire to maintain the overall tax rate of the district when possible.
   - The budget shall reflect the board's desire to not increase the overall indebtedness of the district.
   - The budget shall reflect the board's desire to maintain safe and operationally sound facilities.
   - The budget shall include a reasonable contingency for variable and unanticipated costs.
   - The administration shall identify and present to the board potential efficiencies.
3. Curriculum Goals
   - Improvements to summer school, including online registration.
   - Improvements to summer athletic programs, including online registration.
   - Implementation of performing-arts report recommendations.
   - Identify of *response to intervention* (RtI) structures and procedures.

4. Instructional Goals
   - Average class size of twenty-three (regular level).
   - Provides a full range of course offerings and electives.
   - Provides sufficient extracurricular and athletic opportunities.
   - Maintains and expands support services.
   - Maintains and expands superlative signature programs.

The *decision-making calendar* provides a road map as to when data are needed to make key decisions. For example, decisions regarding new programs, facilities, and staffing are usually needed far in advance of the development of a budget. Legal constraints on school districts with regards to bidding, collective-bargaining agreements, and personnel decisions will dictate when these need to be addressed. Creating a process that allows for these decisions, is transparent, and fosters collaboration is an important element in financial planning. A *decision-making calendar* simply lays out the process and timeline in which these decisions need to be made. It also forces a district to integrate various instructional and facility decisions in to the financial-planning process. Typically, a decision-making calendar would include the components identified in Textbox 2.1.

By working through all of these components, the assembly of the budget should be a fairly routine task since each area has been reviewed and approved. Of course there will always be mitigating circumstances. Things change due to legislative initiatives, the economy, and other unforeseen events. If, however, each area has been thoughtfully reviewed and contingencies considered, it should not result in an undue hardship to revise or adjust the planning document or budget.

Box 2.1. Components of a Decision-Making Calendar

1. Guidelines
2. Facilities
3. New Programs
4. Personnel Decisions
5. Resource Allocations
6. Legislative/Legal deadlines
7. Site Budgets
8.. Special Items (Technology, Capital Items, and Equipment)

DEVELOPING A SCHOOL DISTRICT BUDGET

Public-school districts, like businesses and other enterprises, have experimented with various forms of budget organization. Line item and function/object budgeting are basic to almost all systems. What varies from district to district and school to school is the methodology used to distribute resources through the budgeting and financial planning process (Cooper and Nisonoff 2002). Priority-based budgeting, programming budgeting systems, zero-based budgeting, site-based budgeting, and outcome-based budgeting are attempts to link the budget to goals and objectives while devolving the budgeting process to the school level.

Line-item budgeting or "traditional" budgeting can be defined as "a technique in which line items, or objects of expenditures—e.g. personnel, supplies, contractual services, and capital outlays—are the focus of analysis, authorization, and control" (Mundt, Olsen, and Steinberg 1982). Line-item budgeting as used by many states to report budget data is too general to provide any meaningful data for use by individual schools or school districts.

For example, there may be a line item that represents all the instructional salary expenditures for the school district. It does not provide the details of how much money is being budgeted at each site nor does it indicate what proportion of the salaries are for teachers, aides, or other instructional staff. A second problem with line-item budgeting is the tendency for administrators to just increase each line item by a set percent or dollar amount as opposed to actually determining how much money is needed for that line item. This results in some line items being overbudgeted and some underbudgeted.

Zero-based budgeting (ZBB) is a budgeting process that requires its participants to build each year's budget without regard for what was spent the previous year (Geiger 2001). The premise of ZBB is that school districts start over each year and justify all expenditures in relationship to the organization's goals and objectives. Using ZBB all expenditure proposals would compete annually for an organization's resources on an equal basis. ZBB's popularity peaked in the 1970s when President Carter vowed to use it to balance the federal budget (Mistler 2011). Its popularity resulted from the belief that it would address the concerns that the typical budget simply resulted in incrementally increasing each line item in the budget.

The challenge of using ZBB in public schools is that many costs are fixed on an annual basis—the majority of a school district's expenses are related to salary and compensation costs to provide required educational services. As Hartman (1999) explains, "ZBB . . . forces comparisons of and choices among programs and activities that are often difficult to compare adequately." For example, you can't just have the primary grades compete against the middle school grades. Consequently, like so many theoretical approaches to budgeting, ZBB is often used as part of an overall strategy. In school districts, the most likely use of ZBB is in discretionary spending for building, departmental, and grade level budgets. This involves *zero line-item budgeting* for purchased services, supplies, and equipment.

One of the difficulties in implementing ZBB is that school administrators are reluctant to recommend a decrease in spending levels, fearful that once their budgets have been reduced they will not recapture those funds when they are needed in the future. An additional criticism of ZBB is that it is paperwork intensive. To be successful, administrators would list and justify the expenditures they are proposing in relationship to the district's goals and objectives. The advantages of ZBB are:

- It provides a logical and comprehensive means for cutting a budget.
- Clearly identifies how expenditures relate to an organization's goals and objectives.
- Encourages creativity in how services are delivered.
- Engages all levels of administrators in the budget process.
- Eliminates automatic incremental budget increases.
- Assists in reallocating resources within and between departments.
- Forces administrators to be involved in budget decisions.
- Encourages all levels of the organization to be efficient.

The disadvantages of ZBB are:

- Amount of work to develop decision packages.
- Reluctance of managers to propose decision packages that are less than current spending.
- Does not have a planning process that is separate from budgeting.
- No structured means for considering different service levels.
- Does not have a separate planning process.
- Efficiency gains are not systematic.

Priority-based budgeting (PBB) is designed to bring about a cultural change in the way an organization does its budgeting process so that it's more effective and efficient, results-oriented, and customer-focused. PBB budgets are predicated on the idea that programs support instructional outcomes and/or school-improvement plans. PBB begins with prioritizing its programs and reviewing the costs of its services. A district no longer concentrates on how much money will be needed to maintain the status quo. Another way of looking at PBB is to ask "what are the core competencies you are supporting" and "in what priority should we support them" (Connolly 1994).

There are four basic questions school and/or district administrators need to ask when implementing PBB:

1. Why are we providing this service?
2. What are we buying for these services?
3. Who are we serving?
4. How much does it cost?

The purpose of prioritizing the budgeting process is to bring the district's spending into alignment with policy priorities. It also eliminates repetition of services, establishes economies of scale, and creates parameters for downsizing state government. The point of priority-based budgeting is not change for the sake of change. The goal of PBB is to assist the district in implementing what the stakeholders expect of their schools.

Site-based (school site) budgeting (SBB) gives authority to principals to allocate funds among various line items in a budget (Brimley and Verstegen 2012). To be effective, SBB must involve all stakeholders in the process. It does little good for the district administration to allocate funds on a SBB basis only to have the principal of a school arbitrarily allocate funds without involving other administrators, teachers, and staff. The key to a successful SBB process is to let staff closest to the instructional setting set priorities and allocate funds.

As noted by Odden, Wohlstetter, and Odden (1995, 5), this requires that "teams of individuals who actually provide the services are given decision-making authority and held accountable for results." It also requires the cooperation of all stakeholders. It will not work in an environment fraught with "silos" where the math department is pitted against the English department

Table 2.4. School Site-Based Budgeting

Principals and their school communities receive funds in the following four categories.

Base School Allocation	*Central Office Support*	*Categorical Funds Title I and other federal, state programs*	*School Site Discretionary Funds*
• Principal • Classroom Teacher	• Administrative/ Human resources support • Nurse pool • Security services • Custodial staff, supplies • Network, multimedia tech pool • Elementary prep time • High-school athletics • JROTC program • Special education support • Visiting teacher allowance	Allowed • Instructional materials • Professional development • Substitute teachers • Hourly time • Supplemental teaching positions • Parent involvement Not Allowed • Clerical and support staff • Copier contracts • Noon duty • Athletic equipment • Medical supplies • Campus security • Building improvements • Custodial supplies	• All other campus staffing • Additional teachers for building level programs for at-risk students • Special programs—School/Library block grant, gifted • Materials and supplies • Hourly supervision, extended day stipends • Smaller class sizes

for funds. With decentralization comes the responsibility to work collegially with all stakeholders.

Allocating resources under a SBB must take place horizontally and vertically within the organization (Guthrie 2007). As can be noted in Table 2.4, not all funds can, or need be, allocated to the school. Some funding must be reserved for necessary support services as well as earmarked as restricted due to grants. To understand this concept, examine Table 2.5 titled "School Discretionary Funding." Based on the school type, there is a special allocation and ratio for discretionary funding depending on the type of school. Commonly, discretionary funding is used to promote signature programs, initiate new programs, provide unique co/extracurricular opportunities, and/or provide staff development.

The advantage of SBB is that it empowers administrators by allowing them to make decisions for the allocation of money to programs and positions that directly impact students. The key is to match needs with resources. To

Table 2.5. School Discretionary Funding

Each school's discretionary funding is based on the ratio, amount per pupil, and the projected number of students for the school year. The base level is $400 per student.

For example, a large high school with a projected enrollment of 3,000 students will have a discretionary allocation of $2,040,000 (1.7 x 3,000). For information on the uses for these funds, see the allocation table.

School Type	*Funding Ratio*	*Total*
Small elementary school fewer than 250 students	1.5	$600
Midsize elementary school level 1, 251–399 students	1.2	$480
Midsize elementary school level 2, 400–750 students	1.0	$400
Large elementary school more than 750 students	1.3	$520
Small middle school fewer than 750 students	2.5	$1,000
Large middle school more than 750 students	2.0	$800
Atypical/alternative	2.5	$1,000
K–8 and small high school	2.5	$1,000
Midsize high school up to 2,200 students	1.3	$520
Large high school more than 2,200 students	1.7	$680

do this, SBB cannot stop at the site level. SBB cannot simply be a means of distributing funds throughout a district without regard for how resources are distributed internally at each site. To be truly effective, resources within a site must be distributed equitably. As one might suspect, SBB can be time intensive. Getting all stakeholders together to determine the distribution of funds within a district and within a site requires not only a significant time commitment but also knowledge of how resources impact student achievement.

Outcome-based budgeting represents the desire to tie to educational outcomes and performance to budget allocations (Kedro 2004). Under No Child Left Behind (NCLB) and other federal initiatives the focus is on student performance. To achieve performance increases, many states have moved toward outcome-based education. Outcome-based budgeting requires that school districts have a clear vision, goals, and objectives. Budget allocations are then aligned with those goals, objectives, and outcomes. Unlike other models, where allocations are generally rule driven, outcome-based allocations would be driven by the achievement of outcomes based on performance. In SBB, initial allocations are often determined simply on the number of students, special need students, or other metrics not related to measurable performance data.

The *market dynamics* approach to educational resource allocation is relatively new and untested in the educational field. Market dynamics simply determine what education is worth on the open market to allocate resources and costs. Public schools operated nationally by *educational management organizations* (EMOs) are growing in numbers. As school boards contract out services to EMOs there will inevitably be a comparison of cost and allocation systems. Assuming that EMOs offer an education that meets state and national standards, it is reasonable to assume that EMOs can be used to predict the true costs of an adequate and equitable education. In other words, if an EMO can educate a child for "x" dollars, then why can't a local school system?

SOURCES OF REVENUE

Most, if not all, funds a school district receives are from one of four sources: local, state, flow-through, and federal revenues. Local revenues include receipts from property taxes, fees, interest income, tuition, food service, and so on. Flow-through revenues are funds that are first dispersed to some intermediary educational agency such as a regional service center before they are dispersed to the local district. State revenues can be divided into general and categorical. General state aid is unrestricted, which simply means that it can be used for any purpose. Categorical aid can usually be divided into two groups.

The first is categorical aid that is a reimbursement for expenses already made such as special education, driver's education, and/or transportation. The second is grants that are restricted for a specific purpose such as early childhood education, bilingual education, and/or gifted education. Sometimes states group a number of grants together into what is referred to as a block grant. Block grants usually provide school districts more flexibility in how the funds are spent. Federal revenues can be divided into restricted and unrestricted grants.

The most common type of federal unrestricted revenue is impact aid. Impact aid is provided to school districts in which the federal government has a significant presence. The most common impact is from US military bases. Since military bases do not pay property taxes, impact aid is provided to partially make up for the shortfall in local revenues. Restricted grants include NCLB, the title programs, special education, and/or the national school-lunch program.

Federal Revenues

There is no mention of education in either the US Constitution or its amendments. To fully understand the funding process of schools, it is best to start from the broadest possible scope. By default, the US Constitution bestows the responsibility for K–12 education on each individual state. States are given the task of deciding how to generate and distribute funds to their schools.

Although the US Constitution bestows primary financial responsibility to the state, this is not to say that the federal government is not completely absent as a funding source. Indeed, the government acknowledges the need for high-quality schools across the nation. Because of this, through the legislative process over the years the federal government has found ways to provide assistance that "supplement[s], not supplant[s]" (USDE 2005) state monies devoted toward education. Two major pieces of legislation that support this claim are the Elementary and Secondary Education Act (ESEA 1965) and NCLB (2001).

These initiatives are examples of the federal government's role in assisting the financing of public schools; however, their contributions remain relatively small in comparison to other funding sources. For comparison sake, in total, the federal government provides approximately 8.5 percent of the monies for public schools (USDE 2005), which leaves the remaining 91 percent of the funds needing to be generated from other sources. Therefore, with the federal government offering to fund only a small portion of education, each individual state must shoulder the responsibility of producing the lion's share of needed funds.

Initially, the primary financial responsibility for funding education rested with the states, with the federal government providing minimal funds to "supplant" programs and directives. Because states could not generate sufficient funds for education legislatively, the burden fell on local governments who primarily relied on property taxes.

State Revenues

States have the primary role of providing public education. Each state's constitution varies in its definition of what a free public education is and the state's role in providing it. All of the litigation with regard to school finance centers on the interpretation of the state's constitutional provisions regarding public education. The fact is that most states have not found a methodology to fairly distribute resources. This may be due in part to a lack of funding, the demands of meeting the needs of disaggregated groups, and/or the lack

Table 2.6. Federal Funds for Education and Related Programs: 2005 to 2010

[In millions of dollars (146,207.0 represents $146,207,000,000), except percent. For fiscal years ending in September. Figures represent on-budget funds]

Level, Agency, and Program	*2005*	*2009*	*2010*
Total all programs	146,207.0	163,070.7	(N/A)
Percent of federal budget outlays	5.9	4.6	(N/A)
Elementary/secondary education programs	68,957.7	88,133.6	115,404.3
Department of Education[2]	37,477.6	52,468.1	76,932.5
Grants for the disadvantaged	14,635.6	15,880.5	22,134.3
School improvement programs	7,918.1	19,600.5	34,267.4
Indian education	121.9	118.2	109.9
Special education	10,940.3	12,768.8	16,450.6
Vocational and adult education	1,967.1	2,034.2	1,944.4
Education reform—Goals 2000	-35.0	(X)	(X)
Department of Agriculture[2]	12,577.3	15,273.4	17,277.4
Child nutrition programs	11,901.9[3]	13,714.9[3]	15,500.9[3]
Agricultural Marketing Service—commodities[3]	399.3	1,237.0	1,354.9
Department of Defense[2]	1,786.3	1,907.7	2,048.9
Overseas dependents schools	1,060.9	1,110.5	1,186.6
Section VI schools[4]	401.2	418.5	435.1
Department of Health and Human Services	8,003.3	9,738.0	8,539.3
Head Start	6,842.3	8,499.1	7,235.2
Social Security student benefits	1,161.0	1,238.9	1,304.1
Department of Homeland Security	0.5	2.6	2.9
Department of the Interior[2]	938.5	782.5	784.5
Mineral Leasing Act and other funds	140.0	78.1	74.5
Indian education	797.5	703.4	709.1
Department of Justice	554.5	821.1	882.1
Inmate programs	554.5	820.0	881.0
Department of Labor	5,654.0	6,073,0	7,811.0
Job Corps	1,521.0	1,612.0	1,850.0
Department of Veterans Affairs	1,815.0	919.1	967.2
Vocational rehab for disabled veterans	1,815.0	919.1	967.2
Other agencies and programs	153.2	148.1	158.5

NA = Not available.

X = Not applicable.

[1]Estimated except US Department of Education, which are actual budget reports.

[2]Includes other programs and agencies, not shown separately.

[3]Purchased under Section 32 of the Act of August 1935 for use in child nutrition programs.

[4]Program provides for the education of dependents of federal employees residing on federal property where free public education is unavailable in the nearby community.

of consolidation of school district. Brimley et al. (2012) found that thirty-four states provide additional funding for at-risk students, thirty-seven states provide funding for English Language Learners, and forty-nine states provide additional funding for special education students.

There are two broad categories of state revenue: general state aid and categorical aid. General state aid is calculated based on school-district enrollment, average daily membership, or average daily attendance. States may also weight certain student populations. States that use weighting do so to provide additional funding to special populations such as special education, English Language Learners, or at-risk, or to recognize the additional cost of certain grade levels such as high school.

According to Hightower, Mitani, and Swanson (2010, p. 3), "Five major approaches to state educational funding exist: foundation formulas; equalization methods; local-effort equalization formulas; flat grant funding; and full state funding and states may implement these fiscal mechanisms individually or in combination." They found that twenty-eight states have foundation programs, twenty-two flat grant, twenty-two local-effort equalization, five equalization, and five full state funding in 2008–2009. Furthermore, they identified thirty-one states that had an inadequate funding formula or the funding levels were insufficient.

Flat-grant funding was the most common form of state funding at the start of the twentieth century (Cubberley 1906). Initially, flat grants were distributed without regard to enrollment or other variables such as a community's wealth. Each school system simply received an amount of money to spend for the education of school-age children in their community. Eventually, flat grants were distributed based on student enrollment, average daily attendance, or a census of school-age children.

Flat-grant funding is inherently unfair in that is does not account for differences in the wealth of communities, the various needs of students, or regional cost differences. Philosophically, flat-grant funding was based on the idea that the state should provide an equal amount of funding for every child and that any educational opportunities beyond that minimum should be the responsibility of the local community. The flat grant formula is: *State Aid per Pupil = Total State Revenue/Number of Pupils in the State.* If a public-school district had one thousand students and the flat-grant formula provided for $4,000 per pupil, then the district would receive $4 million in state aid.

Foundation formulas were the next logical evolution from flat-grant funding. The last state to rely on flat-grant funding was Connecticut, which switched to an equalization plan in 1975. One of the problems with flat-grant funding that foundation formulas attempted to address was that states just didn't have enough money to provide an adequate allocation per student. States have generally relied on sales and income taxes to generate funds as opposed to statewide property taxes. Many states did away with their statewide property taxes in the 1930s and replaced them with sales and income taxes as a response to taxpayer revolts (Snell 2009). To determine the amount of money a district will receive under a foundation plan requires a three-step process. That process is as follows:

1. *Total State Guarantee to School District = number of pupils x the guaranteed foundation level of the state plan (constant per pupil)*
2. *Total Local Share provided by the School District = Required (or computational) tax rate x the district's equalized assessed valuation*
3. *State aid entitlement = total state guarantee – local share*

Assuming that the school district had one thousand pupils, the foundation level was $6,000, the required tax rate was $0.015, and the total equalized assessed valuation (EAV) of the district was $250,000,000, the determination of the district's state aid entitlement would like the following:

- 1,000 pupils x $6,000 (foundation level) = $6,000,000 (state guarantee)
- $0.015 (required tax rate) x $250,000,000 (EAV) = $3,750,000 (local share)
- $6,000,000 (state guarantee) – $3,750,000 (local share) = $2,250,000 (state aid entitlement)

Equalization methods is a catch-all for methods that take into account the taxation effort, wealth, and need of local school districts. Two forms are percentage equalizing and power equalizing. Equal access to education and local control are the two basic tenets of percentage equalization. The state provides revenue to each school district based on a ratio of the district's wealth to the average wealth of districts in the state. The resulting factor is applied to the district's budget (Guthrie 2007). *Power equalization* adds the dynamic that school districts can choose the level of program for their communities. The more effort a district makes, the more revenue they receive from the state. The less effort a district makes, the less state revenue. The formula for a district power equalization is:

State Aid Entitlement - local tax rate x guaranteed yield - (local EAV x local tax rate)

Obviously, this formula is more complicated than either the flat grant or foundation formulas. There is no required local effort.

Local Revenues

Local-effort equalization formulas are based on a sharing of costs between the local school district and state. Under these types of formulas, states match the amount of revenue that a school is able to raise through local effort (taxation). Generally, there is a minimum level of expenditures guaranteed for districts that are unable to generate that amount.

A small number of states provide full funding. Those states, such as Hawaii, provide 100 percent of the cost of education. Under full funding, a state determines the total level expenditures for a given district and funds that amount. Wealth is not a factor in determining the amount of money a district receives (Guthrie 2007).

To fund general and categorical state aid, states use a multitude of revenue sources. The two largest sources of state revenue are sales and income taxes. All states except Alaska, Delaware, Montana, New Hampshire, and Oregon collect sales taxes (Federation of Tax Administrators 2012). Delaware collects a *gross receipts tax* (GRT) on businesses (State of Delaware Department of Finance 2012). Some states allow local governments such as cities and counties to add to the sales tax. Exemptions to sales taxes depend on the individual state. Most states exempt prescription drugs, some food and clothing, and some states exempt professional services.

Only seven states do not have a personal income tax (Federation of Tax Administrators 2012). State income taxes fall into two categories: proportional taxes where everyone pays the same percentage regardless of income, or progressive taxes where taxpayers pay a higher percentage as their income increases. Many states with a flat tax attempt to minimize the impact on low-income taxpayers by providing additional exemptions, child credits, and so forth. The problem with states relying on either sales or income taxes is that they are susceptible to swings in the economy. In periods of high unemployment or economic downturns individuals and businesses tend to spend less and make less. That means there are fewer dollars available for the state to allocate for services including education. When that happens, states prorate disbursements or eliminate subsidies based on the revenue available.

States have also come to rely on other sources of revenue, such as lotteries, to fund schools. Lottery revenues have been used in some states to augment education revenues while in other states they have been used to replace revenues earmarked for education. Typically when lottery revenue is used to replace revenues, the additional revenue is shifted to pay social service costs in the state such as healthcare, Medicare, and so on. Other sources of revenue for funding education in the states include liquor taxes, cigarette taxes, oil and mineral taxes and fees, and corporate taxes.

Local Sources

The most important thing to remember about the local role in school finance is that boards of education have no inherent power. They only have those powers provided for and authorized by state government. This is an important fact. When we look at sources of revenue we most often define them in terms of local, state, and federal. The truth is that local and state revenues have been operationally defined by each state. Some states provide for a local property tax but control its distribution. Some states tap into wealthy school district revenues and redistribute them to poorer districts.

In general, local boards of education make decisions regarding tax levies, budgets, salaries, and other services. They approve and set budgets and are charged with creating a vision for their school districts. The reliance of many school districts on property taxes is well documented. The mantra of "local control" of public schools has been ingrained in the United States since its inception (Meyer 2010). It is extremely difficult to imagine a national or state-run school system such as in Hawaii in most of the other states. Consequently, there will always be differences in resource allocation not only between school districts but also between schools in the same district. The concept of intradistrict parity is becoming a bigger issue as the educational community focuses on student standards and outcomes.

The effect of the state shortfalls in funding in recent years has also resulted in school districts seeking additional sources of revenues. These sources, where permitted by state law, have included increased student fees, "pay-to-play" fees for extracurricular activities, outsourcing services, selling the naming rights to facilities, local foundations, school/business partnerships, cooperative, and others (Hoff 2007).

School districts that have not been able to raise revenue have been forced to increase class sizes and reduce programs to balance their budgets. What is and is not permissible to meet the challenges of funding education at the local level is primarily a result of state and federal law. While education is a state function, the reliance of many districts on federal funding dictates they adhere to federal guidelines even when it is not financially to their benefit.

Property taxes are the single biggest source of revenue for many school systems (Meyer 1995). Up until 2008, property values were a very stable source of revenue for most school districts since property values rose year after year. Even though property values have declined since 2008 due to the economic downturn driven by the housing crises, property taxes are still a stable source of revenue when compared to the alternative sources (Fleck 2010). Sales and income taxes are much more sensitive to economic factors than home values (Von Drehle et al. 2010).

There are four variables that affect property-tax revenues. They are the market value of the property and resulting assessment, the tax rate extended, exemptions provided the property owner, and any legal constraints on the district's ability to levy taxes (Sexton 2003). The market value of a property is a fairly simple concept. Assessors use both sales and comparable property values within a given geographical area, such as a neighborhood, to determine the market value of a property. For sales of property the transaction must be between an independent buyer and purchaser. In other words, sales of property between relatives at a discounted price would not be considered for the purposes of establishing fair market value.

For businesses and agricultural property, the process is more difficult. Factors such as profitability, the value of the property based on its best use, and its replacement value minus depreciation are often used in determining the value of these types of property. Once the market value of a property has been established then an assessment rate can be applied. For example, if all property within a state were to be assessed at 33 percent, then a home with a market value of $100,000 would have an assessed valuation of $33,333. Due to variations in assessment practices within a state, a board of equalization may adjust the assessments of property through the use of an equalization multiplier. For example, what if the actual value of our $100,000 home was determined to be $110,000 by the board of equalization?

In order to be fairly assessed, the assessed valuation should be $36,300, not $33,333. In order to correct the underassessment, a factor, or multiplier, of 1.089 would have to be applied to the original assessed valuation of $33,333. The *equalized assessed valuation* (EAV) is then defined as the assessed value ($33,333) times the multiplier (1.089), which equals $36,300.

Tax rates are represented in several ways. They can be expressed as a rate per $100 of EAV or in terms of mills. A mill is one-tenth of one cent. So a mill rate of fifteen is equivalent to 1.5 cents per dollar of EAV. A rate of $1.50 per $100 of EAV is 1.5 percent. The taxing authority for school districts is a function of the state in which they reside. Some states allow school districts to tax for all aspects of school operations while some restrict the levy of taxes to certain purposes. Most have limitations on the maximum tax rate a district can levy.

Exemptions can have a major impact on a school district depending on the community. The most common form of property-tax exemption is the homestead exemption. Homestead exemptions are provided to property taxpayers who live in their own home. Other common types of exemptions are for veterans, seniors, the disabled, long-term homeowners, and nonprofit organizations (Sexton 2003).

As a result of the rapid increases in home values in the 70s and 80s, many states passed legislation to limit the increases in property taxes from one year to the next. The educational community generally refers to these legislative initiatives as "tax caps." Tax caps generally limit the total property taxes extended for school purposes. These limits may be adjusted annually such as through the use of a cost of living adjustment. A cap on the tax rate also may limit them. In Illinois, the Property Tax Extension Limitation Law limits tax extensions to the lessor of the All Urban Consumer Price Index or 5 percent. In 2012, New York implemented a 2 percent cap on tax increases. In order to go over the 2 percent cap, the school districts would need a 60 percent "super majority" of residents voting on the budget. Another key component of the New York law is if voters reject budget approval twice, then the district can't increase taxes at all (Empire Center 2011).

Student fees have been litigated in many states around the notion of what constitutes a "free public education." While there is recognition that low-income or indigent students should not be required to pay fees, nonetheless they are an important revenue stream for many school districts. Student fees include assessments for textbooks, supplies, physical-education uniforms, technology, workbooks, and so forth. In some states these fees have expanded to include "pay for play" fees for students participating in athletics. When faced with the alternative of eliminating a sports team or activity, many schools first consider implementing a fee, if possible, to offset the cost.

As moneys run short, more and more school districts are looking for other sources of funding. The most common alternatives are advertising, fundraising, and the establishment of educational foundations. School districts are, in some cases, selling the naming rights to athletic fields and facilities and/or seeking sponsorships for various activities. Obviously, this is not without debate. The ethical considerations of advertising are a hotly debated topic in some districts.

The involvement of parent/teacher organizations in raising and donating money for programs is also fraught with its own set of problems. A key consideration by some school districts is the equity issues that arise when a school in an economically wealthy area can raise $200,000 to maintain programs and activities while a school in an economically disadvantaged area can only raise $20,000. Another problem with fundraising is its sustainability. Can a school system expect communities to continually come up with donations to maintain programs when they are also paying taxes and supporting the schools through various other means?

In order to preclude these problems, school boards and administrators need to establish guidelines and policies in advance of such fundraising activities. Lastly, a school system may consider the establishment of an educational foundation. Educational foundations are an independent, nonprofit entity that can accept contributions and donations. The boards of foundations can then donate and/or fund various activities in the school district. Foundations can mitigate the economic differences of individual schools by accepting all donations on behalf of the school district and distributing funds fairly between all sites.

In the past, interest income was a significant source of revenue of school districts. Unfortunately, over the past five-to-ten years interest rates have dropped and interest income has plummeted. Other sources of local revenue might include tuition charges to other districts for providing services such as special or vocational education, facility-rental income, donations, and personal property taxes.

TAXPAYER EQUITY

Regardless of the type of tax, property, sales or income, taxpayer equity is an important concept. Taxes can be classified as either proportional, progressive, or regressive. A comparison of these three concepts is shown in Table 2.7.

One of the problems with all of these forms of taxation is what to do with low-income earners. One can argue that all taxes are regressive for low-income earners since they have to spend a larger percentage of their income for basic necessities such as housing, food, healthcare, and transportation. That is why most sales and income taxes have exemptions for prescriptions and food. Of course taxpayer equity must also be put in perspective with the other major stakeholders in an educational system such as students and staff.

Taxpayers are becoming increasingly sensitive to not only the cost of educating students but also the compensation and benefit levels of staff. The burden of funding education has become a significant political issue with regards to teacher pensions. Additionally, with the rising cost of social services such as healthcare, the competition for tax dollars has become a significant issue in many states.

Table 2.7. Comparison of Three Tax Concepts

	Proportional Tax	
Income	*Amount Paid*	*Rate (%)*
$10,000	$500.00	5
$50,000	$2,500.00	5
	Progressive Tax	
Income	*Amount Paid*	*Rate (%)*
$10,000	$250.00	2.5
$50,000	$2,500.00	5
	Regressive Tax	
Income	*Amount Paid*	*Rate (%)*
$10,000	$500.00	5
$50,000	$2,000.00	4.5

Furthermore, many taxpayers as well as districts are looking to parents to assume a greater burden through increases in school fees. This prompts the debate as to what is a "free public education." As US citizens grow older as a result of the "baby boomers" reaching retirement age, the competition of funding will become even more intense.

SUMMARY

A budget is a blueprint that estimates the sources of revenues and expenditures for a school system. A budget should reflect the priorities of the community and address the needs of students. Developing a budget starts with good fiscal planning. Knowing the demographics of the student body is imperative in determining staff needs. Care should be given to include all stakeholders in the process—students, staff, parents, and taxpayers. Funds should be allocated to reflect the goals, objectives, and outcomes desired by the school district.

There are a myriad of approaches to developing a budget from a traditional district-office-centered approach to site-based management, with administrators and staff having significant autonomy. Few, if any school systems, use just one form of budget-allocation system. If in fact more schools are operated by EMOs, the market may dictate how funds are allocated and used in the future.

The two largest sources of revenue for most public-school districts are local and state revenues. The primary source of revenue on the local level is property taxes. The primary source of revenue on the state level is general and categorical aid. Due to shortfalls in state funding and limitations on property-tax revenue, many districts have sought out other forms of revenue. These include fundraising, increasing student fees, and private/public and/or public/public partnerships.

What does the future hold? With the movement toward using student outcomes as an accountability measure, there will be a natural movement toward tracking costs by site level, disaggregated group, and/or even by student. State reporting systems may need to be modified to account for the demand for increased fiscal accountability. At some point, all stakeholders are going to want to know if the inputs (money) result in acceptable outputs (performance). In order for that to happen, new data systems will need to be developed which tie performance to resources.

CASE STUDY 1

"Letter to the Community"

Dear Parents and Community Members,

Last school year we laid the foundation to enhance equity in funding decisions by piloting a system called *student-based budgeting* (SBB) at four schools. SBB allocates dollars directly to schools based on the number of students enrolled and the specific needs of those students. Certain student needs, such as grade levels or at risk learners, will be given a predetermined weight that translates to real dollar amounts. This formula is gaining favor in school districts across the country.

After listening to principals in the pilot group and working through their concerns, we are rolling out SBB this year system-wise. Our district, like many school systems, has traditionally given dollars to schools based on factors such as the number of students and staffing ratios. That formula did little to address students' and schools' diverse needs. It's a simple fact that not every school is the same. This means that now you and your child's school can have greater confidence that money is following students. What this means is that we are literally putting dollars behind our stated goals to empower school leaders.

To address your questions and concerns, your child's principal will contact you in the coming weeks to explain how you can be engaged and involved throughout this process. Our schools are committed to making transparent budget decisions that work in the best interests of all children. We hope that you will be participant in this process.

Best regards,

John D. Superintendent

CASE STUDY 2

"Fundraising Gone Awry?"

Middlebury school system is a K–12 school system with three elementary-school buildings, one middle school, and one high school. In the fall of 2010 the district determined that it would not be able to afford to continue its technology program due to budgetary shortfalls in the upcoming year. Dr. Smith, the principal of West Elementary School, immediately began to lobby his parent–teacher organization to help fund the technology program at his school.

Nearly two years later, West Elementary has a "smart board" and projector in every classroom. The other two elementary-school principals also attempted to solicit the help of their parent–teacher organizations but were unsuccessful due to the impoverished areas in which the schools reside. Parents from the other two elementary schools attended a school board meeting where they indicated their concerns that West Elementary students were being given an unfair advantage going into middle school through their exposure to state-of-the-art technology. Furthermore, they asked the board to adopt a district policy that would create a more equitable environment with regard to individual school fundraising and donations.

EXERCISES AND DISCUSSION QUESTIONS

1. Explain how the current system of federal, state, and local financing of education impacts your school system. Attention should be paid to local, state, and federal sources of revenue. How does the current system promote or inhibit the vision and goals of the district?
2. Does your district have a budget policy? If so, what does it say? If not, what do you believe should be in it?
3. Interview a building administrator (assistant principal or principal) or district-level business administrator. How is the budget developed? Who is involved and what roles do they play?
4. If you were in charge of selecting an approach to developing your school system's budget, which one would you select and why?
5. Read Case Study 1. What questions do you think parents and staff would have after reading the letter in the case study? Do you think that the reaction to the letter would be different for parents of low-income, gifted, or regular-track students?
6. What would a decision-making calendar look like in your district?
7. What are the legal requirements for adopting a budget in your state?
8. Investigate how another state other than your own finances education. What are the similarities and differences? Is there anything that the state you investigated does that could apply to how your state finances education?
9. What types of taxes are used to fund education is your state? Would these taxes be categorized as proportional, progressive, and/or regressive?

10. Read Case Study 2. Do you think that parents of the other elementary schools have a valid case? What steps do you think the school board should take with regard to the parents' request?

REFERENCES

Brimley, V., Garfield, R., and Verstegen, D. (2012). *Financing education in a climate of change.* 11th ed. Boston: Pearson Education.

Connolly, T. (1994). An integrated activity-based approach to budgeting. *Management Accounting: Magazine for Chartered Management Accountants* 72 (3): 32.

Cooper, B., and Nisonoff, P. (2012). *Public school budgeting, accounting, and auditing.* May 15. www.encyclopedia.com/doc/1G2-3403200507.html.

Cooper, K. (2011). Budgeting based on results. *Education Digest* 76 (9): 4–8.

Cubberley, E. (1906). *School funds and their apportionment.* New York: AMS Press.

Empire Center for New York State Policy. (2011). *New York State's property tax cap: A citizen's guide.* November 30. www.empirecenter.org/Special-Reports/2011/11/proptaxcapguide113011.cfm.

Federation of Tax Administrators. (2012). *State comparisons.* www.taxadmin.org/fta/rate/tax_stru.html.

Fleck, C. (2010). Property tax revolt. *AARP Bulletin* 51 (5): 18–20.

Ford, A. (2012). The state of state taxes. *Time* 179 (15): 21.

Geiger, P. (2001). Zero-based budgeting: Reducing costs . . . Improving performance. *School Business Affairs* 67 (11): 54–56.

Guthrie, J., Springer, M., Rolle, R., and Houck, E. (2007). *Modern education finance and policy.* Boston: Pearson/Allyn & Bacon.

Guthrie, J., Hart, C., Ray, J., and Hack, W. (2008). *Modern school business administration: A planning approach.* Boston: Pearson/Allyn & Bacon.

Hartman, W. (1999). *School district budgeting.* Reston, VA: Association of School Business Officials international.

Hightower, A., Mitani, H., and Swanson, C. (2010). *State policies that pay: A survey of school finance policies and outcomes.* Bethesda, MD: Editorial Projects in Education.

Hoff, D. (2007). Should our students pay to play extracurricular activities? *Education Digest* 72 (6): 27.

Kedro, M. (2004). *Aligning resources for student outcomes: School-based steps to success*. Lanham, MD: Rowman & Littlefield.

Meyer, H. (2010). Local control as a mechanism of colonization of public education in the United States. *Educational Philosophy & Theory* 42 (8): 830–845. Doi:10.1111/j.169-5812.2008.00432.x.

Meyer, N. (1995). *The real property tax and K–12 education*. Oak Brook, IL: Farm Foundation.

Mistler, S. (2011). Political pulse: LePage channels Jimmy Carter with zero-based budgeting. *Sun Journal*. August 29. www.sunjournal.com/columns-analysis/story/1079035.

Mundt, B. Olsen, R., and Steinberg, H. (1982). *Managing public resources*. New York: Peat Marwick International.

National Advisory Council on State and Local Budgeting. (1995). *A framework for improved state and local budgeting and recommended budgeting practices*. Chicago: Government Finance Officers Association.

Odden, A., Wohlstetter, P., and Odden, E. (1995). Key issues in site-based management. *School Business Affairs* 61 (5): 2–11.

Ohio Department of Education. (2012). *Ohio schools: Five-year forecasts*. fyf.oecn.k12.oh.us.

Schilling, C. (1998). *Overview of forecasting the budget cycle: A systems approach to financial planning*. Mt. Vernon: IASBO Workshop.

Sexton, T. (2003). The property tax base in the United States: Exemptions, incentives, and relief. *Assessment Journal* 10 (4): 5–33.

Snell, R. (2009). *State finance in the Great Depression*. www.ncsl.org/issues-research/budget/state-finance-in-the-great-depression.aspx.

State of Delaware Department of Finance: Division of Revenue. (2012). *Gross receipts taxes*. revenue.delaware.gov/services/Business_Tax/Step4.shtml.

Von Drehle, D., Hylton, H., Rochman, B., Maag, C., Ball, K., Dias, E., and Steinmetz, K. (2012). The other financial crisis. *Time* 175 (25): 22–29.

3

Accounting, Budgeting, and Reporting

OBJECTIVES

At the conclusion of this chapter you will be able to:

1. Understand the concept of fund accounting (ELCC 3.3, ISLLC 3).
2. Understand the basic accounting structure for budgeting revenues and expenditures (ELCC 3.3, ISLLC 3).
3. Describe the mechanics of budgeting and the importance of encumbrance accounting (ELCC 3.3, 4.3, ISLLC 3, 4).
4. Understand the purpose, use, and accountability of student activity funds (ELCC 3.3, 4.3, ISLLC 3, 4).
5. Recognize the use and accountability issues associated with fundraising activities in schools (ELCC 3.3, 4.3, ISLLC 3, 4).
6. Identify the key concepts that make for a good internal control system (ELCC 3.2, 3.3, ISLLC 3).
7. Recognize the importance of audits and financial statements (ELCC 3.1, 3.2, 3.3, 4.2, 6.2, ISLLC 3, 4, 6).

WHY DO WE HAVE ACCOUNTING SYSTEMS?

The *fund accounting systems* utilized by each state vary according to rules and regulations adopted by individual legislatures and state boards of education. The primary responsibility for implementing fund accounting guidelines usually rests with the state's board of education. In addition, the US

Department of Education has its own chart of accounts that it prescribes for use for federal categorical grants (Allison, Honegger, and Johnson 2009). To ensure public input and review, each state provides rules and regulations for adopting its annual budget. The adoption process usually includes provisions for public input by the way of a public hearing or means. States also regulate the mechanics of the budget-adoption process. Does the budget have to be balanced? If so, what is the definition of a balanced budget?

The budget-adoption process can also serve as a review of the district's financial status (Fisbein 2008). In addition to the budget, some districts may be required to submit some type of budget-reduction plan (i.e., a multiyear plan showing how they intend to meet state guidelines regarding fund balances, deficits, etc.) (IL School Code 105 ILCAS 5/17-1). Most states now require the budget to be transmitted to the state board of education electronically. This allows taxpayers, citizens, and unions instant access not only to current but also past budget information.

Guthrie et al. (2008 pp. 225-226) state that school accounting systems are used to describe "(1) the nature, sources, and amounts of an institution's revenues; (2) the allocation of revenues within the institution to various programs (or funds and accounts); and (3) the actual expenditures in these programs." Accounting systems are also utilized by public schools to:

- Protect public funds from the possibility of loss due to carelessness, expenditure for the wrong purpose, theft, embezzlement, or the malfeasant actions of school officers.
- Provide a systematic way to relate expenditures to the attainment of educational objectives through the operation of a budget and related reports and processes.
- Provide an objective method of appraising the performance of school personnel in obtaining the school's objectives.
- Meet the legal requirements of the state and other governmental units for reporting basic information for comparisons, reports, and reviews, and provide community with information about the fiscal and academic activities and needs of the district.

While there are similarities between business and governmental accounting systems, there are a number of significant differences. Private enterprises are incorporated to make a profit for their owners or stockholders. Governmental entities are not organized to make a profit but to provide critical services to the public. Because governmental entities are not primarily focused on making a profit, the accounting emphasis is on reporting revenues, expenditures, and other uses of funds on operating statements. From a legal perspective, governmental entities are often more regulated than small businesses. Last, but not least, governmental entities use fund accounting (Tidwell 1974).

The *Governmental Accounting Standards Board* (GASB) provides standards for the accounting of funds in school districts and other governmental entities. Local educational agencies must adhere to *generally accepted accounting principles* (GAAP). GASB indicates that school budgets must be reported on a uniform basis (Gauthier 2012). This ensures that the reporting of financial information is comparable from district to district.

Furthermore, in 2001, GASB issued a statement that all reports should include data that compares actual financial results with a legally adopted budget, evaluates the fiscal condition of a school or school district, is compliant with applicable laws, rules, and regulations, and provides insight into assessing the efficiency and effectiveness of the entity's education program and budget (Governmental Accounting Standards Board 2001).

Governmental accounting systems are organized and operated on a fund basis. A fund is a fiscal and accounting entity with a self-balancing set of accounts recording cash and other financial resources, together with all related liabilities and residual equities or balances, and changes therein, which are segregated for the purpose of carrying on specific activities or attaining certain objectives in accordance with special regulations, restrictions, or limitations (Everett, Johnson, and Madden 2012). Often revenue sources are restricted to specific funds such as property taxes, state and federal grants, and locally generated fees. Each fund has its own set of financial statements that include assets, liabilities, fund balance, revenues, and expenditures. Assets can be categorized as either current or fixed.

Current assets are cash or anything that can be converted to cash whereas fixed assets are items such as land, buildings, and equipment. *Liabilities* can be categorized as either current or long-term. A *current liability* is a debt that the district expects to pay for in a short period of time. A *long-term liability* is a debt the district expects to pay for generally over a year or more such as bond issues or warrants. *Fund balance*, or *equity*, is simply the difference between assets or simply the sum of liabilities and fund balance.

(A) Assets = Things you own (cash, investments)

(L) Liabilities = Things you owe (taxes, purchases not paid for)

(R) Revenues = Funds received

(E) Expenditures = Funds paid

Fund balance = A + R – L – E

Examples of *asset accounts* are cash in bank, investments, loans due, and accounts receivable. Examples of liability accounts are accounts payable, payroll payable, loans payable, and contracts payable. Asset and liability accounts are categorized as balance sheet accounts (Everett, Johnson, and Madden 2012).

Basis of Accounting

School districts generally use one of two basis of accounting—*cash basis* or *modified accrual. Cash basis* transactions are recorded based upon actual receipt or disbursement of cash. A district's financial health is often measured on the basis of the size of the district's cash balance. This is sometimes referred to as the reserves a district has on hand. One of the major problems with cash basis accounting is that it fails to disclose the extent to which a district owes money (liabilities) or the degree to which funds are due to the district (receivables).

GAAP utilizes the *modified accrual* basis of accounting. In a *modified accrual* basis of accounting, revenues are recorded when they are known and measurable (receivable) and expenditures when they are due and payable. GAAP is considered a better method of accounting and is recommended by GAFR. The Association of School Business Officials recommends the use of GAAP and has modeled its financial reporting award—the Certificate in Financial Accounting—after it (Heinfeld 2003).

Encumbrance Accounting

Most school districts use some sort of encumbrance accounting. *Encumbrances* are not expenditures and/or disbursements. Encumbrances involve setting aside funds now for the future payment of goods, services or contracts (Guthrie et al. 2008). The most typical form of encumbrance accounting in schools involves the issuance of purchase orders. When a purchase order is issued it adjusts the account budget by the amount of money committed for that purpose (ordered but not paid for). When the order is complete and ready to be paid the amount of the encumbrance is removed and the corresponding amount is expensed against the account the purchase was issued against.

In a *cash basis* system, encumbrances are cancelled at the end of the fiscal year. They are reissued, if necessary, for the next fiscal year. In an accrual basis system, encumbrances are rolled over to the next fiscal year. *Encumbrance accounting* is an important aspect of school district budgeting. It keeps staff from overspending an account by being able to monitor the unencumbered balances. For example, an account for supplies may have a budget of $10,000. The total expenses charged against the account total $3,000, leaving a balance of $7,000. The administrator in charge of the account, however, has approved purchase orders in the amount of $5,000. The unencumbered balance for the account would be $2,000–$10,000 (budget) minus $3,000 (expenses) minus $5,000 (purchases).

Revenues

Local property taxes are usually collected by a local governmental agency that transfers the rightful share to the school district or treasurer. In some states, the school district acts as the collection agency for local property taxes. Tax warrants, state allocations, and other funds are deposited by the state or treasurer into the bank designated by the school board. Funds are either used to cover expenditures or invested to a future date for this purpose.

Expenditures

Expenditures are appropriated through the budget-adoption process. The budget acts as the legal authorization to spend funds on purchases, salaries, benefits, and so forth. Typically authorization comes from the budget and minutes of school board meetings. Board policy dictates what expenditures require preapproval and what expenses can be paid with full accountability to the board—all subject to the adopted budget. All original documentation for payments must be kept for audit purposes.

The Mechanics of School Budgeting

The first step in the accounting cycle for any school district is to have a legally approved budget. Budgets are an estimate of revenues and expenditures for each fund. They are done on a fiscal-year basis that in many cases differs from the calendar year. They include a projection of beginning and ending fund balances as well as information regarding borrowing. Many states require additional information be provided as part of the budget. This may include specific information relative to administrative costs, operating loans, budget-reduction plans for struggling districts, and/or contractual obligations.

Some states such as California require that the budget be revised and submitted several times during the fiscal year to reflect up-to-date information (California Department of Education 2011). Indiana requires that information be reported to the state on a semi-annual basis (State Board of Accounts 2010).

Chart of Accounts

A *chart of accounts* is used in each state to track revenues, expenditures, liabilities, assets, and fund balances. Each state has its own rules and structure for its chart of accounts. A chart of accounts is composed of three types of accounts:

- Revenue accounts that are used to record revenues and receipts
- Expenditure accounts that are used to record the disbursement of funds
- Balance sheet accounts that are used to record assets and liabilities

Fund codes are used to delineate and segregate revenues, expenditures, assets, and liabilities at the highest level. A fund is a fiscal and accounting entity with a self-balancing set of accounts recording cash and other financial resources, together with all related liabilities and residual equities or balances, and changes therein, which are segregated for the purpose of carrying on specific activities or attaining certain objectives in accordance with special regulations, restrictions, or limitations. There are three categories of fund types: *governmental fund types*, *proprietary fund types*, and *fiduciary fund types*. Textbox 3.1 shows the funds recommended by the National Center for Education Statistics (2009).

Box 3.1. Governmental Fund Types

General Fund	To account for all financial resources except those required to be accounted for in other funds. *Example: Education Fund, Operations & Maintenance Fund*
Special Revenue Funds	To account for the proceeds of restricted revenue sources other than expendable trusts or major capital projects where the disbursements are legally restricted for specific purposes. *Example: Transportation Fund, State Pension Funds*
Capital Project Funds	To account for the financial resources used to acquire or construct major capital facilities (not including those financed by proprietary and Trust funds). *Example: Capital Project Fund, Site and Construction Fund*
Debt Services Funds	To account for financial resources for the payment of principal and interests on long-term debt. *Example: Debt Service Fund, Bond Fund*
Permanent Funds	These funds account for resources that are legally restricted to the extent that only earnings, and not principal, may be used for purposes that support the school district's programs.
Proprietary Fund Types	
Enterprise Funds	These funds account for any activity for which a fee is charged to external users for goods or services. *Example: Food service program, the bookstore operation, the athletic stadium, or the community swimming pool*
Internal Service Funds	These funds account for any activity within the school district that provides goods or services to other funds, school district departments, component units, or other governments on a cost-reimbursement basis. *Example: Central warehousing and purchasing, central data-processing and central printing and duplicating*
Fiduciary Fund Types	
Trust Funds	These funds account for assets held by a school district in trustee capacity. *Example: Pension Trust Funds, Investment Trust Funds, Private-Purpose Trust Funds*
Agency Funds	These funds account for funds that are held in a custodial capacity by a school district for individuals, private organizations, or other governments. *Example: Student Activity Fund*

Source: Financial and Accounting for Local and State School Systems: 2009 Edition (NCES 2009-325). National Center for Education Statistics, Institute of Education Sciences, U.S. Department of Education. Washington, DC.

GASB indicates that the number of funds should be kept to the bare minimum necessary to meet the legal and operational needs of the entity. Too many funds result in inflexibility and complex financial administration. Education is a state function; the funds used by schools and school districts must be compliant with the state's chart of accounts.

The education fund would be used to record all instructional and related services. The operations and maintenance fund would be used to record all transactions related to maintaining, cleaning, and operating school facilities. The debt service fund would be used to account for debt issued by the district. The transportation fund would be used to record transactions for transporting students to/from school as well as field trips and extra/cocurricular activities. The retirement fund would be used to record transactions related to employee pension contributions to the state plan. The capital improvement fund would be used to record transactions relative to the improvements, additions, and new school facilities.

The second major category in a chart of accounts is function. A *function* describes the purpose of the transaction. A *revenue function* is a means of recording local, flow-through, state, and federal receipts and revenues. Textbox 3.2 shows an example some of the common revenue functions.

Referring to the chart in Textbox 3.2, along with Textbox 3.1, a state grant for driver's education would be recorded in account 100.3200. Similarly, property-tax revenues for the transportation fund would be recorded in 400.1100. An expenditure function is a means of recording expenses and/or disbursements for instruction, support services, community services, facilities, and debt service. Textbox 3.3 shows an example of some common expenditure functions.

Expense accounts are further broken down by object. An object provides a means of recording the specific nature of the expense and/or disbursement. Object codes are often fairly recognizable to the general public and are therefore used in many districts to explain how funds are expended. Textbox 3.4 shows an example of some general expenditure objects.

A disbursement for classroom teachers' salaries would be recorded in account 100.1000.100 (education fund, regular instruction, salaries). Similarly, a disbursement to pay the bus company for pupil-transportation services would be recorded in 400.2700.300 (transportation fund, transportation services, purchased services).

Box 3.2. Example of Revenue Function Codes

Code	*Description*	*Example*
1000	Revenue from Local Sources	
1100	Tax Levies	Property taxes
1300	Tuition	Summer school tuition
1400	Transportation Fees	Fees paid by parents
1500	Investment Income	Interest on investments
1600	Food Services	Lunch fees
1700	District Activities	Athletic admissions
1800	Revenue from Community Service Activities	Community swim program
1900	Other Revenue from Local Sources	
1910	Rentals	Rental of facilities
1940	Textbook Sales & Rentals	Sale of textbooks
2000	Revenues from Intermediate Sources	Grants from an Intermediate educational agency
3000	Revenues from State Sources	
3100	Unrestricted Grants-in-Aid	General State Aid
3200	Restricted Grants-in-Aid	Driver's Education
4000	Revenues from Federal Sources	
4100	Unrestricted Grants-in-Aid Directly from Federal Government	
5000	Other Financing Sources	
6000	Other Revenue Items	

Source: Financial and Accounting for Local and State School Systems: 2009 Edition (NCES 2009-325). National Center for Education Statistics, Institute of Education Sciences, U.S. Department of Education. Washington, DC.

In its simplest form, *revenue accounts* are composed of a fund and function that indicates the sources—local, intermediate, state, or federal. *Expenditure accounts* are composed of a fund, function, and object that delineates the purpose of the disbursement or expense—instruction, general administration, support services, and so on. The purpose of having a chart of accounts is to provide for standardized reporting and data analysis for all districts within a state.

The sample accounts shown in this chapter for funds, functions, and objects are for illustrative purposes only. A state's chart of accounts is often more detailed and may include other accounting elements such as fiscal year, organization, site or building, program, and/or department. Table 3.1 is a

Box 3.3. Example of Expenditure Function Codes

Code	Description	Example
1000	Instruction	Instruction delivered in/out of classroom
2000	Supporting Services	
2120	Guidance Services	
2320	Executive Administration	
2700	Pupil Transportation	
3000	Operation of Non-instructional Services	
3100	Food Service	
3200	Bookstore	
4000	Facilities & Acquisition	
4300	Architect Fees	
4500	Building Acquisition & Construction	
5000	Debt Service	Payment of principal & interest on bonds

Source: Financial and Accounting for Local and State School Systems: 2009 Edition (NCES 2009-325). National Center for Education Statistics, Institute of Education Sciences, U.S. Department of Education. Washington, DC.

Box 3.4. Example of General Expenditure Codes

Code	Description	Example
100	Salaries	Teacher Salaries
200	Employee Benefits	Health Insurance
300	Purchased Professional & Technical Services	Attorney, Consultant
400	Purchased Property Services	Utility Services
500	Other Purchased Services	Bus Services
600	Supplies	Classroom Supplies
700	Property	Building Renovations
800	Debt Service & Miscellaneous	Bond Payments
900	Other Items	Fund Transfers

Source: Financial and Accounting for Local and State School Systems: 2009 Edition (NCES 2009-325). National Center for Education Statistics, Institute of Education Sciences, U.S. Department of Education. Washington, DC.

Table 3.1. Example of a School-District Budget Summary

RECEIPTS/REVENUES			
Source of Funds	*Amount ($)*	*% of Total*	*Statewide (%)*
State	67,395,703.00	37.87	22.35
Local	75,471,359.00	42.41	65.21
Federal	35,080,969.00	19.71	12.44
Total	177,948,031.00		

EXPENDITURES/DISBURSEMENTS		
Category	*Amount*	*% of Total*
Instruction	89,086,893.00	49.32
General Administration	4,458,518.00	2.47
Support Services	71,429,334.00	39.54
Others	15,664,513.00	8.67
Total	180,639,258.00	
Difference (Revenue – Expense)	–2,691,227.00	

budget summary for a school district. Note the source of funds and categories for expenditures and disbursements. These would be the same for all districts within that state.

While a simple chart of accounts may be acceptable for reporting to the state, it is seldom sufficient for school district budgeting needs. Regardless of whether the state requires it, most districts break down their revenue and expense accounts to more accurately budget and account for specific sources of revenue or expenses as well as to provide a framework for site based budgeting, etc. An example of an *accounting code structure* is shown below:

Fund	Site	Function	Object	Department	Fiscal Year	Program
100	01	1100	100	15	13	3305

In this example the fund would be the education fund, the site would be a specific school, the function is regular instruction programs, the department English, the fiscal year 2013, and the program ESL.

School or *site-level budgets* require that there are sufficient elements in the accounting structure to distinguish between sites, departments, and programs. These budgets may be decentralized based on administrator responsibilities. Depending on the individual school district, budgets may be developed along department, division, grade level, program, and/or a school basis. High-school budgets tend to be organized around departments while elementary budgets tend to be organized around the grade levels (Sorenson, Goldsmith, and Milton 2006).

STUDENT ACTIVITY ACCOUNTS

Student activity funds are both a source of additional revenue for cocurricular and extracurricular programs and an area that is susceptible to misuse and fraud. Although many administrators may consider student activity accounts their own, they nonetheless fall under the auspices and jurisdiction of the school board. Student-generated funds usually involve large amounts of cash. Combined with the fact that activity fund sponsors usually have little financial training, they are particularly vulnerable to problems (Mutter and Parker 2004). Following are just a few examples of what can happen when things go wrong.

- A respected principal has been charged with theft and fraud on allegations he took nearly $90,000 from a high-school student activity fund. The Great White school account held funds from student fundraising, as well as parents' payments for field trips, school uniforms, and student planners, among other things.
- The Pacific School District says "tens of thousands of dollars" were stolen by four of its employees in the form of lunch money accounts, activity and library fees, among others.
- Suspended teacher John Doe has requested a jury trial on charges he stole $2,104 from student activity accounts at Seal Middle School.
- A middle-school employee was charged in federal court on Tuesday with stealing money from student fundraisers, submitting bogus timesheets, and filing false tax returns.

By definition, student activity funds are those that are managed by clubs, organizations, and associations that are either cocurricular or extracurricular. A cocurricular activity is one that is an extension of work begun in a class for which the student received academic credit. Examples of cocurricular activities would include debate, band, student newspaper, and Spanish club. Athletics would be an example of an extracurricular activity. Student activity accounts can also include convenience accounts, which are used for the convenience of faculty, staff, parent organizations, or similar nonstudent groups.

Examples of convenience accounts would include a scholarship fund, faculty coffee fund, flower fund, and faculty–parent organization.

The school board should approve all student activity accounts. As part of their oversight, school boards should set policies for student participation and adult supervision, approve the collection of monies, establish a system of accounting, appoint a treasurer, authorize the closure of accounts, authorize the investment of idle funds, distribute earnings, and designate depositories. Since student activity funds are easily liquidated, adequate controls should be established to prevent fraud and waste, promote the adherence to stated policies, and ensure conformity with application laws (Brimley, Verstegan, and Garfield 2012).

The most common sources of revenue for student activity funds include ticket sales, fundraising, concessions, publications, advertising, school stores, interest, gifts, and transfers of funds from inactive accounts. It is not uncommon for revenues from some sources to be thought of as student activity accounts. They would include lunch programs, athletic programs, towel and locker fees, student insurance, sales of district supplies, and restricted grants from state/federal sources.

Activity funds are especially susceptible to control problems (Thiel 2008). Those problems are usually a result of: incomplete documentation, failure to keep records, sponsors not turning money in daily, sponsors not reconciling fundraising activities, paying bills from statements instead of invoices, not bonding employees, or not keeping funds safe (Cuzzetto 1999). Student activity funds cannot be used for any purpose that represents an accommodation, loan, or credit to a board member or other employee. Postdated checks should not be accepted and the fund should not be used to cash checks for anyone.

Board members and employees may not make purchases through student activity funds to take personal advantage of purchasing privileges such as tax exemption. Furthermore, student activity funds should not be used for either the deposit of regular district funds or for paying regular district expenses. In other words, checks should not be written against district accounts and deposited into the activity fund to spend or to insure they are "carried over" to the next fiscal year. Another common mistake is the payment of employee compensation via student activity fund checks. All employee compensation should be processed through payroll.

FUNDRAISING

Fundraising is any activity permitted under the school board's policy to raise money or other resources that is approved by the school principal, supported by the school board or a school fundraising organization operating in the name of the school and for which the school provides the administrative processes for collection. Such activities may take place on or off school property. Fundraising policies should outline the compliance requirements related to fundraising activities and provide examples of acceptable and unacceptable activities (Mutter and Parker 2004). The development of a distinct board-wide fundraising policy will ensure consistency and transparency in the collection and distribution of funds and should reflect the following principles:

- Complementary to Student Education
  - The purposes for which funds are collected should be consistent with the school board's mission and values.
  - Activities should support student achievement and not detract from the learning environment.
  - Funds raised for school purposes are used to complement regular educational activities.
- Voluntary
  - Participation in fundraising activities is strictly voluntary for staff and students. Parental consent should be required for student participation for students under the age of eighteen.
  - Privacy should be respected. The personal information of staff, students, or other individuals should not be shared for the purposes of fundraising without prior consent.
- Safety
  - The safety of students must be a primary consideration in all fundraising activities.
  - In addition to parental consent, student fundraising activities require supervision and should be age-appropriate.
- Accountable and Transparent
  - Fundraising activities should be developed and organized with advice and assistance from the school community, including students, staff, parents, parent involvement committees, school councils, and community organizations.

- Board of Trustees (School Board) should have a separate and distinct policy for fundraising, which addresses the use of fundraising proceeds and accounting for school-generated funds. This policy should be available on the school board's website.
- A fundraising activity must not result in any staff or volunteer benefiting materially or financially from the activity.
- Fundraising should have a designated purpose and the proceeds should be for that purpose, as intended. Transparent financial reporting practices to the school community should be in place.

Additionally, school boards need to consider the extent and number of fundraising activities at each school each fiscal year. The concept of equity must be considered with regard to fundraising. Schools located within a wealthy area of a district may be able to generate more funds than schools located in poorer neighborhoods. This may result in some schools having programs, equipment, and technology that other schools cannot afford.

Care should also be given to any proposed capital project for which fundraising is the main source of revenue. School districts need to consider whether they are willing to assume the future maintenance and repairs. Lastly, school districts need to ensure the stewardship of monies generated through fundraising. This includes, but is not limited to, the responsibilities of sponsors, compliance with board policies, collection and disbursement procedures, and reporting requirements.

Internal Controls

Internal controls are procedures that ensure the integrity of the accounting system. Internal controls can be divided into two categories: *administrative controls* and *accounting controls* (Illinois State Board of Education 1993). Administrative controls assure that the proper authorizations are obtained prior to the issuance of purchase orders, hiring of personnel, and disbursement of funds. They also serve as authorization for the recording of accounting transactions. Regardless of the authorization process utilized by the school district, the ultimate approving authority for all disbursements is the board of education. Accounting controls are designed to protect the assets of the district and ensure the integrity of the financial statements issued by the district.

In order to protect the district against fraud and embezzlement, there should be adequate staffing to ensure that there is a segregation of duties with regard to the approval and issuance process. Segregation of duties simply means more than one employee should be involved in the accounting process. Proper segregation involves three key concepts: custody (who receives or disburses checks or receipts), authorization (who approves the receipt or disbursement), and transaction recording (who enters it into the accounting system) (Cuzzetto 1993).

This is often more difficult to achieve in a small district with limited personnel resources than in larger districts. Consider the issuance of a check to a local vendor. A single employee should not approve a purchase order, approve the invoice, issue the check, mail it to the vendor, and reconcile the accounting transaction. In this example there is no segregation of duties or internal control of the process. The process clearly is susceptible to misuse. Likewise, there should be the same due diligence with regard to the hiring of personnel. At least two levels of authorization, including the board of education, should be required. The payroll department should not set up an employee's contract and pay the contract.

FINANCIAL STATEMENTS

Financial statements in the private sector are basically composed of income statements, balance sheets, statements of cash flow, and statements of owner's equity or retained earnings statement. Obviously, in the private sector shareholders, investors, and lenders use financial statements. As such, they are closely monitored by rating agencies, analysts, and the public. School-district financial statements are rarely monitored with the same scrutiny as private business but that is changing in the aftermath of the 2008 economic recession. School districts are basically monitored by an elected board whose members seldom have in-depth financial in-fund or governmental accounting. Compounding the problem is the fact that school districts aren't supposed to be "for profit" organizations.

First and foremost, timely *monthly financial statements* provide an internal control with regard to the receipt of funds and disbursement of funds. In order to have accurate financials districts must have timely reconciliation of all accounts. Falling behind on reconciling and reporting can be a very serious deficiency in the eyes of an auditor. Financial statements provide internal stakeholders such as the board of education, administration, and staff with information about the organization's financial position. They provide external stakeholders such as the public with information about the organization's financial position (Mead 2001).

Interim financial statements are usually required in most states. There are several types of statements that should be utilized to accurately report a district's financial activity (Chase and Triggs 2001). They are:

- Statement of position
- Budget reports
- Cash flow and investment activity

A *statement of position* should include both a combined balance sheet of all fund types and account groups, and a combined statement of revenues, expenditures, and changes in fund equity. For districts that report on a modified accrual basis of accounting, statements should be categorized by governmental fund type such as general, special revenue, debt service, and capital project (see Table 3.2) (Siegel et al. 2010).

A monthly schedule of revenues and expenditures provides a district with information as to how it is doing against its legally adopted budget. Under GASBE this would include a summary by fund type and account groups. Information that should be included:

- Original budget
- Amended (adjusted) budget (reflects budget journal entries)
- Current year's expenditures/revenues
- Unexpended balance
- Encumbrances
- Unencumbered balances

Budget reports should provide a "meaningful" picture of a district's financial position. It is not necessary to list every account in the working budget. Revenues should be broken down into major sources—property taxes, fees, state aid, and so on. Expenditures should be broken down by function (see Table 3.3). Reports that show totals by object (salaries, benefits, etc.) are also helpful (Everett, Johnson, and Madden 2012).

Table 3.2. Sample Statement of Position – Governmental Funds

	General	*Special Revenue*	*Debt Service*	*Capital Projects*	*Total Governmental Funds*
ASSETS					
Cash and investments	33,000,000	–	9,000,000	26,000,000	68,000,000
Restricted cash and investments	–	–	1,000,000	–	1,000,000
Property taxes receivable–net of allowance for uncollectible of $3,000,000	1,200,000	1,500,000	300,000	200,000	3,200,000
Other receivables					
Local	500,000	200,000	–	100,000	800,000
State	700,000	1,400,000	–	–	2,100,000
Federal	800,000	500	–	–	800,500
Prepaid items	1,000,000	–	–	–	1,000,000
Inventories	500,000	–	–	–	500,000
Total Assets	$37,700,000	$3,100,500	$10,300,000	$26,300,000	$77,400,500
LIABILITIES					
Book overdraft of cash account	–	500,000	–	–	500,000
Accounts payable	600,000	5,000	–	3,000,000	3,605,000
Salaries payable	1,200,000	–	–	–	1,200,000
Deferred revenues	1,500,000	900,000	400,000	50,000	2,850,000
Total Liabilities	$3,300,000	$1,405,000	$400,000	$,050,000	$,155,000
FUND BALANCES					
Nonspendable					
Prepaid items	1,000,000	–	–	–	1,000,000
Inventory	700,000	–	–	–	700,000
Restricted					
Federal grants	800,000	–	–	–	800,000
Teacher salaries and benefits	–	1,695,500	–	–	1,695,000
Debt service	–	–	9,900,000	–	9,900,000
Capital improvement	–	–	–	17,250,000	17,250,000
Assigned					
Other capital projects	–	–	–	6,000,000	6,000,000
Student activities	3,500,000	–	–	–	3,500,000
Unassigned	28,400,000	–	–	–	28,400,000
Total Fund Balances	$34,400,000	$1,695,500	$9,900,000	$23,250,000	$69,245,500
Total Liabilities and Fund Balances	$37,700,000	$3,100,500	$10,300,000	$26,300,000	$7,400,500

Table 3.3. Sample Budget Report

	Budgeted Amounts			
	Original	*Final*	*Actual*	*Variance from Final Budget*
Revenues				
Local	63,000,000	64,000,000	65,100,000	1,100,000
County	1,800,000	1,800,000	950,000	(850,000)
State	5,500,000	4,800,000	4,400,000	(400,000)
Federal	4,200,000	3,300,000	4,200,000	900,000
Interest	600,000	300,000	325,000	25,000
Other–student activities	3,500,000	3,500,000	3,250,000	(250,000)
Other–cost reimbursements	2,800,000	4,000,000	2,750,000	(1,250,000)
Total Revenues	$81,400,000	$81,700,000	$80,975,000	$(725,000)
Expenditures				
Current				
Instruction	6,000,000	6,500,000	8,400,000	(1,900,000)
Student activities	4,100,000	4,150,000	3,800,000	350,000
Attendance	400,000	500,000	425,000	75,000
Guidance	700,000	650,000	675,000	(25,000)
Health services	2,100,000	2,100,000	2,150,000	(50,000)
Improvement of instruction	2,600,000	2,500,000	2,450,000	50,000
Professional development	—	10,000	6,000	4,000
Media services	900,000	925,000	775,000	150,000
Board of education services	500,000	550,000	500,000	50,000
Executive administration	1,500,000	1,500,000	1,475,000	25,000
Building level administration	9,100,000	10,000,000	9,200,000	800,000
Operation of plant	24,000,000	23,200,000	23,025,000	175,000
Pupil transportation	8,200,000	8,500,000	8,800,000	(300,000)
Food services	6,100,000	6,100,000	6,250,000	(150,000)
Business and central services	10,000,000	11,100,000	10,900,000	200,000
Security services	1,300,000	1,200,000	1,100,000	100,000
Adult basic education	800,000	900,000	950,000	(50,000)
Adult continuing education	1,000,000	900,000	875,000	25,000
Community services	1,800,000	1,900,000	1,975,000	(75,000)
Debt Service				
Principal retirement	200,000	400,000	525,000	(125,000)
Interest	10,000	20,000	14,000	6,000
Other	—	—	75,000	(75,000)
Total Expenditures	$81,310,000	$83,605,000	$84,345,000	740,000
Excess of revenues over (under) expenditures	90,000	(1,905,000)	(3,370,000)	(1,465,000)
Other financing uses				
Transfers		(5,000,000)	(5,000,000)	—
NET CHANGE IN FUND BALANCE	$90,000	$(6,905,000)	$(8,370,000)	$(1,465,000)
Fund balance at July 1, 20xx	$40,000,000	$40,000,000	$40,000,000	
Fund balance at June 30, 20xx	$40,090,000	$33,095,000	$31,630,000	

Cash flow and *investment activity* reports provide a school district with a snapshot of future resources. *Cash flow reports* indicate:

- Whether or not a district will have sufficient cash-on-hand to meet ordinary and extraordinary expenditures.
- Provides a mechanism by which the district can plan future investments.

Investment activity reports provide assurance that funds that are not needed are being invested in a timely fashion. They show not only the types of investments but indicate the rates of return. There are a number of techniques that can be applied to financial statements to analyze or convey a district's financial status. Those include:

- Management discussion and analysis
- Notes to financial statements
- Variance analysis

Financial statements should be presented with a management discussion and analysis. This is no more than an interpretation of the statements by the district for the public. This would include a discussion of:

- Significant changes in financial position
- Assessment of revenue and expenditure trends against previous years or projections
- Significant events that will affect future statements (maybe the state will be postponing state aid two months, etc.)
- Analysis of significant variations in expenditures and/or financial statements should be presented with notes.

Financial statements should be presented with notes. A note is a general disclosure and/or clarification of a district's fiscal policy, management, or an interpretation of the information. Auditors routinely examine variances in expenditures and revenues. They do this to account for differences and shortfalls. This technique can be used to assist nonfinancial personnel (such as board members) in understanding financial statements through one of two ways.

- By looking for and reporting reasons for variances between what is budgeted and actual, and
- By looking for and reporting reasons for variances over time—that is why there is a 10 percent decrease in property taxes this year versus last, and so on.

Since a budget is no more than an estimate it is not unreasonable to think there will be some sort of variance between actual and budget on every account. The "trick" is to pick a level of variance that is meaningful—say 10 percent or 15 percent. One of the most difficult tasks is conveying information to the public in an easily understandable format. This is also true of analyzing trends. Revenue and expenditure cycles in school districts are not neat—they don't follow a pattern where you can divide everything into twelve monthly segments and test how you're doing month by month. Monthly budgeting for a school district would be almost impossible. One technique a school district can use is to analyze trends in revenue and expenditures. Keeping historical information by month would allow a district to see how it's doing against this year's budget compared with other years. Variances may assist in identifying potential problems, shortfalls, or windfalls.

AUDITS

The auditor's primary responsibility is to render an opinion on the fairness of the financial statements in accordance with GAAP. The auditors work for the board of education. The board may request the auditors to submit the audit report directly to the board without the review of district business personnel. The auditors are expected to report to the board as to their findings. Management letters issued by the auditors are addressed to the board of education. District business personnel will be required to respond to the management letter and should propose methods of addressing the auditors' concerns. Auditors issue the following types of reports:

- Independent auditor's report
- Notes to financial statements are required to explain the numerical presentation of data
- Independent auditors' report on internal control structure based on an audit of financial statements performed in accordance with government auditing standards

- Independent auditor's report on compliance based on an audit of financial statements performed in accordance with government auditing standards
- Management letter (if applicable)
- Annual federal financial compliance report-single audit act
- Annual state financial report (varies by state)
- Other

As part of their responsibilities, auditors issue an opinion. Those opinions can possibly include:

- *Unqualified (Clean)*—Most common; Auditor is satisfied that the financial statements are fairly presented in conformity with GAAP. An immaterial departure from GAAP does not preclude an unqualified opinion. Cash basis is not GAAP. GAAP requires a separate paragraph notation in the opinion but does not preclude an unqualified opinion.
- *Qualified*—Auditor reports that the financial statements are fairly presented *except for* some material item(s) (i.e., auditor was unable to test fixed assets).
- *Adverse*—Auditor gives an opinion that the financial statements are not fairly presented in conformity with GAAP.
- *Disclaimer*—Auditor is unable to provide an opinion (i.e., no accounting records to be tested).

Receipt of Audit Report

Once the audit report is received, it should be:

1. Reviewed by the business manager and accounting director for accuracy.
2. Tied out to district financial reports.
3. Sent to the audit committee for review, if applicable. If the district does not have an audit committee, then there may be some other type of review process prior to the board discussing and approving it.

Prior to final approval by the board of education, any changes should be submitted to and discussed with auditors.

SUMMARY

Accounting, budgeting, and reporting are all key components of safeguarding public funds. A legally prepared budget becomes the authorization for the encumbering and disbursing of funds. School districts should use GAAP accounting. The two most common accounting methodologies in schools are cash and modified accrual. The modified accrual basis of accounting is preferred because it best discloses all factors affecting the district—liabilities, receivable, and so on.

School districts use fund accounting. Unlike businesses, which are concerned with the results of operations to make profits, schools are more concerned with accounting for revenues and expenditures and services they provide. A chart of accounts provides the account structure for recording revenues, expenditures, liabilities, assets, and fund equity. Charts of account are state-specific, although the National Center for Education Statistics has published a suggested account structure.

School districts should be cognizant of the inherent problems that student activity funds and fundraising activities pose. Both these activities should be governed by board policy and adequate control procedures. Administrators should be careful to ensure that the funds are being appropriately used for the benefit of students. Activity funds must not be used for normal school-district activities.

Internal controls are important in ensuring that receipts and expenditures are properly authorized and recorded. To that end, it is important that districts segregate the approval and accounting functions as much as possible to prevent fraud and other problems (Locigno 2008). Financial statements should be issued on an interim and annual basis. Financial statements not only serve as an internal control but also provide information regarding the district to various stakeholder groups such as taxpayers, bond holders, and state agencies. Audits are a means to check that internal controls have been followed, accounting entries have been recorded appropriately, and that the financial statements issued by the entity accurately reflect its position.

CASE STUDY

"Chart of Accounts for a New School Building"

Justin School District is located in the suburbs adjoining a large urban district. For the past five years the district has been seeing significant increases in its enrollment. After much debate, the district's board of education has decided to open a new elementary school. The superintendent has appointed you as the new principal for the soon-to-be Sycamore Elementary School. Your first job is to develop an expenditure budget for the school and submit it to the superintendent and Board for approval. You have determined that you have the following expenses:

Classroom Teachers	
Teachers (K)	50,000
Teachers (1–2)	100,000
Teachers (3–4)	100,000
Teachers (5–6)	100,000
Substitutes	4,200
Aides (K–6)	67,500
Supplies	5,000
Textbooks	38,000
Overhead Projectors	12,500
Computers	10,000
Special-Education Teachers	
Teachers	250,000
Substitutes	3,600
Aides	89,500
Supplies	1,200
Textbooks	2,250
Athletics	
Coaches	9,500
Supplies	2,800

Bilingual Education	
Teachers	50,000
Aides	22,500
Supplies	100
Textbooks	250
Security	22,500
Improvement of Instruction	
Substitutes	100
Media Center	
Teachers	60,000
Substitutes	600
Secretary	35,000
Aides	22,500
Copier Rental	25,000
Books	24,500
Computers	1,000
Building Administration	
Principal	90,000
Assistant principal	75,000
Secretary	35,000
Copier rental	5,000
Fax machine	400
Supplies	100
Custodians	25,000
Buses for field trips	250

Box 3.5. Case Study Chart of Accounts

Fund	*Description*
100	Education Fund
200	Operations and Maintenance Fund
400	Transportation Fund

Function	*Description*
1100	Instruction
2210	Improvement of Instruction
2220	Library/Media Services
2230	Instruction-Related Technology
2410	Office of the Principal
2710	Operation of Buildings
2660	Security
2700	Student Transportation

Object	*Description*
111	Administrators
131	Teacher Salaries
132	Extra Compensation Paid to Teachers
139	Substitute Teachers
151	Instructional Aide Salaries
161	Custodians
181	Clerical Staff
443	Rental of Equipment
510	Student Transportation Services
610	General Supplies
640	Books/Textbooks
730	Equipment

Program	*Description*
110	Instruction K–6
120	Special Education
150	Athletics
221	Improvement of Instruction
222	Media Services
223	Instructional Technology
241	Principal's Office
261	Building Cleaning
266	Security
272	Field Trips

Using Textbox 3.5, develop a budget for your new school.

EXERCISES AND DISCUSSION QUESTIONS

1. Obtain a copy of your school district's budget. Does your district use cash or modified accrual accounting? What are the major components of the

budget—that is, fund, function, object, and so on? Does the legally adopted budget differ from the budget that is used internally by the school district?
2. Obtain a copy of your district's audit. From a taxpayer's perspective, how easy is it to understand?
3. Interview the staff member responsible for finances in your school district. What are the biggest challenges in putting together the annual budget for the school and/or school district?
4. Interview a building principal. What is the role of fundraising in generating revenue for the school? What are the pros and cons to fundraising from his/her perspective? What has been the most difficult issue he/she has to address with regard to fundraising?
5. Determine the internal controls put in place for your school district relative to activity funds. Assess whether they are sufficient to safeguard school funds.
6. Using the case study, prepare a budget for a new school.

REFERENCES

Allison, G., Honegger, S., and Johnson, F. (2009). *Financial accounting for local and state school systems: 2009 edition* (NCES 2009-35). Washington, DC: National Center for Education Statistics, Institute of Education Sciences, US Department of Education.

Brimley, V., Verstegen, D., and Garfield, R. (2012). *Financing education in a climate of change.* 11th ed. Boston: Pearson Education.

California Department of Education. (2011). *California school accounting manual.* Retrieved from www.cde.ca.gov/fg/ac/sa/documents/csam2011complete.pdf.

Chase, B., and Triggs, L. (2001). How to Implement GASB 34. *Journal of Accountancy* 192 (5): 71.

Cuzzetto, C. (1993). *Internal auditing for school districts.* Reston, VA: Association of School Business Officials.

——. (1999). *Student activity funds.* New York: Rowman & Littlefield and Association of School Business Officials International.

Everett, R., Johnson, D., and Madden, B. (2012). *Financial and managerial accounting for school administrators: Tools for school.* Lanham, MD: Rowman & Littlefield Education.

Fisbein, J. (2008). *Preparing high quality budget documents for school districts.* Chicago: Government Finance Officers Association.

Gauthier, S. (2012). *Governmental accounting, auditing, and financial reporting* (GAAFR). Chicago: Government Finance Officers Association.

Governmental Accounting Standards Board. (2001). *Codification of governmental accounting and financial reporting standards.* Norwalk, CT: Financial Accounting Standards Board.

Guthrie, J., Hart, C., Ray, J., Candoli, C., and Hack, W. (2008). *Modern school business administration: A planning approach.* Boston: Pearson Allyn and Bacon.

Heinfeld, G., and Association of School Business Officials International. (2003). *Financial reporting under GASB statement no. 34 and ASBO international certificate of excellence in financial reporting*. Lanham, MD: Scarecrow Education.

Illinois School Code (105 ILCS5/17-1).

Illinois State Board of Education (ISBE). (1996–2009). *Illinois progam accounting manual.* Springfield, IL.: The Board.

Locigno, M. (2008). New auditing standards help district guard against fraud. *School Business Affairs* (November): 34–36.

Mead, D., and Financial Accounting Federation. (2001). *The quick guide to school district financial statements*. Norwalk, CT: Governmental Accounting Standards Board.

Mutter, D., and Parker, P. (2004). *School money matters: A handbook for principals.* Alexandria, VA: Association for Supervision and Curriculum Development (ASCD).

National Center for Education Statistics. (2009). *Financial accounting for local and state school systems: 2009 Edition* (NCES 2009-325). Washington, DC: Institute of Education Sciences, US Department of Education.

Siegel, J., Levine, M., Qureshi, A., and Shim, J. (2010). *GAAP 2011: Handbook of policies and procedures.* Chicago: CCH Inc.

Sorenson, R., and Goldsmith, L. (2006). *The principal's guide to school budgeting.* Thousand Oaks, CA: Corwin Press.

State Board of Accounts. (2010). *Accounting and uniform compliance guidelines manual for Indiana public school corporations.* www.in.gov/sboa/2405.htm.

Thiel, W. (2008). Managing student activity funds: Basic guidelines. *School Business Affairs* (May): 28–31.

Tidwell, S. (1974). *Financial and managerial accounting for elementary and secondary school systems.* Chicago: Association of School Business Officials.

4

Managing Resources for Higher Performance and Productivity

OBJECTIVES

At the conclusion of this chapter you will be able to:

1. Understand the relationship between student achievement and funding (ELCC 3.3, ISLCC 3).
2. Understand what education resources are (ELCC 4.3, ISLLC 4).
3. Describe the relationship between educational resources and achievement (ELCC 3.1, ISLLC 3).
4. Articulate strategies for allocating resources for higher performance and productivity (ELCC 3.3, 4.3, ISLLC 3, 4).
5. Describe what core and noncore functions of a school are (ELCC 3.2, ISLLC 3).
6. Understand various approaches to identifying efficiencies in a school or school district (ELCC 3.3, ISLLC 3).
7. Understand the impact of educational choice on public-school finance (ELCC 3.3, 4.3, 6y.1, ISLLC 3, 4, 6).

WHAT ARE EDUCATIONAL RESOURCES?

In 1983, the National Commission on Excellence in Education published *A Nation at Risk*, a document stressing the need for education reform in the midst of academic underachievement of American schools when compared to schools worldwide. One aspect of this publication focused on the financial state of schools across the nation, especially schools located in socioeconomically disadvantaged areas. Since this publication, much research has resulted in an effort to determine the correlation between school budgets and program success (Guthrie et. al. 2007).

Public-school leaders across the country appear to be nearing consensus about the necessary characteristics of successful schools. Class size, advanced in college-preparatory curriculum, teacher professional development, and differentiated instruction are key factors in helping all students learn (Newstead, Saxton, and Colby 2008). However, implementing these programs is not a cost-neutral endeavor. On the other hand, authors like Stephen Brill note that "if school systems stopped adhering to class size limits now that we know that class size counts less than the quality of the teacher in front of the class" they could invest more in teacher salaries (Brill 2011).

Additional funding may be an important remedy to help low- and middle-income schoolchildren, but certainly not the only remedy. Arnie Duncan, the Secretary of the Department of Education, also indicates the great importance of improving the quality of instruction. Providing students with high expectations begins with teachers being able to develop those high expectations and meeting them as well (Klein 2009; Karoly and Bigelow 2005).

The importance of parents providing a safe and encouraging home environment can be a key influence in helping students succeed at school. Unfortunately, students living in poverty-level housing are often at a distinct disadvantage when it comes to school achievement. The implications for school finance are numerous. While research has shown that an early start for the students in preschool programs and full-day kindergarten can have a significant impact in their achievement, not all school districts or states require such programs (Heckman 2011). Consequently, it is critical that school districts and states be able to target educational resources in the most efficient and effective manner to improve student achievement.

Educational resources come in many forms. Tying those resources to standards and student outcomes is important not only to have an effective program but an efficient one. What is equally important is how those resources are targeted within a state, school district, and/or school building. Table 4.1 shows the pupil–teacher ratio for elementary and secondary schools from 1970 through 2009. Note that the overall ratio has dropped approximately seven students per teacher during this time period.

Table 4.1. Elementary and Secondary Schools—Teachers, Enrollment, and Pupil-Teacher Ratio: 1970 to 2009

[In thousands (2,292 represents 2,292,000), except ratios. As of Fall. Dates are for full-time equivalent teachers. Based on surveys of state education agencies and private schools; see resource for details)

	Teachers			*Enrollment*			*Pupil–Teacher Ratio*		
Year	*Total*	*Public*	*Private*	*Total*	*Public*	*Private*	*Total*	*Public*	*Private*
1970	2,292	2,059	233	51,257	45,894	5,363	22.4	22.3	23.0
1975	2,453	2,198	255	49,819	44,819	5,000	20.3	20.4	19.6
1980	2,485	2,184	301	46,208	40,877	5,331	18.6	18.7	17.7
1984	2,508	2,168	340	44,908	39,208	5,700	17.9	18.1	16.8
1985	2,549	2,206	343	44,979	39,442	5,557	17.6	17.9	16.2
1986	2,592	2,244	348	45,205	39,753	5,452	17.4	17.7	15.7
1987	2,631	2,279	352	45,487	40,008	5,479	17.3	17.6	15.6
1988	2,668	2,323	345	45,430	40,189	5,242	17.0	17.3	15.2
1989	2,713	2,357	356	45,741	40,543	5,198	17.0	17.2	15.7
1990	2,759	2,388	361	46,451	41,217	5,234	17.0	17.2	15.6
1991	2,797	2,432	365	47,728	42,047	5,681	17.1	17.3	15.6
1992	2,827	2,459	368	48,500	42,823	5,677	17.2	17.4	15.4
1993	2,874	2,504	370	49,133	43,465	5,668	17.1	17.4	15.3
1994[1]	2,925	2,552	373	49,898	44,111	5,787	17.1	17.3	15.5
1995	2,974	2,598	376	50,759	44,840	5,918	17.1	17.3	15.7
1996[1]	3,051	2,667	384	51,544	45,611	5,933	16.9	17.1	15.5
1997	3,138	2,746	391	52,971	46,127	5,944	16.6	16.8	15.2
1998[1]	3,230	2,830	400	52,525	46,539	5,988	16.3	16.4	15.0
1999	3,319	2,911	408	52,876	46,857	6,018	15.9	16.1	14.7
2000[1]	3,366	2,941	4,24	53,373	47,204	6,169	15.9	16.0	14.5
2001	3,440	3,000	441	53,992	47,672	6,320	15.7	15.9	14.3
2002[1]	3,476	3,034	442	54,403	48,183	6,220	15.7	15.9	14.1
2003	3,490	3,049	441	54,639	48,540	6,099	15.7	15.9	13.8
2004[1]	3,536	3,091	445	54,882	48,795	6,07	15.5	15.8	13.7
2005	3,593	3,143	450	55,187	49,113	6,073	15.4	15.6	13.5
2006[1]	3,622	3,166	456	55,307	49,316	5,991	15.3	15.6	13.2
2007	3,634	3,178	456	55,203	49,293	5,910	15.2	15.5	13.0
2008[1]	3,674	3,219	455	55,235	49,266	5,969	15.0	15.3	13.1
2009[2]	3,617	3,161	457	55,282	49,312	5,970	15.3	15.6	13.1

[1]Private-school numbers are estimated based on data from the Private School Universe Survey.

[2]Projection.

Source: US National Center for Education Statistics. *Digest of Education Statistics*, annual, and *Projections of Educational Statistics*. See also www.nces.ed.gov/annuals.

Schools tend to reallocate funds differently than other organizations due to funding constraints, union contracts, and other factors. A school can define its priorities but that does not guarantee that the funds can or will be distributed to those areas. In order to assure a proper reallocation of resources the principal should be the responsible party that leads a team in researching the trouble areas of the school to determine whether it is possible for the reallocation. The Center for Comprehensive School Reform and Improvement (2009) observed that:

> The complexity of the task of allocating resources within a school is directly related to the quantity and type of resources available for reallocation. It is easier to allocate money than it is to reallocate, which requires taking hold from one area of the school to provide in another. Before starting the process, school leaders should examine the situation in which they will be working to determine if the context is conducive to school-level resource allocation. Addressing problems in this area in advance is helpful because changes in school district resource allocation and accountability processes may be needed before the work can proceed.

By following this procedure, the school leader can make better decisions on how and what should be reallocated with documented support through the research process to reduce possible school inequities.

THE RELATIONSHIP BETWEEN RESOURCE ALLOCATION AND ACHIEVEMENT

When considering the funding of public schools, there are a multiple of factors influencing the distribution of resources. Considering that the primary reason schools exist is the education of young people, the majority of the financial resources should go toward the instructional process, namely the teachers and tools for teaching. Everything else is, in the strictest sense, in support of the instructional process. Just how much money is needed for schools to operate effectively is unknown. Hanushek and Lindeth (2009) found that the court remedies in Kentucky, New Jersey, and Wyoming yielded virtually no change in patterns of achievement. As noted by Golab (2010):

> Elementary students in Bannockburn had the fourth-highest test scores in Illinois last year, but that achievement wasn't reflected in the pay of their teachers, whose average salaries ranked 242nd among elementary school districts statewide.
>
> The north suburban school district is one example of the wide disparity between teacher pay and student achievement that a *Chicago Sun-Times* analysis has found is common throughout Illinois.
>
> Just seven of the top 25 elementary districts for highest-paid teachers also made the top 25 in student achievement scores.

On the other hand, Ferguson (1991) demonstrated that expenditure levels make a difference in increasing performance. He found that the biggest difference occurred when expenditures were targeted at instructional processes. His research suggests that allocating resources on such things as higher quality teachers generates the most significant increases in achievement. Darling-Hammond, in her book *The Flat World and Education* (2010) noted that there are five obstacles that prevent the equal and adequate distribution of resources. They are:

- The high level of poverty and low level of social supports for low-income children's health and welfare, including their early learning opportunities.
- The unequal allocation of school resources, which is made politically easier by the resegregation of schools.
- Inadequate systems for providing high-quality teachers and teaching to all children in all communities.
- Rationing of high-quality curriculum through tracking and interschool disparities.
- Factory-model school designs that have created dysfunctional learning environments for students and unsupportive settings for strong teaching.

What can be said, at best, is the jury is out on whether money matters. Hanushek (1989) indicated that there was no strong relationship between school expenditures and student performance. Hedges, Laine, and Greenwald (1994) challenged that concept. They noted that money does matter. In fact, to reach their conclusion, they relied on the same data most often used to demonstrate the opposite. One of the most often cited research regarding "does money matter" is that of Hanushek (1981, 1986, 1989). He looked at data from thirty-eight different articles and books using regression coefficients to determine the effect inputs on student performance. Picus (1995) summarized his conclusion as follows:

- There was no conclusive statistical evidence that pupil–teacher ratio or teacher education resulted in increased student achievement.
- There was a positive correlation between teacher experience and salaries and student achievement. Hanushek noted that neither of these relationships was particularly strong.

- Per-pupil expenditures were not a significant variable in determining student performance.
- Administrative inputs did not have a systematic relationship to student achievement and there was little relationship between the quality of school facilities and student performance.

The National Working Group on Funding Student Learning (2008) postulates that there are some inherent problems with the current way that finance systems target and link resources. They look at five different attributes of financing systems: resource target, the linkage between resources and educational programs, the resource-management process, accountability, and the link between resources and student outcomes. What they observe is that in conventional finance systems resources are directed toward district goals and that there is no link between resources and education programs, spending is governed by categories, accountability is a matter of compliance, and the link between resources and outcomes is missing.

In what they have termed *learning-oriented finance systems*, resources are targeted toward students, integrated with educational programs and effectively used for continuous improvement. Accountability is a function of student learning and the link between resources and student outcomes is transparent (National Working Group on Funding Student Learning 2008).

In 2012, the Albert Shanker Institute issued a new report "*Revisiting the Age Old Question: Does Money Matter in Education?*" (Baker 2012). Baker basically looked at three questions:

1. Are there differences in aggregate school funding reflected in differences in short- and long-term measured outcomes?
2. Are the differences in measured outcomes a result of differences in specific school programs and/or resources?
3. Does redistributing money or increasing the level of funding through state finance reforms lead to improvements in the distribution of student outcomes?

The answer to each question, according to Baker, is "yes." Baker noted that Hanushek's 1986 student has been the basis for the belief by many that money does not matter. He notes that African American and other subgroup scores on the National Assessment of Educational Progress rose over time as school spending increased.

A review of literature on productivity and the link between resources and achievement still creates more questions than answers. Even so, it is clear that the focus of the educational community is now centered on student outcomes. This will inevitably lead to more discussion on how to align financial resources with student outcomes in the most productive and efficient manner. In order for this to happen there will need to be a greater emphasis on data analysis and evaluation. Hanushek noted in 2003 that:

> If educational policies are to be improved, much more serious attention must be given to developing solid evidence about what things work and what things do not. Developing such evidence means that regular high quality information about student outcomes must be generated. In particular, it must be possible to infer the value-added of schools. Improvement also would be advanced significantly by the introduction and general use of random assignment experiments and other well-defined evaluation methods. Without incentives and without adequate evaluation, there should be no expectation that schools improve, regardless of the resources added to the current structure. (Hanushek 2003)

ALLOCATING RESOURCES FOR HIGHER PERFORMANCE AND PRODUCTIVITY

School administrators are constantly challenged to meet the academic and socializing goals for the students they educate. Whereas private businesses seek to minimize overhead and increase profits, public schools tend to maximize the utilization of budgets in support of increasing achievement. In economically challenged times, businesses reduce expenses and increase efficiency to stay in business and attempt to stay profitable. For businesses, productivity is the key. School districts are not used to thinking of productivity in the same terms as private businesses. Schools tend to think of efficiency as simply making "cuts" to balance their budget. However, making certain "cuts" can be counterproductive. Basically, there are only three methods of balancing a school budget: cut spending, increase revenues, or a combination of both (Wong and Casing 2010).

Unfortunately for most public school districts, the only viable alternate is to cut spending. Spending is the only thing a school district has total control over. So with these challenges, how do we allocate resources for higher performance and productivity in public schools? As Daggett (2009) notes, school districts need to focus "resources and accountability around specific tools, strategies, professional development, procedures, and policies that can be documented to improve student performance." He goes on to state that this is a subtle change from what currently exists—it shifts the focus from inputs (programs) to outputs (student performance). Education Resource Strategies, Inc. has developed five strategies to help low-performing schools improve their chances for success (Baroody 2011). Those strategies are:

1. Understand what each school needs.
2. Quantify what each school gets and how it is used.
3. Invest in the most important changes first.
4. Customize the strategy to the school.
5. Change the district, not just the school.

Increasing performance and productivity are dependent on many variables. The key to implementing any plan is to first identify the parameters, needs, and options available. This process should be done in collaboration with staff, taxpayers, and other stakeholders. The second step is to identify the strategies that are available for achieving the outcomes. Outcomes include not only those related to the academic achievement of students but the fiscal health of the organization and maintenance of a safe and secure learning environment. Following are some suggested steps in this process (Schilling 2010):

- Establish broad goals
- Establish financial parameters
- Confirm educational needs
- Confirm facilities needs
- Develop approaches and strategies
- Make choices

Establish broad goals. Establishing broad goals that promote sustainability and scalable success in student achievement over time is crucial to allocating resources. The natural inclination for most school boards and administrators is to address the most immediate needs of the organization. This, of course, ignores planning for the long-term success of the school district. The goal of every school board should be to provide equity over time and have a means of measuring it. Financially, this may be as simple as ensuring expenditures for instruction are adjusted annually based on enrollment and the cost of living.

Academically, it may mean developing criteria to insure that test scores and student outcomes are met over time. This is especially important when protecting the school's ability to address the needs of students from low-income families, English learners, and students with disabilities from the impact of budget cuts. The key to establishing broad goals is the involvement of all stakeholders in the process. Collaborative and meaningful engagement of all stakeholders is important in insuring the successful implementation of goals.

Establish financial parameters. Each school and school district needs to establish its own financial parameters. Financial parameters provide a basis for how funds are to be distributed as well as benchmarks for the fiscal wellbeing of the district.

How a budget is developed and who is responsible for deciding how resources are allocated is an important decision. No matter how much the board, superintendent, and other central office administrators are involved, the ultimate decision is made at the school-building level. School personnel know where resources are needed and are responsible for achieving the goals of the school. A significant portion of the resource allocation authority should reside with the principal and his or her staff.

Data-driven resource models are just as important at the school and school-district level as they are at the state level. Ensuring intradistrict equity and adequacy for students and schools creates a level playing field. Simply dispersing funds based on the number of students in each school does not serve the best interests of anyone. The method of dispersing funds should

Box 4.1. Example of Finance Parameters

- Reserves in operating funds kept above 10% of the next year's operating budget.
- Maintain safe and operationally sound facilities.
- Building fund balances in the Site and Construction Fund for major capital projects using pay-as-you-go approach to the majority of capital improvements or rely on borrowing?
- Establish capital replacement cycles for major purchases such as printing, technology, etc.
- Provide for staff and operating expenses to meet instructional and enrollment changes before funding other new programs or facility improvements.

Table 4.2. School District Pupil Weighting Allocation System Example

Category	*Weighting*
Grade Level—Regular Instruction	
• Early Childhood Education	1.10
• Primary	1.10
• Intermediate	1.00
• Middle Schools	1.00
• High school	1.20
Special Education	1.40
Bilingual	1.15
Low-income	1.15
At-risk (see note)	1.05
Gifted	1.05

Note: At-risk refers to students failing or at risk of failing. Weighting numbers are for illustrative purposes and do not represent any research based figures.

depend on the make-up of the student body and the challenges instructing them pose. This would include language barriers and socioeconomic class.

As discussed in chapter 2, there are several approaches to distributing and managing resources. In addition to those reviewed, school districts can also develop their own weighting system. For example, special-education students could be given a weight of 1.5, low-income 1.25, and English-as-a-second-language learners 1.15, for example. This would automatically direct funds to schools with higher concentrations of "at risk" students.

According to Snell (2009) there are a number of "best practices" associated with weighted-student formula budgeting. They are:

- Redirect central office resources to the schools.
- Use school-level academic plans to align resources and achievement goals.
- Publish detailed school-level budgets.
- Use foundation grants to support small schools.
- Charge schools actual salaries to increase equity.
- Devolve district-restricted funds into the weighted student formula.
- Connect student weights to academic achievement rather than poverty.
- Use hold-harmless strategies to phase-in equitable school-level budgets.
- Allow schools discretion over purchasing of central office services.
- Implement weighted-student formula to help with enrollment fluctuations.

The allocation of resources also needs to take into account the basic services all schools provide. Most every school needs a principal, a secretary, a copier, and so on regardless of its size. Therefore, part of the equation needs to include an allocation for fixed costs. Last but not least are adjustments for cost and enrollment. Annual increases in the cost of living may need to be made to maintain the purchasing power of the school for new supplies and materials. Likewise, as enrollment fluctuates, staffing should be adjusted whenever possible.

Class size is probably the biggest driver of educational resources. In a small elementary school with only two sections of each grade level, losing two students per grade probably doesn't mean you're going to have any significant savings. On the other hand, in a large school with multiple sections you may find that you can increase class size by a few students, not affect achievement, and realize staffing reductions and savings. Again, all of this is affected by the composition of the class. In the final analysis, most districts, when faced with budget reductions, will closely guard class sizes as opposed to other nonessential support services.

Confirm educational needs. Like most bureaucracies, schools and school districts tend to maintain programs already in existence and have difficulty eliminating those that no longer are effective. Demographics change as well as best practices and student needs. Confirming educational needs is important in that it forces organizations to reevaluate programs in light of student outcomes. The result of such a process is that resources can be reallocated and realigned to promote student achievement in a productive and efficient manner.

Care should be exercised to comply with all legal requirements. Most categorical programs such as special education, response to intervention (RTI), and bilingual programs have specific requirements set but the state. RTI, which focuses on research-based interventions and instruction for general education students, has been adopted by a growing number of states (Zirkel 2011). RTI, which focuses primarily on reading improvement, may hold the promise of reducing costs by implementing early interventions.

There are several strategies to confirm an organization's current instructional needs. Among these are reviewing information that will shed light on which practices, programs, and policies have been effective and produced measurable improvements in student achievement and/or outcomes. Simply put, invest in what works. This is especially important in times of limited educational resources. Shifting resources from less effective to more effective programs and strategies will most likely result in the least amount of harm to students.

To achieve effectiveness, schools and school districts must have data systems from which to draw evidence and conclusions. One method of doing this is establishing a set of "Dashboard Reports" that shows achievement trends over time. Figure 4.1 shows an example of a performance dashboard.

As part of the process of confirming educational needs, require that new courses, programs, and instructional strategies contain a fiscal analysis or business plan. Commit the organization to evaluating new initiatives from both an instructional and fiscal basis. Determine if there is evidence that the results achieved are cost effective or could the resources designated for the new initiative be better spent on investing in current programs and services. Often we just look at the cost of staff and textbooks. A better approach would be to include all costs: staff, benefits, professional development, supplies, textbooks, equipment, digital materials, facilities, and so on. How many students will the initiative serve? Will there be a need for indirect resources such as counselors, media specialists, technologists?

Schools and school districts can utilize a more structured and systematic approach to confirming instructional needs (Cook 1979). The *Educational*

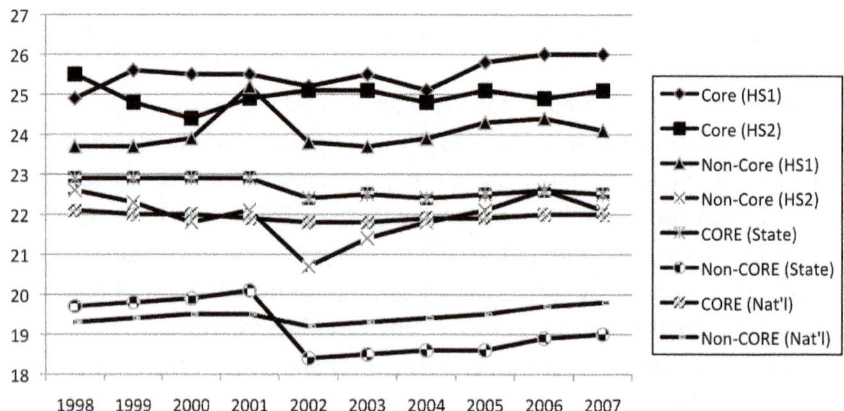

FIGURE 4.1
An Example of a Performance Dashboard

Program Review Technique (EPRT) provides school districts with a means of comparing programs and functions within their system on several levels—priority, impact on achievement, and cost (Fox and Prombo 2010). How does EPRT work? Basically it involves reviewing and evaluating programs on their effectiveness. Program plans are submitted at various funding levels outlining expected outcomes, activities, and evaluation techniques at each level. In the case of Community Unit School District 300 in Illinois, those levels are about 10 percent reduction, status quo, and an increase of about 10 percent (Fox and Prombo 2010). Once all the data is acquired, programs are then ranked based on whether they should be reduced, stay the same, or receive more resources.

Confirm facilities needs. Facilities are an integral part of the operation of a school or school district. Other than instructional and support services, maintaining facilities can be a significant cost to school districts. In times of financial restraint and challenges, schools often settle for just "doing the minimum." Unfortunately, that can have devastating consequences for a school district in the long-term. Not fixing a water leak now for $25,000 may result in a $500,000 mold problem in a year or two.

Another consideration in any renovation of school facilities is what changes can be incorporated to save energy costs. Not all savings are equal. The key indicator of whether or not to include these is the "payback period." The payback period refers to the length of time that the cost of the energy savings improvement takes to pay for itself. For example, a project with a cost of $100,000 with an annual savings of $10,000 would take ten years to pay for itself. Chapter 6 will discuss the process of confirming facility needs and energy considerations.

Develop Approaches and Strategies. The primary purpose of schools and school systems is to educate children. In accomplishing that purpose, a number of services are necessary that have nothing to do with student achievement or outcomes. Those services could be referred to as noncore functions of the school as opposed to the core competencies of academic preparation. In private industry, if a function is not generating a profit, it is usually considered a noncore function and organizations seek to look for the most efficient ways of providing the service. In schools and school districts, the noncore functions that come to mind quickly are transporting students, custodial and maintenance services, food service, security, and other similar auxiliary services.

Not all states allow for the outsourcing of these services or have passed stringent rules protecting work done by union employees from arbitrarily being outsourced. However, in states where outsourcing is legal it can lead to substantial savings in these noncore functions. Whether these services are provided internally or externally they should be reviewed periodically to ensure they are being provide in the most efficient and cost effective manner. Schools and school districts need to adopt an entrepreneurial mindset in this regard. They need to ask four key questions (Schilling 2006):

1. Why am I doing this?
2. If I don't do this, what's the consequence?
3. Can somebody else do it better?
4. Is it a core competency?

The key to managing staff efficiently and effectively is to have an effective position-control system. Simply, a position-control system defines every position within an organization, attaches every employee to a specific position, and then tracks all costs associated with these positions including vacancies. Why is this important? Approximately 75 to 85 percent of all school-district expenditures are associated with personnel costs—salary and benefits (Beyne and Bedford 2009). Position control

- Assists with staff planning and hiring, budgetary control, and position monitoring,
- Ensures staff are only assigned to authorized positions,
- Eliminates payments to staff that are not authorized in the budget,
- Provides accountability by department and activity for positions hired, maintained, and funded.

Process mapping is another strategy that can be used to streamline operations and increase efficiency. A process map defines how an organization performs work, the steps and sequence involved, who is responsible for each step, and how various groups interact (Beyne and Bedford 2011). One Gartner study suggests that the simple exercise of getting employees together to jointly map their processes, with no subsequent process improvement efforts, can result in productivity improvements of 12 percent or more. Figure 4.2 shows an example of a process map for a school-district business function.

Figure 4.3 shows the purchasing process after it was revised. Notice how many fewer steps there are in the process. This results in both efficiency and productivity gains by just changing "how things are done."

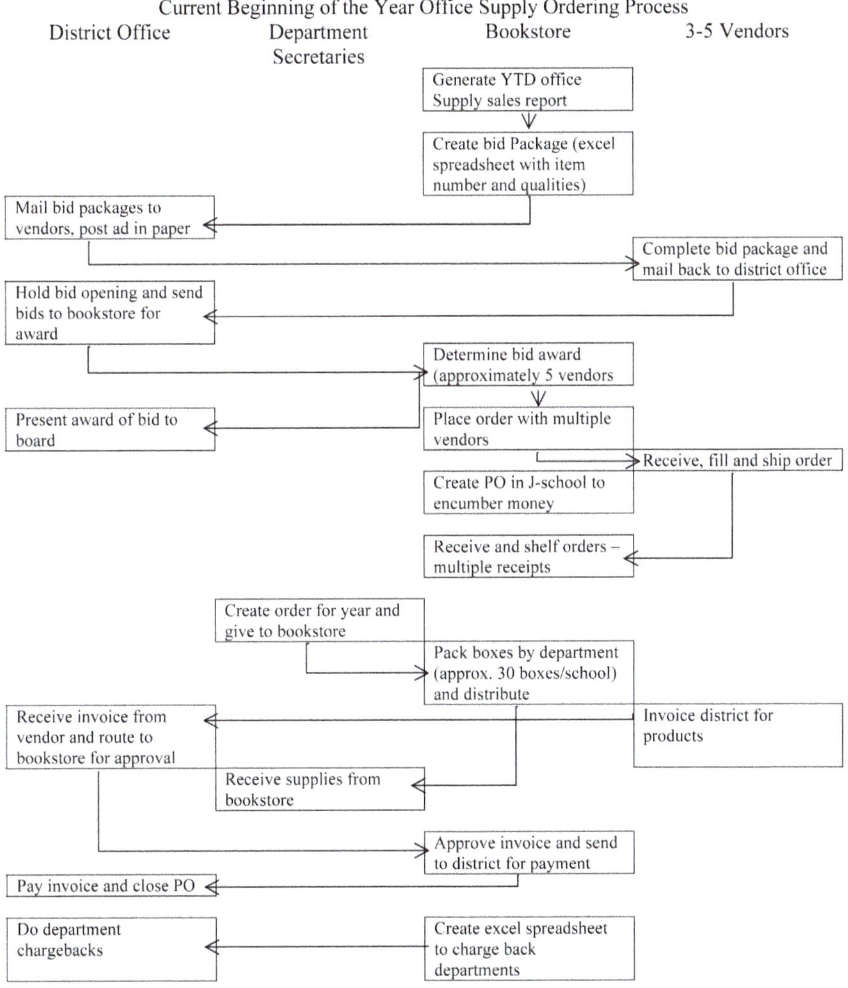

FIGURE 4.2
Example of Process Mapping

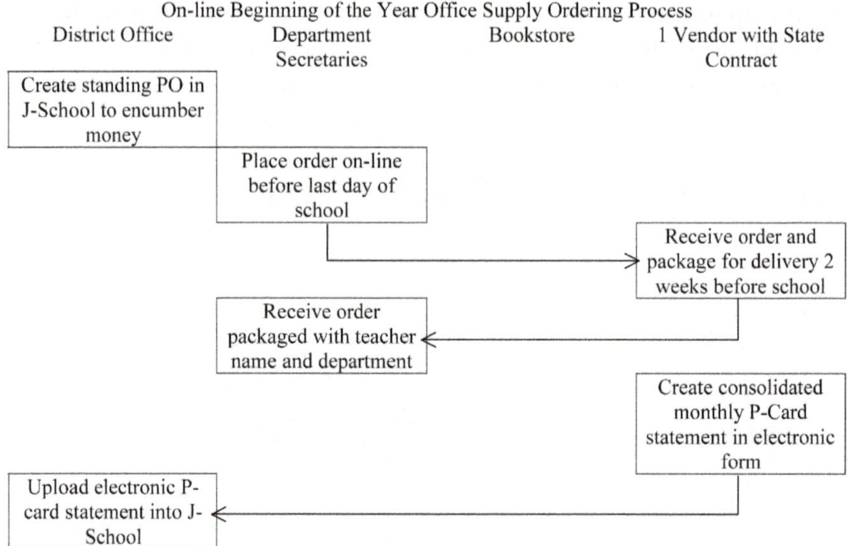

FIGURE 4.3
Example of a Final Process Map

Common sense would tell us that we should only pay for what we need. Practically, however, this is not always the case. Many school districts consider a full-time employee to be eight hours per day for 260 days, or 2,080 hours per year. The following example shows how just a small change in those contracts can result in a substantial savings.

BEFORE: The district has one hundred secretaries working eight hours per day for 260 days. Those secretaries are entitled to an average of fifteen holidays and ten days of vacation. They are scheduled for winter and spring break. The average salary is $30,000 per year. Total cost to the school district: $30,000 × 100 = $3,000,000.

AFTER: The district identifies a core of twenty secretarial positions that need to work full-time over the winter and spring breaks and during the summer. For the remaining positions the district eliminates work over the winter break (ten days), spring break (five days), and during the summer; these positions only work a four-day work week for eight weeks (eight days). The result is that staff will work only when they are needed. The district can also possibly negotiate or reduce the amount of vacation time since the staff will be off the equivalent of about five weeks. Furthermore, the district could implement the change as positions open. Total cost to the school district after changes: $30,000 × 20 = $600,000, plus $27,346 times 80 = $2,187,680 for a total of $2,787,680—an annual savings of $212,320 or 7 percent.

School districts can seek to find alternative service delivery modes. Maybe the local Park District would be willing to maintain the school grounds in return for access to the facilities. Tapping into community resources for the delivery of services is another possibility. Piggy backing on a village's bid for renovating streets and parking lots could result in a cost savings for the district. Districts are working with other governmental bodies to have after-school and before-school programs. What partnerships are available is strictly a matter of the creativity and cooperation of the public bodies. School districts can also seek contributions and grants from charitable organizations to fund key programs. Toward that end, many school districts have set up foundations to raise money to provide resources for value-added programs and services in their schools.

Technology can play a significant role in increasing productivity at every level of the education system. Educators can utilize open sourced software, digital textbooks, and other technology-based resources that can provide low-cost and up-to-date materials. Digital materials can be used to provide additional online learning programs for students, be modified to meet a variety of student and teacher needs, and create new opportunities for students in rural areas. Of course, school districts need to be cognizant of insuring that all students have access to the technology. School districts also need to assess the total cost of ownership of technology. That includes not only the cost of the equipment but software, supplies, maintenance, and depreciation.

Another strategy that schools and school districts can utilize is shared services. Consolidating purchasing, insurance, or other services has resulted in cost savings and efficiencies in many states. Intergovernmental agreements for the delivery of low-incidence special-education students and vocational-education cooperatives are also common. In some states investment pools, cooperative bidding, state-purchasing cooperatives, and shared fiscal services have also resulted in savings. Small school districts in particular that have limited purchasing power, small staffs, and fewer funds to invest are most likely to be the biggest beneficiaries of cooperative or shared-services ventures. Following is a list of possible shared services in which school districts may engage:

- Curriculum planning
- Custodial services
- Employee benefits
- Energy procurement
- Food services
- Insurance
- Investment pools
- Legal services
- Professional development
- Purchasing and procurement
- Special education
- Staff recruitment
- Technology services
- Transportation services
- Vocational education

A more comprehensive approach to looking for efficiencies and increased productivity is the use of a performance audit. Performance audits can be used to determine how economical each of the school district's operations is and their efficiency. They can also be utilized to identify weaknesses in the system as well as compliance issues. Auditing firms or consultants familiar with the overall operations of school systems and their compliance issues most often execute performance audits.

EDUCATIONAL CHOICE

Educational choice proponents argue that students should be given a greater choice in the schools they attend. As recently as June 2012, presidential candidate Mitt Romney indicated that if he was elected he would "expand parental choice in an unprecedented way" (Gabriel 2012). There are several choice options according to the Education Commission of the States (2012). They are magnet schools, open enrollment, charter schools, vouchers, tax credits and deductions, and homeschooling.

The original purpose of magnet schools was more political than educational. Magnet schools were seen as a vehicle for voluntarily reducing racial segregation in schools. Magnet schools operate as a part of the school system in which they reside (Chen 2007). They are different from other public schools in that they usually offer a different educational setting or experience. They may be a math and science academy, a school for the arts, and so on. Magnet schools make up the largest percentage of educational choice schools in the United States (Siegel-Hawley and Frankenberg 2012).

School districts can implement their own form of choice by simply allowing for open enrollment (intradistrict). For example, the Pasadena Unified School District in California allows for open enrollment as well as neighborhood schools. The choice of whether to apply for a nonneighborhood school is strictly up to the parents (PUSD 2012). On a regional basis, districts could allow for open enrollment between school districts and their schools (interdistrict). Minnesota has generally been recognized as a leader in this type of choice. Minnesota law allows children to attend schools outside their district as long as there is room and it does not have an adverse effect on desegregation.

Charter schools are not without their controversy. By providing families with an alternative they impact both resource allocation and effectiveness of public schools (Moore 2006). By 2010, approximately 1.4 million students were enrolled in about 4,600 charter schools (Ravitch 2010). According to Odden and Busch (1998) there are several methods that are used to fund charter schools: state funding, flow-through from the local district to the charter school, locally negotiated funding, or not specified in state law. Charter schools often are challenged to provide the same educational outcomes without the same financial resources (Publicover 2011). In Chicago, charter schools get on average 23 percent less funding than other district schools (Eaton 2007).

In 2011, Indiana created the nation's most comprehensive voucher system. What makes Indiana's voucher program significant is that it is available to all families with an income up to $60,000—not just low-income, special-needs students in failing schools (Martin 2011). At the same time, Milwaukee schools were coming under fire for a failed voucher program. In Milwaukee, after twenty years of vouchers there is no evidence that any significant improvement has occurred for the neediest students (Ravitch 2010).

Nobel Laureate economist Milton Friedman first proposed vouchers. He saw vouchers as a mechanism to give parents a greater control over their children's education. Attempts at passing state-wide voucher programs have failed in a number of states (Minnesota, 1978; California, 1980 and 2000; and Michigan, 2000). In 1992, the US Supreme Court upheld the use of vouchers at sectarian schools (*Zelman v. Simmon-Harris* 2002). Since the Zelman decision a number of states have passed voucher-type legislation. The Colorado Supreme Court held Colorado's attempt in 2003 unconstitutional in 2004. Similarly attempts in Florida (2006) and Arizona (2009) were held unconstitutional by their state supreme courts. With all of the other choices available, vouchers have not been significant in providing alternatives for large numbers of students.

Tax credits and deductions are viewed by most public schools as no more than a state subsidy for private and religious schools. As of May 2012, nine states have tuition tax credit programs (NCLS 2012). Those states are Arizona, Florida, Georgia, Indiana, Iowa, Oklahoma, Pennsylvania, Rhode Island, and Virginia. Four of these states allow both individual and corporate tax credits for contributions to scholarship-granting organizations. Arizona allows credits for taxpayers that pay extracurricular public-school fees. Illinois and Iowa allow individuals with a nonrefundable tax credits for qualified K–12 education expenses. Louisiana provides for a tax deduction for qualified K–12 education expenses for public, private, or homeschool expenses. Illinois, Iowa, and Arizona courts have upheld the constitutionality of their laws.

It is estimated that 1.5 million students or slightly less than 3 percent of the K–12 student population were homeschooled in the United States in 2007 (NCES 2008). Homeschoolers can be divided into two groups: those who provide all educational services and those who access the public schools for part of their child's education. The laws regarding homeschooling vary from state to state. California, Indiana, and Texas, for example, treat homeschooling as a type of private school. New Jersey and Maryland rely on the wording of their compulsory attendance laws. Other states such as Maine have their own statutes regarding the requirements for homeschoolers. A minority of states have statutes that require public schools to give homeschoolers access to district resources. Access to extra and cocurricular programs such as athletics also varies from state to state.

SUMMARY

For resources to support higher performance and productivity there must be participation and collaboration of all stakeholders. There is research that both supports and refutes whether or not educational resources make a significant impact on student achievement and the attainment of outcomes. What is critical is that educational resources are targeted in an efficient and productive manner to improve student achievement and attainment of outcomes.

School districts are continually being challenged to do more with less. The 2008 economic downturn has only exacerbated that fact. In order to obtain higher performance and productivity, school districts need to allocate resources where they make the most impact being thoughtful to maintain intradistrict equity and adequacy. In order to accomplish this, school districts should:

1. Establish broad goals.
2. Establish financial parameters.
3. Confirm educational needs.
4. Confirm facilities needs.
5. Develop approaches and strategies to obtain its goals.
6. Make choices regarding the best alternatives.

To maintain intradistrict equity school districts may want to use a *weighted-student allocation system*. To insure decisions reflect the needs of each school, some type of site-based budgeting should be implemented and principals should be given as much autonomy as possible over the budgeting decisions that affect their buildings. There are a number of strategies and techniques to increase efficiency and effectiveness. They include position control, process mapping, focusing on core competencies, looking for alternative service-delivery models, using technology expeditiously, participating in shared services, and possibly engaging in a performance audit.

There are a number of educational choices which parents can make that affect public-school systems. The alternative can affect the resources public-school districts receive and/or the amount of funds allocated internally within the district. Of all these alternatives, magnet schools make up the largest percentage of these choices. As of 2007, charter schools served about 3 percent of the US student population. Charter schools differ from magnet schools in that they usually aren't subject to the same rules and regulations with the district. State courts have generally held voucher programs unconstitutional. The most aggressive voucher plan was approved in 2011 by the state of Indiana. Indiana's program allows families with household incomes up to $60,000 to have access to school vouchers. Tuition tax credits and deductions are another option that has been approved in a number of states. As of 2007, homeschools served about 3 percent of the US student population. The rules and laws regarding homeschools vary from state to state.

The future of public-school education in the United States is dependent on school districts and administrators finding more productive and effective means for obtaining educational outcomes (which have basically evolved to standardized tests). The economic challenges most Americans have faced these past few years only highlights the cost of education, staff salaries, benefits, and pensions. It is incumbent on the school community to demonstrate that "money matters." To do that, educators need to find what works and invest in it.

CASE STUDY

"Aligning Student Outcomes with Educational Resources"

Thunderbird School District is facing some tough times. Home values have fallen and revenues are predicted to be flat at best for the foreseeable future. Thunderbird School District serves about 7,500 students in grades K–12. Most of the parents in the district work in the local automobile plant. About 25 percent of the students in the district qualify for free and reduced lunches. Academically, the district has struggled. Only about 60 percent of the students meet or exceed state outcomes in math and science and only 54 percent meet standards in English/language arts and social studies. The superintendent has asked you to chair a committee to determine what reductions the district should make to save money. Those possible reductions are indicated in table 4.3.

EXERCISES AND DISCUSSION QUESTIONS

1. Do higher teacher compensation and/or lower class sizes result in improvements in student achievement? Provide at least three reasons for and against the proposition.

Table 4.3. Possible Budget Reductions

OPTION ONE

Item	*Savings*	*Cost of Replacement*	*Net Savings*
Staff Positions			
Eliminate middle-school assistant principal position; add full-time office staff	$135,563	$29,148	$106,415
Supplies			
District:			
– Reduce annual supply allocation from $575 to $400 per teacher	$15,225		$15,225
– Reduce hard copies of formal communication to a minimum—replace with electronic copies; parent/student handbook, Annual Report, etc.	$15,824	$500	$15,324
– Eliminate board of education recognition of staff (holiday party, beginning of school year welcome-back gifts, etc.)	$3,000		$3,000
– Reduce administrative supplies annual allocation by 50% (including $1,500 for general recognition)	$6,650		$6,650
– Reduce psychologist supplies annual allocation from $2,075 to $1,275	$1,275		$1,275
Elementary School:			
– Parent fees: Have parents pay for field trips, bus, and activity; exceptions include student travel between schools and between schools and high schools	$17,400		$17,400
– Grades 5–8 band program: have parents pay for band competitions. Have parents pay band fees	$6,315		$6,315
– Increase price of yearbook to include stipend, printing, and binding	$15,087		$15,087
– Have parents pay for student magazines—add to textbook fee	$20,200		$20,200
– Evening family activities: eliminate middle-school Medieval Night	$3,500		$3,500
– Student competitions: eliminate Gifted Program competitions	$18,500		$18,500

(continued)

Table 4.3. ***(Continued)***

OPTION TWO

Item	*Savings*	*Cost of Replacement*	*Net Savings*
Staff Positions			
Elementary:			
– Eliminate learning-center assistant (rely on volunteers; close down learning center when teacher is at lunch and on breaks)	$25,450		$25,450
– Replace science lab teacher with full-time assistant (responsible for set-up and tear-down of labs)	$63,799	$25,000	$38,799
Middle School:			
– Eliminate two special-education assistants	$58,970		$58,970
Supplies			
Elementary:			
– Reduce supplies/discretionary items annual allocation form $8,000 to $4,000	$4,000		$4,000
Middle School:			
– Reduce supplies/discretionary items annual allocation from $11,000 to $5,500	$5,500		$5,500
Programs			
Elementary:			
– Eliminate extra/cocurricular activities, including substance abuse program	$23,492		$23,492
Middle School:			
– Eliminate extra/cocurricular activities including substance abuse program (not including sports)	$85,670		$85,670
Technology			
– Eliminate next phase of Technology Plan: rely completely on PTC and Education Foundation	$158,225		$158,225

OPTION THREE

Item	*Savings*	*Cost of Replacement*	*Net Savings*
Improvement of Instruction			
– Eliminate all school-improvement activities (ex: committees)	$103,395		$103,395
– Eliminate all substitute teachers needed for committee work	$26,500		$26,500
– Reduce summer work to items necessary to reopen school year (ex: technology maintenance and student health related work)	$29,685		$29,685
– Reduce professional development for teachers, administration, and board	$33,888		$33,888
Staff Positions			
District:			
– Reduce speech and language pathologist FTE from 2.6 to 2.0	$45,200		$45,200
– Reduce social worker FTE from 2.0 to 1.0	$74,668		$74,668
– Reduce psychologist FTE from 2.0 to 1.0	$67,406		$67,406
– Reduce literacy specialist FTE from 4.0 to 2.0	$120,000		$120,000
Elementary:			
– Eliminate five grade 1 assistants	$42,264		$42,264
– Eliminate two kindergarten assistants	$48,640		$48,640
– Eliminate four special-education assistants	$100,917		$100,917
Programs			
Middle School:			
– Eliminate all sports	$80,000		$80,000
– Reduce/eliminate band	$96,016		$96,016
– Reduce/eliminate art	$135,986		$135,986
– Reduce/eliminate music	$154,372		$154,372
– Reduce/eliminate family consumer science	$70,021		$70,021
– Reduce/eliminate applied technology	$92,048		$92,048

2. In the school system you work or reside, how are resource allocation decisions determined? Is there a process for evaluating whether resources result in increased student performance?
3. Referring to the case study, generate a list of $500,000 in reductions. Write one to two paragraphs on how your proposed reductions would affect:
   - An effective instructional program: describe how your financial recommendations will affect the effectiveness of the instructional program provided to students.
   - Management of the organization: describe how your financial recommendations will affect the administration and supervision of students.
   - Collaboration with families and community: prepare a statement to the community that describes the budget as meeting the community desire that the school "live within its means" while you solicit their input, involvement, and collaboration. Identify potential school, business, community, and social-agency partnerships.
   - Student diversity: state how you combined impartiality and sensitivity to student diversity in preparing the budget.
   - The larger context: prepare a statement for your state legislator advocating for equitable funding for all students regardless of their socioeconomic background.
4. In your professional life, what choices have you made with regard to allocating resources to improve achievement? How did you determine whether they were successful?
5. What should be the role of the principal, superintendent, and board of education in allocating resources and evaluating their effectiveness?
6. Pick a program or function with which you are familiar. Using the EPRT, develop a proposal at various funding levels, outlining expected outcomes, activities, and evaluation techniques at each level. Assume that the funding levels are 10 percent less, 10 percent more, and the status quo.
7. If faced with the task of having to significantly reduce the expenditures in a school or school district, how would you go about it?
8. What are the pros and cons of giving principals control over a school's operating budget?
9. If you were designing a weighting system for the allocation of resources based on the characteristics of each student, what would be your criteria?

10. Do you think paying teachers more money produces better quality teaching?

REFERENCES

Baker, B. (2012). *Revisiting the age-old question: Does money matter in education?* Washington, DC: The Albert Shanker Institute.

Baroody, K. (2011). *Turning around the nation's lowest performing schools.* February. www.americanprogress.org/issues/2011/02/five_steps.html.

Beyne, S., and Bedford, M. (2009). Business and HR integration through position control: The information technology interface. *DataBus* (Winter).

Beyne, S., and Bedford, M. (2011). Bending the trend: Lowering personnel expenditures for K–12 schools. *California School Business News* (May).

Brill, S. (2011). *Class warfare: Inside the fight to fix America's schools.* New York: Simon & Schuster.

Center for Comprehensive School Reform and Improvement, The. (2009). *Reallocating resources for school improvement = Context for resource allocation.* www.centerforcsri.org/pubs/reallocation/context/html.

Chen, G. (2007.) What is a magnet school? *Public School Review.* www.publicschoolreview.com/articles/2.

Cook, D. (1979). *Program evaluation and review technique: Applications in education.* Washington, DC: University Press of America.

Daggett, W. (2009). *Effectiveness and efficiency framework: A guide to focusing resources on student performance.* April. www.leadered.com/pdf/EE%20%20White%20Paper%20website%203.25.09.pdf

Darling-Hammond, L. (2010). *The flat world and education: How America's commitment to equity will determine our future.* New York: Teachers College Press.

Eaton, F. (2007). Civic group finds Illinois charter schools don't drain resources. *Heartlander.* October 1. news.heartland.org/newspaper-article/2007/10/01/civic-group-finds-illinois-charter-schools-dont-drain-resources.

Education Commission of the States. (2010). *Equipping education leaders, advancing ideas, 2009.* www.ecs.org/html/issue.asp?issueid=22.

Ferguson, R. (1991). Paying for public education: New evidence on how and why money matters. *Harvard Journal on Legislation* 28:465–98.

Fox, F., and Prombo, M. (2010). *Program cuts.* Illinois Association of School Business Officials Update Magazine Winter 2010 v. 18 i. 02, pp. 32-35.

Gabriel, T. (2012, June 11). Vouchers unspoken, Romney hails school choice. *New York Times.* June 11. www.nytimes.com/2012/06/12/us/politics/in-romneys-voucher-education-policy-a-return-to-gop-roots.html?_r=1&pagewanted=all.

Golab A. (2010). High teacher pay no guarantee of results. *Chicago Sun-Times.* www.highbeam.com/doc/1N1-12F31B7FE4BB7140.html.

Guthrie, J., Springer, M., Rolle, R., and Houck, E. (2007). *Modern education finance and policy.* Boston: Pearson/Allyn & Bacon.

Hanushek, E. (1981). Throwing money at schools. *Journal of Policy Analysis and Management* 1:19–41.

Hanushek, E. (1986). The economics of schooling: Production and efficiency in public schools. *Journal of Economic Literature* 24:1141–77.

——. (1989). The impact of differential expenditures on school performance. *Educational Researcher* 18 (4): 45–65.

——. (2003). The failure of input-based schooling policies. *Economic Journal* 113 (485): 64.

Hanushek, Eric A., and Lindseth, Alfred A. (2009). *Schoolhouses, courthouses, and statehouses: solving the funding-achievement puzzle in America's public schools.* Princeton: Princeton University Press.

Heckman, J. (2011). The economics of inequality: The value of early childhood education. *Education Digest: Essential Readings Condensed for Quick Review* 77 (4): 4–11.

Hedges, L., Laine, R., and Greenwald, R. (1994). Does money matter? A meta-analysis of studies of the effects of differential school inputs on student outcomes. *Educational Researcher* 23 (3): 5–14.

Karoly, L., Bigelow, J., and Labor and Population Program. (2005). *The economics of investing in universal preschool education in California.* Santa Monica, CA: RAND Corp.

Klein, A. (2009). Nothing but praise for Duncan in senate hearing. *Education Week*. January 13. www.edweek.org/login.html?source=http://www.edweek.org/ew/articles/ 2009/01/13/18duncan.h28.html&destination=http://www.edweek.org/ew/articles/2009/01/13/18duncan.h28.html&levelId=2100.

Martin, D. (2011). Indiana lawmakers approve nation's largest school voucher program. *Huff Post Education*. April 27. www.huffingtonpost.com/2011/04/27/indiana-education-reform_n_854575.html

Moore, T. (2006). How much is tuition? Charter schools defined. *Illinois Loop*. September. www.illinoisloop.org/charter.html.

National Conference of State Legislatures (NCSL). (2012). *Tuition tax credits*. www.ncsl.org/issues-research/educ/school-choice-scholarship-tax-credits.aspx.

National Institute for Education Statistics (NCES). (2008). *1.5 million homeschooled students in the United States in 2007*. (NCES 2009030). Washington, DC: US Department of Education.

National Working Group on Funding Student Learning. (2008). *Funding student learning: How to align education resources with student learning goals*. Seattle, WA: School Finance Redesign Project.

Newstead, B., Saxton, A., and Colby, S. (2008, June 06). Going for the gold: Secrets of successful schools. *Education Next* 8 (2): 38–45.

Odden, A., and Busch, C. (1998). *Financing schools for high performance*. San Francisco, CA: Jossey-Bass.

Pasadena Unified School District (PUSD). (2012). *Open enrollment*. 2012. openenrollment.info/.

Picus, L. (1995). Does money matter in education? A policymaker's guide. In *National Center for Education Statistics: Selected papers in school finance 1995*. Washington, DC: US Department of Education.

Publicover, J. (2011). National study shows dramatic inequity in charter school funding. *PR Newswire*. www.prnewswire.com/news-releases/national-study-shows-dramatic-inequity-in-charter-school-funding-95128829.html.

Ravitch, D. (2010). *The death and life of the great American school system: How testing and choice are undermining education*. New York: Basic Books.

Schilling, C. (2006). General session presented at the Jamaican Association of School Bursars Annual Meeting: *Entrepreneurship in education*. November. Jamaica.

——. (2010). Funding our vision: A five-year plan to provide excellence and opportunity for all. Consultant presented to West Northfield School District 31. Northbrook, IL.

Siegel-Hawley, G., and Frankenberg, E. (2012). *Reviving magnet schools: Strengthening a successful choice option*. February. civilrightsproject.ucla.edu/research/k-12-education/integration-and-diversity/reviving-magnet-schools-strengthening-a-successful-choice-option/MSAPbrief-02-02-12.pdf.

Snell, L. (2009). *Weighted student formula yearbook 2009*. April 30. Los Angeles: Reason Foundation. reason.org/files/wsf/yearbook.pdf

Wong, O., and Casing, D. (2010). *Equalize student achievement: Prioritizing money and power*. Lanham, MD: Rowman & Littlefield Education.

Zelman v. Simmons-Harris, 536 U.S. 639, 2002.

Zirkel, P. (2011). State laws and guidelines for RTI: Additional implementation features. Communique. http://www.nasponline.org/publications/cq/39/7/professional-practice-state-laws.aspx

5

Managing Human Resources

OBJECTIVES

At the conclusion of this chapter you will be able to:

1. Understand the human-resources-planning process (ELCC 3.3, ISLLC 1, 3).
2. Define critical laws and executive orders of the Equal Employment Opportunity Commission (ELCC 6.1, 6.2, 6.3, ISLLC 3, 6).
3. Describe how EEOC laws and regulations impact human resources planning (ELCC 6.1, 6.2, 6.3, ISLLC 3, 6).
4. Describe employee compensation and evaluation programs (ELCC 3.3, ISLLC 3).
5. Understand basic collective-bargaining process (ELCC 3.3, ISLLC 3).

PLANNING STAFFING NEEDS AND ENROLLMENT PROJECTIONS

One of the most important resources of any organization is the employees. While there are many facets to managing human resources, the foundation begins with proper planning. There is an old adage that states, "Those who fail to plan, plan to fail." Planning in human resources involves assessing organizational needs, predicting the future, establishing and communicating operational goals, conducting job analyses, and identifying key positions needed by the organization (Marler 2009).

Human resources planning ensures that an organization has the correct number of people in the right places at the right time who have the necessary skills and performance to complete the institution's objectives. An organization cannot accomplish any goals without qualified people. Proper planning allows administrators to ensure successful transitions and ensure that people can accomplish the tasks needed of an organization in a smooth and harmonious manner. While some school districts approach human resources planning differently, all administrators need to be involved in human resources forecasting to ensure that there are capable people performing the necessary tasks of the organization (Earley et al. 2009).

The foundation of human resources planning is *projecting student enrollment*, which helps determine the amount of employees needed for a school district, and helps administrators plan for future finances, facilities, and human resources. Forecasting student enrollment is like looking into a crystal ball, but not having 100 percent accuracy. Administrators can use several methods to help predict student enrollment, such as quantitative statistical analysis and qualitative techniques. Quantitative statistics involve calculating the number of children in an elementary-school district and determining the number likely to enroll in high school. Specific trends in elementary-school enrollment over two- to four-year periods of time can be used to help predict enrollment trends. In addition, feedback from local realtors and statistics from the planning commissions of local municipalities can provide statistics on housing trends and residency.

Qualitative measures consist of administrators using inductive analysis to make conclusions based upon discussions with people through the local chamber of commerce, identifying potential new businesses coming or leaving the area, residential and commercial developments that are being planned, the general economy in the area, and geographical potential for expansion. For example, some school districts may be within a community that is land-locked or has older residents and has decreasing numbers of children in school. Also, new emerging communities that have high growth and new residential and commercial developments can provide valuable clues as to the direction of enrollment trends. However, all this information must be perceived with caution because a community may be rapidly growing but suddenly, due to economic reasons, the development can come to a halt, leaving school buildings empty and future plans for school expansion dormant.

The human-resources-planning strategy essentially involves matching the school's human resources needs with the projected student enrollment. Administrators must make a good-faith effort in determining this match in order to avoid shortages, overstaffing issues, or employing teachers who have the wrong people with the wrong certifications needed for the students. For example, if a community is experiencing a high growth in foreign immigrants, the necessity for bilingual and English-as-a-second-language (ESL) programs may be more critical than other areas. Likewise, nothing may be worse for an administrator than to overstaff a district and then experience a drastic decline in enrollment. This may necessitate a *reduction in force* (RIF). Recent legislation regarding desegregation and affirmative action has supported other means than using seniority as the basis whenever possible (Ray, Baker, and Plowman 2011).

EMPLOYMENT LAWS

There are a myriad of federal and state laws and executive orders that impact human resource planning and employment (Hirsh and Kornrich 2008). These laws cover a wide range of employment practices ranging from planning human resources, recruiting, interviewing and selection, writing job descriptions, compensation, placement and induction, career development, mentoring practices, professional development, employee evaluation, collective bargaining, managing conflict, handling grievances, and termination and reduction in force (see table 5.1).

While there are many federal laws impacting education, there are also specific laws unique to individual states and school district policies. While federal laws tend to trump state and local laws, all of these laws must be understood and practiced by administrators. Also, state laws and regulations generally specify certification and licensing regulations. Local school boards may establish higher standards than state regulations but generally cannot legally establish lower standards. An administrator must be well informed and seek local counsel in understanding the interrelationship of federal, state, and local school-board laws and regulations.

For example, school boards may have the authority to set policy as long as the policy does not conflict with state laws. Also, there may be state laws that are not clearly defined by federal laws and statutes. For example, the state of Illinois added an anti-sexual-orientation discrimination to the Illinois

Table 5.1. Major Federal and EEOC Laws and Executive Orders

Law	*Basic Description*
Title VII of the Civil Rights Act of 1964 as amended	Prohibits discrimination on the basis of race, color, religion, national origin, and gender, or pregnancy, childbirth, and retaliation.
Equal Pay Act of 1963	Prohibits pay discrimination against males and females who perform equal work that is substantially the same.
Occupational Safety and Health Act (OSHA) of 1970	Enforces standards for workplace safety and health to prevent work-related injuries, illnesses, and death. Provides regulatory safety guidelines to ensure safe work environment.
Title IV of the Education Amendments of 1972	Prohibits discrimination against males and females in activities and programs receiving federal funding and grants.
Rehabilitation Act of 1973 sections 501 and 505	Prohibits discrimination against qualified disabled people who can perform the major functions of a job and affirmative action to employ and promote qualified disabled people.
Vietnam Era Veterans' Readjustment Act of 1974	Requires employers with federal contracts to provide affirmative action for Vietnam-era veterans to prevent discrimination for disabled Vietnam war veterans.
Pregnancy Discrimination Act of 1978	Provides EEO protection for pregnant women and new mothers that they be treated like any other disability for employment matters.
Family and Medical Leave Act (FMLA) of 1993	Requires employers to provide male and female employees up to twelve weeks a year in unpaid leave for qualified medical and family illness, military situations, pregnancy, foster care and adoption, or personal serious illness.
Title VII, Section 1604, Sexual Harassment Act	Prohibits unwelcome sexual advances, requests for sexual favors, and other verbal or physical conduct of a sexual nature that creates a hostile or offensive work environment.
Age Discrimination in Employment Act 1967 (ADEA)	Protects people who are forty or older from age discrimination or retaliation for filing a complaint.
Title I Americans with Disabilities Act of 1990 (ADA)	Protects disabled people from employment discrimination or retaliation for filing a complaint.

Source: US EEOC, www.gov/laws, 2011.

Human Rights Act. Essentially this act states that it is unlawful to discriminate against sexual orientation as defined as "actual or perceived heterosexuality, homosexuality, bisexuality or general related identity, whether or not traditionally associated with the person's designated sex at birth" (Illinois Department of Human Rights 2010).

This addition to the Human Rights Act has created controversy within many public schools and local school-board opinions regarding sexuality and employment practices within a school district. State laws may also provide different employment work and compensation safeguards for teachers and staff. For example, some states forbid school districts from waiving their rights granted by state law in matters concerning housing, compensation, cost-of-living adjustments, and contractual placement of teachers. Understanding the many federal and state laws is critical to reduce potential distress, financial burden, and legal vulnerability for the school district (Morgan and Vardy 2009).

Many of the federal laws have originated based upon societal movements (Huffman, Cohen, and Pearlman, 2010). During the late 1800s there were little federal laws that protected employees in the workplace. However, the Human Relations Era began in the 1930s, which strongly influenced the passage of several federal legislative acts. For example, in 1935 the National Labor Relations Act (NLRA) was established to prohibit discrimination against union members with regard to employment and apprenticeship practices. There have been many additions to the Fair Labor Standards Act since 1938. Many of these provisions relate to child labor law, minimum-wage requirements, overtime provisions, meals and breaks, travel, training, as well as additional guidelines for exempt employees.

The Labor Management Relations Act (LMRA) was established in 1947. This act, which is also known as the Taft-Hartley Act, was significant in outlining specific employment practices. This act was an offshoot to the original National Labor Relations Act and contains additional provisions and guidelines regarding employees' right to free speech and collection of union dues. Also during this time the Federal Mediation Conciliation Service (FMCS) was established to help resolve management and union disagreements.

As an outgrowth of the civil rights movement of the 1960s, the Equal Employment Opportunity Commission (EEOC) was established by Title VII of the 1964 Civil Rights Act. The original act prohibited discrimination on the basis of race, color, relation, national origin, and gender. This law covered all aspects of employment including planning, hiring, supervising, compensation, job classification, promotions, training, retirement, and termination. While the Civil Rights Act primarily covered all employers and public and private institutions with fifteen or more employees, the act provided the basis for bringing litigation against institutions that practiced discriminatory acts. This federal law created protected classes of employees which mainly consisted of women, African Americans, Asians, Hispanics, Indians, and Eskimos.

Subsequently, amendments have been made to the act, which include protecting individuals above the age of forty, disabled people, and pregnant women. Also, in 1978, the EEOC adopted other guidelines to protect claims of reverse discrimination practices as an outgrowth of affirmative action. Essentially, the act stated that organizations should avoid selection policies that have an adverse impact on hiring or employment opportunities because of race, gender, or ethnicity unless there is an organizational necessity for the practice.

The penalties associated with Civil Rights Act violations can be severe. The law allows individuals who have been discriminated against to seek compensatory and punitive damages for both willful and intentional acts of discrimination. Compensatory damages generally address harm to an employee for pain and emotional suffering. Punitive damages can be assessed against an employer, which serves as punishment and a deterrent for others. There are some limitations for judgment awards depending upon the size of an organization. In addition to the EEOC, violations of discrimination are also enforced and judgments can be awarded by state human-rights commissions. For example, the state of Illinois has a Department of Human Rights Commission that is responsible for protecting individuals from discriminatory practices.

Both the EEOC and state human-rights commissions have the authority to assess monetary penalties and both of these agencies have established time frames in which a claim can be filed. For example, the state of Illinois typically allows for 180 days from the occurrence and the EEOC allows three hundred days. Not only can an organization incur financial costs for acts of discrimination but they can also incur significant emotional pain, legal costs, work disruption, wasted time, and resources defending claims. Therefore, organizations are wise to follow legal practices and avoid claims of discrimination.

The Equal Pay Act of 1963 was an outgrowth to the Fair Labor Standards Act. This law prohibits compensation discrimination between people who have the same skills and experiences and are performing the same job. However, there can be several exceptions to pay differences, such as bonuses for higher performance, seniority, merit, working conditions, geographic differences, and quality and quantity of work. The law primarily serves to protect differences in pay between men and women who are substantially doing the same work and have the same qualifications, performance, and seniority.

The Occupational Safety and Health Act (OSHA) was established in 1970. This act included mandatory safety and health standards for all employers. The objective of the act is to prevent occupational injuries and illnesses by enforcing standards of workplace safe practices. The law is enforced by the OSHA Agency, a division of the US Department of Labor. This agency, in addition to implementing investigations for work-related injuries, also initiates proactive inspections to organizations when there is a possible hazard or danger to people. This law has had a major impact on school-district facilities and requires administrators to ensure that the facilities are safe and do not impose health risks and illnesses on staff and students.

The agency has the power to impose monetary fines and require facility improvements. The agency also provides significant safety regulations involving permissible exposure limits, personal protective equipment, hazard communications, safety management, blood-borne pathogens, evacuations, exposure to asbestos, and in some cases mandatory training for safety and health practices.

Title IV of the Education Amendments Act of 1972 prohibits discrimination on the basis of gender for educational programs by recipients of federal financial assistance. The act states that "No persons in the United States shall, on the basis of sex, be excluded from participating in, be denied the benefits of, or be subjected to discrimination under any program or activity receiving Federal financial assistance" (US Equal Employment Opportunity Commission 2011). This law requires school districts to maintain internal procedures for federal grants and resolving complaints of discrimination. In addition, Title IV also applies to programs of a school district regardless of whether the program is federally funded.

The Rehabilitation Act of 1973 serves to promote equality for employees with disabilities. This law requires that employers take affirmative action to recruit, hire, and promote qualified disabled people. The law serves to protect disabled persons who can perform the main functions of the job with reasonable accommodations. While the law has good intentions, some administrators may have difficulty interpreting exactly what "reasonable accommodations" means. The law does not mandate that accommodations be made if doing so imposes a significant hardship or monetary expense that is unreasonable for a school district. However, in most cases administrators can accommodate disabled employees through actions such as modifying work schedules and providing ergonomic devices and other special equipment or modifications to support a disabled person in performing the primary functions of a job.

Examples of accommodations might include installing entrance ramps for people in wheelchairs, providing special seat cushions for back pathologies, wrist splints for accumulative trauma disorders, and special lighting for people with eye-related diseases. It should be noted that a school district is not required to hire a disabled person who is less qualified than nondisabled people. The intention of the law it to prevent discrimination against disabled people who can perform the major functions of the job.

The Vietnam-Era Veterans' Readjustment Act of 1974 followed the Vietnam War. This act mandates that employers take affirmative action to recruit, hire, and promote Vietnam War veterans and disabled veterans. Definitions of veterans of the Vietnam War include US military, ground, naval, or air service military people who served during the period of 1964 through 1975. The regulations of the law are intended to prevent employers from discriminating against protected Vietnam War veterans.

This law mainly impacts contractors or subcontractors receiving federal funds. In addition, employers are required to keep records for at least two years. However, employers who have fewer than 150 employees are only required to maintain records for one year. Examples of records include job descriptions, job advertisements, interview notes, applications, résumés, employment policies, human resource files, and any related employment forms and records.

The Pregnancy Discrimination Act of 1978 provides protection for pregnant women and new mothers so that they are treated like another disability for employment matters. This act was an amendment to the Title VII Civil Right Act and impacts organizations with at least fifteen employees. This law provides protection for pregnant women in hiring, promotion, and terminating practices.

The Family and Medical Leave Act of 1993 (FMLA) prohibits discrimination against male and female employees who desire to take twelve weeks of unpaid leave because of the birth of a child, adoption or foster care of a child, or caring for a family member who has a serious health condition. This law is administered by the Wage and Hour Division of the US Department of Labor. The law supports people who have qualified medical and family situations, leaving decisions to the discretion of the employer. Interpretation of the law is not always clear cut and while guidelines have been provided by the federal agency, questions regarding what medical situations qualify remain. For example, the federal FMLA does not recognize many part-time workers who desire unpaid leave, or certain employers with fewer than fifty employees. Also, employees who desire to take unpaid time off for illnesses of relatives, pets, personal short-term illness, or other routine medical care are generally excluded.

Other related FMLA state statutes may apply as well. For example, the state of California recognizes domestic partners and children of domestic partners. Connecticut, on the other hand, recognizes parent-in-laws of civil union partners and the state of Hawaii recognizes grandparents of employees.

The EEOC included a sexual harassment amendment in 1980 to the Title VII Civil Rights Act. This law prohibits *sexual harassment* in the workplace. The law states that sexual harassment involves "unwelcome sexual advances, requests for sexual favors, and other verbal or physical conduct of a sexual nature—when such conduct has the purpose or effect of unreasonably interfering with an individual's work performance or creating an intimidating, hostile or offensive working environment" (US Equal Employment Opportunity Commission 2011).

There are several types of sexual harassment discrimination in this amendment (Perry 2008). *Adverse impact discrimination* involves unintentional actions that have negative or detrimental effects against a person or group of people. This discrimination might involve requiring certain height requirements that could unintentionally discriminate against people of a certain ethnicity. *Adverse treatment discrimination* involves the intentional act of treating people differently. An example of this discrimination could be asking different interview questions for men versus women during an employment interview. *Retaliation* is an intentional discrimination when an employer commits an adverse action against the employee because he or she has complained against discrimination or filed a discrimination claim. Another type of sexual discrimination is called *quid pro quo*. This harassment (also called "this for that" or "in exchange for") involves requesting sexual favors in exchange for some type of employment benefit.

An example of quid pro quo might be a school administrator requesting sexual favors from a teacher in exchange for a good performance rating or promotion. A type of sexual harassment discrimination that addresses to *environmental sexual harassment* is called *hostile working environment*. This type of harassment involves any unreasonable actions with a sexual basis that interfere with an employee's work performance. Examples might include verbal, physical, and visual sexual actions, patently offensive conduct, harassment of individuals because of their gender, displaying inappropriate sexual pictures, physically touching people, or sending e-mails with sexually based content.

Sexual harassment complaints have significantly increased over the past several years. School administrators are required to post sexual harassment policies, conduct investigations when complaints have been received, take action against offenders, provide training for employees, and provide an employee-complaint mechanism or grievance system. Many state laws have similar provisions to the Federal Title VII amendment. Sexual harassment discrimination has become a complex law and requires school administrators to consult legal counsel.

The Age Discrimination in Employment Act (ADEA) of 1967 was designed to prohibit age discrimination for employees over forty years of age in planning, recruiting, selection, training, promoting, transferring, compensating, and other practices of employment. The intention of the law is to prevent companies from discharging or refusing to hire older workers based upon the workers' age (Jusko 2011). In 1986 this act was amended to prohibit discrimination in retirement for people above forty years of age. An example of this law would include a school district that forced a competent sixty-year-old teacher to retire against his or her will in order to hire a twenty-two-year-old teacher with the intention of saving money for the school district. It should be noted that this law protects people who are forty years of age or older but does not protect people who are under the age of forty. It is never a good practice to hire or fire people based upon age rather than performance factors and needs of the school. Also, because of this law many school districts have offered early retirement programs in an effort to encourage retirement and reduce costs.

The Americans with Disabilities Act of 1990 (ADA) Title I was established to prevent discrimination against disabled individuals who can perform the essential functions of a job with reasonable accommodations. This law generally applies to employers who have fifty or more employees. This law has had significant impact on school districts given that it covers such a wide range of medical conditions such as HIV, mental illnesses, learning disabilities, alcohol and drug addiction, and other physical ailments. This law is executed under the Equal Employment Opportunity Commission and was subsequently amended to prohibit school districts from discrimination regardless of the number of employees.

EMPLOYEE EVALUATION AND COMPENSATION PROGRAMS

Performance evaluations are conducted at virtually all school districts. The State Department of Education, local school district policies, union contractual agreements, and federal programs such as the No Child Left Behind Act are some of the proponents of performance evaluations (Milanowski 2011). The use of performance evaluations has increased because of the emphasis on performance accountability and standards. Using the performance-evaluation process can be an important tool in helping improve the performance of all teachers and staff within the school district.

There are many types of performance-evaluation systems, such as narrative appraisals, formative and summative assessments, 360, rating systems, and goal-based evaluations. Some organizations utilize an *open narrative evaluation*, especially for high-level administrators and managers. In this system the subordinate is asked to write a narrative regarding how well he or she performed during the year. This narrative is then used as a basis for performance review session. This type of system is a more informal approach and is infrequently used.

The *formative assessment* is often used to support the summative evaluation process. During the formative assessment informal feedback is given to the employee by the supervisor and this information is not used as part of the employee's permanent evaluation record. The whole idea of formative assessment is to give informal feedback without the fear of the information negatively impacting the employee's performance. However, it is sometimes difficult to entirely disregard the information when preparing a summative report.

The *summative evaluation* is the most popular approach and consists of a combination rating assessment and narrative section on the evaluation form. The evaluation forms can consist of a paper copy and filed in a cabinet or an electronic copy and stored in a computer. The *360 performance evaluation* is a system that uses a multirater feedback process to obtain an evaluation about an employee. The feedback is generally provided by multiple supervisors, peers, support staff, community members, and possibly students. This system began during the 1950s in the corporate world and gradually gained popularity with human resources professionals. However, the system has been somewhat controversial in that it requires extensive time to collect the feedback and some people feel that the information is not always accurate or used exclusively for developmental purposes.

The 360 feedback may require gaining information from up to six to ten people. Each one of these individuals needs to complete an assessment of the employee. Sometimes the employee is allowed to choose the raters in addition to the supervisor. There are many decisions to be made in using a 360 approach, such as the selection of the type of feedback instrument, number of raters, how the raters are selected, the process to be used, degree of confidentiality, anonymity of the raters, and how to integrate the information into the performance-management system. One advantage of the 360 process is that the employee receives multiple assessments. This may be more valuable than simply obtaining feedback from one supervisor. Also, when feedback is received from multiple stakeholders, a more diverse and comprehensive assessment can be obtained (Cleveland and Murphy 1995).

The traditional *combination rating* and *open-comment evaluation* is still probably the most popular rating form (Milanowski 2011). The evaluation of an employee is generally conducted on a semiannual or annual basis. Nontenured teachers are generally evaluated on a semiannual basis and tenured teachers are evaluated annually. Conducting evaluations on a semiannual basis provides a good opportunity to obtain regular feedback, although this can be time-consuming for both the employee and supervisor. Typically, the annual review is the requirement by school districts and state departments of education. Also, the use of computer software has greatly increased the efficiency in completing and storing the evaluation forms into one database.

There are many different types of compensation plans used in organizations today. Some of these consist of profit sharing, gain sharing, merit based, bonus based, noncash recognition programs, deferred compensation, pay for performance, and so on. There is no one best compensation system and school districts need to establish what works best for their exempt and nonexempt people employees (Billinger 2007). Also, people do not work for pay alone and other rewards should be considered as part of the entire compensation package.

For example, intrinsic rewards such as having a career progression, job enrichment, the work itself, and full appreciation for the work being done can have significant motivational impact for employees. On the other hand the absence of good working conditions, benefits, and supervision can demotivate employees as well. All of these factors should be taken into consideration. In other words, simply paying people more money may not guarantee higher performance or good results with student learning (Callier 2010).

A report completed by the *World at Work Compensation and Practices Research* (2010) revealed some interesting statistics:

- There is a wide variety of pay practices and compensation systems, and nine out of ten companies subscribe to a compensation philosophy with over 60 percent having a written policy and 29 percent having an unwritten policy.
- Forty-two percent of employees indicate that they do not understand their company compensation philosophy, and for the employees who understand the philosophy they believe a written policy has a positive effect on employees' understanding.
- There is a higher attrition rate associated with companies who have unwritten compensation policies, suggesting that clearly establishing salary schedule and policies have benefits for employee retention.
- Nearly all organizations give a pay increase with a promotion and award merit increases for good performance (World at Work Compensation Programs and Practices Research Report 2010).

The objective of merit compensation plans is to coordinate an employee's performance with their compensation (Sawchuk 2010). Many believe that providing merit pay based on performance provides an incentive to perform well and is a fairer compensation structure that may have a more direct impact on quality of work and student learning. However, determining merit pay requires subjectivity and these plans are often criticized because of supervisory favoritism, disparities in amounts of money available, poor performance-appraisal evaluations, and small differentiations between merit pay and performance. Unless there is a sufficient pool of merit pay to distribute, this plan may create employee dissatisfaction.

For example, if an average performer receives a 2 percent merit pay and an exceptional performer receives a 3 percent pay raise, the difference may not be worth the additional work. Therefore, establishing a larger differentiation in merit pay among the levels of performance may be more motivating and fair to employees. Also, some compensation experts believe that the merit-pay system in itself can produce aggressive competition among employees and undermine collaboration and teamwork. Employees soon realize that their merit pay is determined based upon their performance as compared to other employees. Also, employees may not be motivated by money alone and may not have a desire to work significantly harder to obtain more money. Some employees may be content with their current pay rate and level of job performance. Table 5.2 illustrates a typical teacher salary schedule.

Table 5.2. Example of a Teacher Salary Schedule

YEARS	*BA*	*BA+15*	*MA*	*MA+15*	*MA+30*	*MA+45*
1	$43,000	$45,900	$48,906	$49,560	$51,225	$52,455
2	$46,244	$47,465	$50,583	$51,812	$53,786	$55,018
3	$47,919	$49,250	$53,686	$54,574	$56,349	$57,680
4	$50,137	$51,468	$56,349	$57,680	$59,011	$60,342
5	$52,375	$53,686	$59,111	$60,342	$62,117	$63,004
6	$54,574	$55,905	$61,673	$63,004	$64,779	$66,110
7		$58,123	$64,335	$65,666	$67,541	$68,772
8			$66,997	$68,328	$701103	$71,434
9			$69,659	$70,990	$72,765	$74,096
10			$72,321	$73,653	$75,427	$76,578
11			$74,987	$76,315	$78,089	$79,421
12			$77,646	$78,977	$80,752	$82,083
13			$80,308	$81,639	$83,514	$84,745
14			$82,970	$84,301	$86,076	$87,851
15			$86,276	$87,407	$89,182	$90,956

A gain-sharing compensation program is another option. The idea behind this program serves to reward employees who take responsibility and meet or exceed organizational goals. The program often works when clear organizational goals are established and employees then strive to meet or exceed these goals. An advantage of this type of program is that it helps organizations achieve sustained increases in results, employees have more accountability in achieving organizational goals, they share in the benefits, and there may be enhanced commitment for collaboration and teamwork and school-district support. However, there can be many disadvantages to this type of program, such as not all employees are able to directly impact the accomplishment of goals, goals are not always easily measured, federal and state Fair Labor Standards Act guidelines may conflict with the plan, and the formulas for determining gain sharing may be complex. However, the combination of gain-sharing plans when constructed in a simplified manner can be beneficial for increasing motivation and productivity in achieving organizational goals of a school district.

COLLECTIVE BARGAINING

The process of collective bargaining can be an intense negotiating process. The process often begins with a number of activities such as:

- Reviewing of existing agreements and goals of the negotiation process.
- Establishing the time and location for negotiating and participants to be involved.
- Establishing the roles of participants, procedures for negotiating, and target dates.
- Examining past and present grievances on record by administration or union officials.
- Agreeing to ground rules in negotiations, such as video or audio recording, policies on press releases, and impasse procedures.

Typical negotiations involve assembling the school-board team, which might consist of the school board president, superintendent, and local school counsel. This team would need to conduct extensive planning and preparation including such items as financial conditions, cost analysis, bargaining issues, work policies, roles of each member (e.g., spokespeople, observer, recorders), as well as negotiation ground rules. Likewise, the union representatives would outline their ground rules and bargaining issues. Textbox 5.1 lists some typical bargaining issues between labor and management.

The negotiation process ideally should be a collaborative win-win process. All parties should demonstrate professional behavior and negotiate in good faith. Some of the positive behaviors in negotiating include:

- Respecting all members and listening to their concerns
- Controlling emotions and remaining calm
- Taking good notes
- Staying alert and being a good participant
- Keeping on the subject and not getting off on tangents
- Being open-minded and cooperative, and
- Avoiding premature judgments and distractions such as using smartphones and cell phones.

If an impasse is encountered during negotiations, some of the common remedies include the use of *mediation* and *arbitration*. Mediation involves securing a mediator to act as a facilitator to attempt to broker agreement between the two parties. Generally this process is not binding and is only an attempt to persuade each party to resolve the bargaining issues. Arbitration is similar to mediation but generally involves securing a third-party "arbitrator" who will review the overall bargaining issues and render a decision that becomes binding (Maciejewski 2007)

Often when agreement is reached between the two parties a ratification vote by the members and the board is necessary. If both parties are able to approve the agreement with their constituents the agreement is consummated. It is not unusual for one of the parties not to achieve agreement and they

Box 5.1. Examples of School Board and Union Bargaining Issues

Salary and benefits	Procedures on student discipline and attendance
Teacher professional development	Privacy and leave policies
Professional safety and security	Class size requirements
Extracurricular duties	Work conditions and hours of work
Grievance procedures	Impasse procedures
Other issues in current contract	

need to go back to the bargaining table for additional rounds of negotiation. It should be noted that the arbitration can be voluntary or compulsory.

Some states utilize compulsory arbitration as determined by state law. Other ways to resolve negotiation disputes can be done through the use of the Federal Mediation Conciliation Service (FMCS). This is an agency created by the federal government with the primary goal of promoting labor–management collaboration (Martomez-Pecino et al. 2008). The office of this agency is located in Washington, D.C., and it contains a list of many arbitrators who are available throughout the country.

The FMCS was created in 1947 and has more than seventy field offices. The FMCS provides both mediators and arbitrators. When a mediator is used, some of the strategies provided include reestablishing negotiation ground rules, clarifying issues and disputes, helping parties define problems, keeping the negotiation process moving along, promoting communications and exchange of information, and managing conflict (Federal Mediation Conciliation Service 2011). In addition, the FMCS provides a number of different services, such as creating annual reports and providing audits of financial statements, performance and accountability reports, annual employee surveys, and congressional matters relevant to labor–management collective bargaining (Lawson 2011).

Unfortunately if labor–management negotiations break down then a strike may occur. A strike is one of the final and deadliest weapons in the union's arsenal that can be used against a board of education. However, strikes come with a price and are often detrimental to student learning and cause employee loss of pay, disruption in the workplace, community dissatisfaction, and animosity among all school stakeholders. Generally the State Education Labor Relations Board requires a *notice of intent to strike* for union bargaining units. Therefore, the use of the strike provision should be a last resort.

Unions often use the strike as a last resort to gain concessions and reach agreement from the school board. It is possible by law that when employees participate in a strike they may be eligible for termination by the school board for failure to carry out contractual responsibilities. A specialized type of strike is called the "wildcat" strike. This is a strike that is unauthorized by state legislation and serves the intention of creating a work stoppage by union employees. Regardless if the strike is authorized or not, it may or may not be announced by union officials prior to striking. Tactical advantages for making an announcement or not can be determined by union leadership.

SUMMARY

The compensation of employees for a school district represents approximately 80 percent or more of the school district's total budget. Human resources administrators need to carefully examine all the factors that motivate employees for good performance other than only relying upon pay and benefits. There are many different types of compensation programs, which include pay for performance, skills based, knowledge based, gain sharing, and merit plans, that can be successfully utilized by the school board.

All these programs should be considered when improving and existing school-district compensation program. The school-district compensation program, however, can be one of the most important factors for recruiting, retaining, and motivating employees. Therefore the importance of remaining competitive with other school districts is a common goal for human resources administrators.

Besides compensation, the collective-bargaining process is of equal importance. The negotiation process should not be done by unskilled representatives. Skillful negotiators need to thoroughly understand compensation contracts, working conditions, tactics of negotiations, federal and state laws, and the psychology of human interactions. All these areas can contribute to the success during the collective-bargaining process. However, if both parties cannot reach agreement, outside facilitators may need to be secured. Mediators and arbitrators are commonly used to assist in these matters. Both are considered third-party facilitators.

Mediation is generally not binding and serves to help the parties reach agreement, while arbitration can either be voluntary or involuntary but often is considered binding in nature. The collective-bargaining process should be approached by all parties with good-faith intentions. When both parties utilize a win-win collaborative negotiation process they are more likely to reach an amicable agreement, which best services all stakeholders of the school district.

The primary goal of human resources planning is to forecast the future needs of an organization and to ensure that all resources are obtained. Proper planning entails understanding the goals of the organization, anticipating changes in staffing, understanding and staying current with federal and state laws as well as local district policies, and working with school administrators to match future needs and current organizational resources with future resources.

There are many responsibilities in managing human resources, such as administering evaluation and compensation programs, collective bargaining, dealing with disciplinary problems, and forecasting to satisfy future organization. Proper planning allows for all administrators to develop a framework to recruit, select, hire, mentor, and develop future employees to meet staffing needs. There is no one strategy that can guarantee a perfect prediction of all human resource needs since the planning process is a dynamic one and must adapt to the changing needs of the organization.

Therefore, the human-resource planning process is matching the needs of a school with available people. The bottom line is that "the trains must leave on time" and all operations and staffing need to be in place to best service the educational needs of the students.

CASE STUDY

Washington Magnet School—Creating a Ninety-Day Entry Plan

Washington School is a magnet school in an urban environment serving about 1,600 students from early childhood to eighth grade. The school specializes in the language arts and is recognized throughout the city as being a good academic institution. The school is searching for a new principal since the recent termination of the last principal for poor performance.

There is a myriad of problems at the school, which include:

1. Low test scores
2. Low staff morale
3. High attrition rate of teachers
4. Frequent complaints from parents regarding curriculum, instruction, and school policies
5. Several recent filings of sexual harassment complaints against female teachers by male teachers, and
6. Employee complaints about compensation and past performance evaluation.

In addition to these issues, the district has made several recent policy changes that have impacted the school. These policies will increase the student enrollment at the school over the next two years. This increase in students will put a strain on the school's capacity and there will be a need to expand the facilities of the school in order to accommodate this increased enrollment. Also, additional staff must be hired to accommodate these new students.

The school board is in the process of hiring a new principal who could start immediately to address these issues and plan for the future. You are a candidate for the principal position and the school board has asked you to prepare "a ninety-day entry plan," outlining what you would do as a new principal during your first ninety days on the job. The school board would like for you to prepare this written, comprehensive, ninety-day entry plan and present it at the next board meeting. It should include detailed human resource planning, communication, facilities, legal concerns, staff morale, budget and finance, instruction and curriculum, enrollment projection, and any other factors deemed important.

EXERCISES AND DISCUSSION QUESTIONS

1. Investigate different employee evaluation programs and identify positive and negative aspects.
2. Research different compensation programs and suggest the best ones for teachers.
3. Interview a school administrator and outline the process for human resources planning that is being used.
4. Interview a school administrator and identify some of the major legal issues confronting the school, including recent complaints and lawsuits.
5. List and describe at least six different EEOC laws or executive orders.
6. Outline the grievance or complaint procedure for a staff member to follow in filing a sexual harassment claim at the school.
7. Explain the history and process of the EEOC.
8. List and explain the laws that protect people on the basis of race, sex, religion, national origin, age, and disability.
9. Research and list some laws unique to your state and how they support federal laws.
10. Explain the 360 performance evaluation program.

REFERENCES

Billinger, S. (2007). Principals as agents? Investigating accountability in the compensation and performance of school principals. *Industrial & Labor Relations Review* 61 (1): 90–107.

Caillier, J. (2010). Paying teachers according to student achievement: Questions regarding pay-for-performance models in public education. *Clearing House* 83 (2): 58–61. doi:10.1080/00098650903386451.

Cleveland, J., and Murphy, K. (1995). *Understanding performance appraisal: Social, organization, and goal-based perspectives*. Thousand Oaks, CA: Sage.

Earley, P., Weindling, D., Bubba, S., and Glenn, M. (2009). Future leaders: The way forward? *School Leadership & Management* 29 (3): 295–306. doi:10.1080/13632430902793791.

Federal Mediation & Conciliation Services. (2011). www.fmcs.gov

Hirsh, C., and Kornrich, S. (2008). The context of discrimination: Workplace conditions, institutional environments, and sex and race discrimination charges. *American Journal of Sociology* 113 (5): 1394–432.

Huffman, M., Cohen, P. N., and Pearlman, J. (2010). Engendering change: Organizational dynamics and workplace gender desegregation, 1975–2005. *Administrative Science Quarterly* 55 (2): 255–77.

Illinois Department of Human Rights. (2011). State of Illinois. www2.illinois.gov

Jusko, J. (2011). EEOC Underestimates impact of ADA amendments act. *Industry Week*, 260 (5): 18.

Lawson, N. (2011). Is collective bargaining pareto efficient? A survey of the literature. *Journal of Labor Research* 32 (3): 282–304. doi:10.1007/s12122-011-9112-y.

Maciejewski, J. (2007). Broadening collective bargaining. *District Administration* 43 (7): 34–39.

Marler, J. (2009). Making human resources strategic by going to the net: Reality or myth? *International Journal of Human Resource Management* 20 (3): 515–27.

Martomez-Pecino, R., Munuate, L., Median, F., and Euwema, M. (2008). Effectiveness of mediation strategies in collective bargaining. *Industrial Relations* 47 (3): 480–95. doi:10.1111/j.1468-232X.2008.00530.x.

Milanowski, A. (2011). Strategic measures of teacher performance. *Phi Delta Kappan* 92 (7): 19–25.

Morgan, J., and Vardy, F. (2009). Diversity in the workplace. *American Economic Review*, 99 (1): 472-585. dot:10,1257/aer.99.1.472.

Perry, P. (2008). Jut say no to harassment. *Restaurant Hospitality*, 92(11),44–48.

Ray, J., Baker, L., and Plowman, D. (2011). Organizational mindfulness in business schools. *Academy of Management Learning & Education* 10 (2): 188–203.

Sawchuk, S. (2010). Merit-pay model pushed by Duncan shows no achievement edge. *Education Week* 29 (33): 1–21.

United States Equal Employment Opportunity Commission. (2011). www.eeoc.gov/laws.

World at Work Compensation and Practices Research. (2010). www.worldatwork.org.

6

Managing Facilities for Higher Performance and Productivity

OBJECTIVES

At the conclusion of this chapter you will be able to:

1. Understand the current state of school facilities in the United States (ELCC 3.1, ISLLC3).
2. Understand the relationship between environmental factors in public schools and student achievement (ELCC 3.1, 3.2, ISLLC 3).
3. Describe how facilities impact teaching and teacher retention (ELCC 3.3, ISLLC 3).
4. Describe what a high-performance school is (ELCC 3.3, ISLLC 3).
5. Identify strategies for implementing energy savings in public schools (ELLC 3.1, 3.2, ISLLC 3).
6. Understand the environmental laws and practices that apply to public schools (ELLC 3.2, 6.2, ISLLC 3.6).
7. Understand the components of good facility management (ELLC 3.3, ISLLC 3).

SCHOOL FACILITIES IN THE UNITED STATES

It has been estimated that over six billion gross square feet of building space and one million acres of land have been dedicated in the United States to public schools (The 21st Century School Fund 2011). Filardo, Bernstein, and Eisenbrey (2011) note that:

- The average public school is forty years old.
- There is conservatively about $270 billion in deferred maintenance and repairs needed to the nation's public schools.
- If one included the cost of updating these buildings to today's environmental standards, the cost could exceed $500 billion.

Clearly, the recession of 2008 has contributed to the lack of funding for school facilities. Also contributing to the problem is the fact that many schools built between 1950 and 1970 were "low bid" schools that were rapidly built to meet growing enrollments. A survey conducted by the Council of Great City Schools in 2011 revealed that the sixty-five member urban school districts had about $100.5 billion in total facilities needs. Of the $100.5 billion, $20.1 billion was for new construction and the remaining $80.4 billion was for renovation, updating, repair, and deferred maintenance (Casserly, Lachlan-Hache, and Naik 2011).

Public schools face a myriad of facility issues. They include not only aging buildings that are in need of repair but buildings that were never designed to accommodate today's environmental, safety, technology, and teaching needs. Furthermore, the enrollment of public-school children is not decreasing; it is increasing and shifting geographically. Student enrollment, preschool through grade 12, is projected to increase through 2019 according to the National Center for Education Statistics (NCES 2011).

Some areas of the nation are faced with growing enrollment and the need for new school facilities. In Nevada, the nation's fastest growing state from 2000 to 2010, the Clark County School District could not open schools fast enough to keep up with the growth in enrollment. Due to the recession, however, the district's current enrollment is about the same as it was in 2007–2008 and it has no new schools under construction (Clark County School District 2012). Several other factors have influenced the maintenance, renovation, and design of school facilities: energy costs, environmental issues, increased use of technology in schools, safety and security issues, and Title IX.

A survey conducted by the American Association of School Administrators (AASA) in 2008 revealed that 99 percent of respondents thought rising fuel and energy costs were having a significant impact on their school system. According to the report, the top five actions school systems were considering to address the rising cost of energy were implementing energy conservation measures (59 percent), cutting back on student field trips (44 percent), cutting back on heating and air-conditioning use (37 percent), consolidating bus routes (35 percent), and limiting staff business travel (34 percent) (AASA 2008). For many public school districts, the cost of energy is the largest reoccurring operating expense outside of staff and benefit costs.

Concern over the environment has increased over the years as more scientific research and evidence links various products, chemicals, and so on with health issues. Public schools have come under scrutiny as well with regard to the healthiness of their environment. Children are often more susceptible to the effects of environment contaminants than adults. Asbestos removal has been the "the biggest environmental project in US history" at an estimated cost of $50 billion (Cauchon 1999).

In some cases, public schools were forced to cut services and expenditures to pay for the removal. Today, schools deal with a multitude of environmental laws (to be discussed later in the chapter) and concerns. They include mold; air quality (particularly indoor); water quality; industrial toxic-waste disposal with ground and water pollution; structure-related diseases; sick building syndrome (SBS); building-related illnesses (BRI); volatile organic compounds (VOCs); contact, inhalation, and ingestion of irritants, allergens, toxins, infectious agents, carcinogens, and molds/fungi; noise exposure; radiation and radon exposure; lead exposure; asbestos exposure; and other toxic-compound exposure.

Parents send their children to public schools assuming they will be safe. Starting with Columbine in 1999, a series of high-profile school shootings brought safety and security in school facilities to the forefront. From July 1, 2005, through June 30, 2006, for example, there were fourteen homicides and three suicides of children at school (NCES 2007a). Trump (2009), reflecting back on the ten years since Columbine noted that many schools have added surveillance cameras to monitor entrances, upgraded their building infrastructure to support better communications, and incorporated security reviews in their planning process for new and/or renovated facilities. In fact, Trump notes that schools are adapting concepts from crime prevention through environmental design (CPTED). These concepts are resulting in improved main entrances, line-of-sights in hallways, washroom design, lighting, surveillance, and other detection methods (Trump 2009).

In the early twentieth century no one could predict what schools would be like in a hundred years. Unfortunately, while we admire the beauty and construction of some of these older schools, their thick masonry walls, inflexible spaces, and general lack of outlets, and so on are now a liability when implementing and using technology. At the very least, these old buildings pose a challenge to designers' intent on using wireless networks and other state-of-the-art technology in their classrooms and buildings. The rapid rate at which technology is changing means designers must be more flexible in designing space and avoid highly specialized rooms and equipment that may become obsolete.

According to the US Department of Education and its publication "Title IX: 25 Years of Progress," the number of girls and women who participated in high-school athletics grew from less than three hundred thousand in 1971 to over 2.4 million in 1997. In 1991, very few school athletic facilities were designed to accommodate both boys and girls sports.

For many school districts, the addition of women's sports meant using the same practice facilities late into the evening to accommodate all of the practices. Significant disparities in the quality of facilities can lead to legal challenges and whether the school's athletic program has directly overseen facility development.

In *Daniels v. School Board of Brevard County* (1985 F.Supp. 1458 [M.D.Fla. 1997]), new bleachers, an announcer's booth, a scoreboard, a batting cage, restrooms, and lights for night boys' baseball games were funded by the booster club at Merritt Island (Florida) High School, while the girls' softball diamond had none of these features. The father of two of the girls who participated on the softball team filed suit against the school. The school claimed it did not have enough money to make similar improvements to the girls' softball field so it started to dismantle the baseball field improvements. The US District Court in Orlando ordered the district to cease the dismantling and directed it, instead, to make improvements to the softball diamond. The Wilkes County schools must improve facilities and equipment for women's athletics at North Wilkes, East Wilkes, West Wilkes, and Wilkes Central high schools and take other action under an agreement reached between the Wilkes Board of Education and the federal Office for Civil Rights (OCR).

The agreement follows a federal investigation that included months of interviews with Wilkes high-school students and staff after a complaint was filed against the Wilkes school system on July 28, 2009. The complaint, filed with the OCR, claimed the civil rights of North Wilkes High softball and volleyball players were being violated on the basis of gender. Again, the largest issue was that the girls' softball practice and competitive facilities weren't equivalent to those of the boys' baseball teams. The complaint also stated that the girls' volleyball team wasn't provided open gym sessions while boys' teams had multiple open gym sessions (Hubbard 2010).

FACILITY DESIGN AND STUDENT ACHIEVEMENT

There is a growing body of research that suggests that the quality of public-school facilities can directly impact student outcomes, achievement, behaviors, and attitudes. Results confirmed a link between the quality of school facilities and student achievement in English and mathematics (Uline and Tschannen-Moran 2008). A Carnegie Foundation (1988) report on urban schools concluded that students are only aware of their physical environment but that it can influence their conduct too.

Furthermore, there is growing evidence that the quality of school facilities also affects teacher attitudes, behaviors, and retention. In regards to teacher attitudes, behavior, and performance, there is evidence that teachers really care about, and are influenced by, the spaces within which they teach. In a recent study of 531 California elementary teachers, Horng (2009) utilized forced-choices questions to determine how these teachers decided where they would teach, and what factors influenced these decisions. In fact, facility quality factored significantly into their decisions about where they would choose to teach.

A survey of public-school principals published in 2007 by the US Department of Education (NCES 2007b) asked what environmental factors in their buildings interfered with the delivery of instruction. Table 6.1 shows the results of that survey which displays the percentage distribution of public elementary and secondary schools and which environmental factors interfered with the ability of the school to deliver instruction.

Overall, 56 percent of the principals reported that, when taken as a whole, environmental factors did not interfere with the ability to deliver instruction in their school building. There are two ways to look at this data. While the

Table 6.1. Environmental Factors and Education Impact

Environmental Factor, by Type of Building	*Not at All*	*Minor Extent*	*Moderate Extent*	*Major Extent*	*Not Applicable*
Permanent buildings					
All factors, taken together	56	33	9	1	–
Artificial lighting	76	18	5	1	–
Natural lighting	73	18	5	1	3
Heating	63	24	10	3	1
Air conditioning	46	21	10	6	17
Ventilation	66	22	8	3	–
Indoor air quality	69	21	7	3	–
Acoustics or noise control	61	27	9	3	–
Physical condition of ceilings, floors, walls, windows, doors	71	19	8	3	–
Size or configuration of rooms	64	23	9	4	–

Source: US Department of Education, National Center for Education Statistics (2007), *Public School Principals Report on Their School Facilities: Fall 2005* (NCES 2007-007).

perception of most principals is that the impact of environmental factors had no impact on the delivery of instruction, 44 percent perceived it did.

Do principals' perceptions match what evidence there is regarding the impact of environmental factors on instruction? A study of the District of Columbia school system found, after controlling for other variables such as a student's socioeconomic status, that students' standardized achievement scores were lower in schools with poor building conditions. Students in school buildings in poor condition had achievement that was 6 percent below schools in fair condition and 11 percent below schools in excellent condition (Edwards 1992).

Similarly, Hines' (1996) study of large, urban high schools in Virginia also found a relationship between building condition and student achievement. In fact, Hines found that student achievement was as much as 11 percentile points lower in substandard buildings as compared to above-standard buildings. Picus et al. (2005) noted that if the quality of facilities can influence student achievement then some children may always be at a disadvantaged. The inference being that school funding systems need to address both disparities in funding as well as facilities. Substandard facilities can also be perceived by the community as a lack of commitment to high-quality schools (Rydeen

2009). Following is a brief overview of the research regarding facility features and conditions that have been shown to influence student achievement.

Air-conditioning and heating systems appear to be very important, along with special instructional facilities (i.e., science laboratories or equipment), and color and interior painting in contributing to student achievement (McGuffey 1982). Shaughnessy et al. (2006) found that children tended to achieve higher scores on standardized math and reading tests when they were in classrooms with high outdoor-air ventilation rates than those that were poorly ventilated. Research suggests that children, especially under the age of ten years old, are more likely to be affected by contaminants (asbestos, radon, formaldehyde) than adults. The evidence further suggests that quality of indoor air in school buildings may significantly affect students' ability to concentrate (Andrews and Neuroth 1988).

Daylighting refers to the concept of providing as much effective natural light as possible to classrooms. Of course, there are other design considerations relative to daylighting for it to be effective such as controlling glare, heat gain, the view, and so on. Unfortunately, both the advent of air conditioning in the 1960s and energy crisis of the 1970s caused many new and renovated schools to be built without windows.

A number of studies, however, have linked student health and test-score improvement to improved ventilation, indoor air quality, and daylighting. In 1999, the California Board for Energy Efficiency analyzed test data for more than two thousand classrooms and twenty-one thousand students in Orange County, California; Seattle, Washington; and Fort Collins, Colorado. What the researchers found was that in Orange County, California, students with the most daylighting improved 20 percent faster on math tests and 26 percent faster on reading tests in one year than students with the least amount of daylighting.

Furthermore, they found that student with the largest window areas progressed 15 percent and 24 percent faster in math and reading. One other effect according to the report was that students who were in classrooms where windows opened progressed 7 to 8 percent faster than students in classrooms with fixed windows (regardless if the room had air conditioning) (California Energy Commission 2003).

Movement and circulation through school facilities, positive outdoor learning spaces, large group meeting rooms, and the organization of the school building where teachers are placed in close proximity to each other so that they have the ability to communicate readily with each other have been shown to have a positive effect on achievement (Tanner and Lackney 2006). Additionally, ample building entrances, exits, and views to the outside have been shown to be strongly related to student learning and achievement (Tanner 2009).

Cleanliness and maintenance of facilities has been shown to impact achievement in several ways. A review of building-investigation reports suggests that regular heating, ventilation, and air conditioning (HVAC) maintenance can have significant impact on health and performance (Sieber et al. 1996, 2002). Routine maintenance that results in improvements in a building's environment can lead to increases in test scores (Schneider 2002; Earthman, Cash, and Van Berkum 1995). A strong cleaning program that includes disinfecting bathroom surfaces, combined with alcohol-based hand rubs, can reduce absences from gastrointestinal infections by 10 to 15 percent as well as improve student and staff health (Sandora and Goldman 2008).

Impact on Teaching and Teacher Retention

Lowe (1990) interviewed State Teachers of the Year to determine which aspects of the physical environment affected their teaching the most, and these teachers pointed to the availability and quality of classroom equipment and furnishings, as well as ambient features such as climate control and acoustics, as the most important environmental factors. In particular, the teachers emphasized that the ability to control classroom temperature is crucial to the effective performance of both students and teachers. A study of working conditions in urban schools concluded that the physical conditions of facilities can have either a positive or negative effect on teacher morale, their perception of personal safety, how they view their own effectiveness in the classroom, and on the learning environment (Corcoran, Walker, and White 1988).

According to Corcoran, Walker, and White (1988), building renovations in one district led teachers to feel "a renewed sense of hope, of commitment, a belief that the district cared about what went on in that building." They found that in dilapidated buildings in another district, the atmosphere was punctuated more by despair and frustration, with teachers reporting that leaking roofs, burned out lights, and broken toilets were the typical backdrop for teaching and learning. When conditions were serious enough, they found there were higher levels of absenteeism, lower classroom effectiveness, and low morale. Conversely, when working conditions were good, the results were just the opposite.

What are High-Performance Schools?

Facilities that improve the learning environment and save money, resources, and energy are referred to as *high-performance schools.* Sustainable technologies like ground-source heat pumps, photo-voltaic cells, windmills, wind turbines, and rainwater collection and energy-management systems are but some of the energy strategies being explored in high-performance schools. Daylighting, floor coverings, indoor air quality, flexible building space, sustainable building materials, and improvements that enhance the environment are also key considerations in high-performance schools. In designing new schools, Black (2007) suggests that schools should consider:

1. Learning spaces with daylighting, flexible furniture, and room for group projects.
2. Use of atriums and learning streets to promote social interaction (instead of corridors or hallways).
3. Project rooms for creative thinking and inventing.
4. Areas for multiage groups that mix students of similar interests and aptitudes.
5. Use of outside facilities within the community.
6. Community-use facilities such as meeting rooms, exercise rooms, and meeting rooms.
7. Workrooms for staff that encourage collaboration.
8. Quiet areas.
9. A variety of technology to include distance learning, online classes, wireless networks, and so on.
10. Adaptable classrooms that can be reconfigured as instructional strategies and technology change.

SCHOOL-FACILITY PLANNING

School facilities can, if planned correctly, have an influence on student achievement and behaviors. The cost of energy is, in many cases, the largest operating expenditure schools make on an annual basis after salaries and benefits. Furthermore, design improvements can be made to new or existing school facilities that improve the safety and security of students. Consequently, it is important that all of these factors be considered in developing a short- and long-term facility plan.

There are a number of variables that can affect short- and long-term facility planning. Those variables include enrollment growth/decline, building capacity, building age, and facility utilization. Sometimes the simplest change can have a major impact on building capacity. Consider, for example, a high-school building with an eight-period day with lunch outside the school schedule. If a school decided to change to an eight-period day with lunch included as one of the periods, it would basically lose one-eighth of its building capacity or 12.5 percent. Demographics are equally as important as they result in school closings, renovation, new construction, or a change in use (such as high school to middle school).

The first step in developing any facility plan is to perform a *space inventory*. This should include the number of buildings, usage, classrooms, multipurpose rooms, special-purpose rooms, common areas, storage, office space, and outdoor facilities. Once a complete inventory has been accomplished, the next step is to compute the ideal and maximum building capacities of each school facility. The ideal capacity should be based on class-size standards established by the district as well as the ideal utilization of classroom and school space. This may mean that some space designed for classrooms is utilized for other purposes such as drop-in tutoring, and so on.

The maximum capacity should be based on maximum class sizes authorized by the district. It must also take into account the movement of students in hallways and other common areas. In either ideal or maximum enrollment capacity calculations, it is not unusual to find certain facilities will restrict the size of the building. For example, the lack of science labs or the capacity of cafeteria may restrict the overall capacity of the building.

Short- and long-term facilities planning should be integrated. Assume that a short-term plan is three to five years. The short-term plan should blend into a longer term plan that may range from four to ten years. With the help of an architect or engineer, school districts should be able to estimate the lifecycle of building infrastructure and expected replacement costs. Facilities plans should be updated every year—preferably early in the fiscal year to allow ample time for determining needs, budgeting for them, and preparing the necessary specifications and bids. From a practical perspective, school personnel need to be involved in:

- Updating the space inventory—is there an updated inventory of all space, its use, and capacity?
- Classroom design needs—does the design or number of classrooms or space impede or adversely affect how the instructional program is delivered? Is there a program or schedule that can't be offered because of building restrictions/deficiencies?
- Special area needs
- Office space—is there enough space for the administration, teachers, specials (psychologists, social workers, nurses, etc.) sufficient?
- Comfort issues—are there any concerns regarding temperature, air quality, or lighting?
- Security—are there any concerns regarding the security of the building and safety of students?
- Fixed equipment—is there any old, malfunctioning or missing fixed equipment needed for instructional purposes? Examples would be kilns, science hoods, and so on.
- Outdoor space—is the outdoor space sufficient? Are there any deficiencies with playground space, playing fields, and so on?
- Parking/roadways—is the drop-off area for parents safe and efficient? Is their sufficient parking space for staff, students, parents, and visitors?
- District administration—is there adequate space for staff, district operations, and record storage?

After collecting this information from staff, the services of an architect should be employed to put it and other building information into a formal plan. The formal plan should include information regarding:

- Building envelope—roofs, walls, doors, windows, security
- Interior systems—walls, finishes, ceilings, flooring, hardware, signage, furniture, fixed equipment, elevators
- Capital planning—facilities inventory, planning, utilization, funding
- Operations and maintenance—computerized energy- and equipment-monitoring systems, routine repairs, supplies

- Instruction/technology—space design and flexibility, electrical, networking
- Auxiliary services—transportation, kitchen, and athletic facilities

Part of the facilities master plan developed by a school district should be an attempt to standardize systems whenever possible. Standards can equate to operational savings in training, repairs, and purchasing. The types of items that can be standardized are floor coverings, paint, mechanical systems, HVAC-control systems, security-control systems, and signage systems. A portion of a five-year facility master plan is displayed in Table 6.2. Note that it includes the following information: the item, location, year schedule, and estimated cost. What isn't shown is the funding source. The funding source for most projects is identified in the school budget.

Managing School Facilities

Managing school facilities has changed in complexity over the years. Looking back at the 40s, 50s, and 60s it was fairly simple. There were few, if any, environmental rules and regulations. Most states, if they did have rules and regulations, were directed toward building codes and safety issues. Facility management centered around custodial, maintenance, and grounds operations as well as utility costs, in-house pest control, playground equipment, roofs, safety, school closings, and vandalism. By the 1970s the number of issues were expanding due to concerns over the environment, rising energy costs, aging buildings, and changes in instructional technology. Some of the current facility-management issues are listed in Textbox 6.1.

ENVIRONMENT ISSUES

With increasing frequency, school districts encounter health and environmental issues. Beginning in the 1970s, legislative bodies at the state and federal levels recognized the need to start regulating how hazardous and nonhazardous materials are dealt with by private and public entities. Some of the regulations such as the Asbestos Hazardous Emergency Response Act and Lead Contamination and Control Act directly affect school districts. Other statutes have more indirect consequences. Throughout the 1980s, Congress amended and enhanced environmental acts as a matter of public policy and to keep up with improvements in cleanup technology. In the 1990s the emphasis changed from policy generation to policy enforcement. Enforcement

Table 6.2. Example of Five-Year Facility Plan

Life Safety Survey Projects				*5-Year Plan—$4,251,000*		
SOUTH HIGH SCHOOL	*IS Survey*	*2007/08*	*2008/09*	*2009/10*	*2010/11*	*2011/12*
Architectural Items						
Roofing Repairs/Replacement	A-1	7,000	7,000	283,000	9,000	675,000
Masonry Repairs	A-2	200,000		200,000		200,000
Metal Panels over Masonry Walls	A-1	21,000				
Window Replacement	A-4	312,500		234,000		227,500
Architectural Subtotal		540,500	7,000	717,000	9,000	1,102,500
Mechanical Items						
Air Handler Replacement	M-1					
–Gym				900,000		
–Sp. Ed. ($175,000)						
–CPA						480,000
Mechanical Subtotal				900,000		480,000
Plumbing Items						
Shower Replacement—Main Lockers	P-1	115,000				
Bubbler Removal/Drinking Fountain	P-2	5,000				
Vacuum Breakers—Miscellaneous Areas	P-3	5,000				
Storm Sewer Repairs	P-6	250,000				
Sanitary Sewer Repairs	P-4	45,000				
Plumbing Subtotal		420,000				

Box 6.1. Current Facility Management Issues

1. Custodial operations
2. Maintenance operations
3. Grounds operations
4. Electrical/gas utility
5. Pest control (in-house)
6. Playground equipment
7. Roofs
8. Safety (general)
9. School closings
10. Vandalism
11. Mold
12. Asbestos (AHERA)
13. Lead in paint
14. Labor law issues
15. Purchased services management
16. Protective equipment and clothing
17. Radon management
18. Carbon dioxide testing
19. Lead in water
20. Natural gas/electric volume purchasing
21. Budget planning
22. CMMS
23. Emergency/disaster plans
24. Energy education/management
25. Environmental issues
26. Rentals, community use
27. ADA
28. Indoor air quality
29. Hazardous waste removal
30. Relocatable classrooms
31. Right to Know Act
32. Underground storage tanks
33. Computerization - technology
34. Bloodborne pathogens

is primarily a function of the US Environmental Protection Agency (USEPA). Following is a partial listing of some of the statutes that have been enacted with respect to the environment:

- The Clean Air Act (CAA)
- The Federal Water Pollution Control Act (Clean Water Act) (CWA)
- The Toxic Substances Control Act (TSCA)
- The Comprehensive Environmental Response Compensation and Liability Act (known as the Superfund)
- The Safe Drinking Water Act (SDWA)
- The Asbestos Hazard Emergency Response Act (AHERA)
- The Indoor Radon Abatement Act (IRAA)
- The Lead Contamination and Control Act (LCCA)

Asbestos has been identified as a known human carcinogen capable of producing lung cancer. Asbestos is a naturally occurring fibrous material that can be found in such products as fireproofing and insulation. The Asbestos Hazard Emergency Response Act (AHERA) stipulates a school district's liability from exposure to asbestos by students, staff, and/or the general public. Regulations require both inspection and management plans for each school building. School districts have responded to AHERA by either removing or encapsulating "asbestos-containing building materials."

School districts are required to inspect facilities they own, lease, or use for "asbestos-containing building materials." An accredited inspector must be used. School districts must generate an asbestos-management plan for each school building. The plan must include a description of the inspection, recommendations, and name of a "designated person" required to oversee the management plan.

School districts must generate and institute an operation and maintenance (O&M) program for each building. The O&M program must include short-term maintenance operations, worker protection, and cleaning techniques. Maintenance and custodial staff working in a school building must receive instruction regarding asbestos-containing building materials. Asbestos-containing building material (ACBM) is regulated by the US Environment Protection Agency. Anytime an ACBM is discovered, the school district must institute a response action. All work done, including project management, air sampling, and removal must be by accredited personnel.

The *Report to Congress, Management of Hazardous Wastes from Educational Institutions* (1989) laid out the regulatory and statutory guidelines for the management of hazardous wastes in the school districts. A waste is any solid, liquid, or contained gaseous material no longer in use, recycled, thrown away, or stored until treatment or disposal. The types and quantities of wastes generated by school districts affect the manner and legality in which storage, treatment and disposal methods are used.

Hazardous waste can be subject to regulation in two ways: (1) if the waste is listed in the Resource Conservation and Recovery Act (RCRA) regulations, or (2) it exhibits ignitability, corrosiveness, reactivity or toxicity characteristics even though not on the RCRA list. Most school districts are small-quantity generators or conditionally exempt small-quantity generators. A small-quantity generator produces between one hundred and one thousand kilograms of nonacute hazardous waste per month. Exempt small-quantity generators create no more than one hundred kilograms (about twenty-five gallons) of hazardous waste per month and no more than one kilogram of acutely hazardous waste in any calendar month. Acutely hazardous waste includes, for example, certain pesticides and dioxin-containing wastes. Conditionally exempt small-quantity generators (most school districts) are required to:

- Identify all hazardous waste generated
- Send waste to a hazardous waste facility or landfill, or other approved facility

It is important to note that both the carrier and owner of hazardous waste can be held liable should it not be disposed of properly.

The Lead Contamination Control Act was passed by Congress in 1988. The act was passed to address the growing concern about lead levels in drinking water. At the time the act was passed, the USEPA estimated that up to 241,000 children under age six were exposed levels high enough to impair their intellectual development. The USEPA has issued testing protocols and information to assist schools in evaluating drinking water for possible lead contamination. States are required to also disseminate guidelines and information to school districts. Local education agencies (LEA) are required to notify parents, teachers, and employee organizations of lead-testing results. School districts are required to make copies of test results available to the general public and notify parents, teachers, and employee groups that results are available. Notification can take the form of a printed notice in newsletters or letters to organizations that the results are available.

In recent years, *indoor air quality* (IAQ) has probably received the greatest amount of attention in schools. The primary reason for this is the discovery of mold in a number of schools across the nation. Mold is the result of moisture and is usually found in areas with high humidity. In some cases, mold is the result of deferred maintenance. Specifically, leaky roofs, pipes, windows, and anything that allows for water infiltration in a building can be a cause of mold. Brick, where the mortar has decayed, is a perfect entry point for water infiltration. Unfortunately, mold is not always discovered before it becomes expensive to remove. In some cases, entire school buildings have had to be closed to remediate indoor air quality issues (Masterson 2011).

School districts can obtain guidance regarding indoor air quality from the USEPA but the best defense is to routinely have indoor air quality tested and visually inspect all areas that would be susceptible to mold. Schools can use the *IAQ Tools for Schools Action Kit* from the USA EPA to get started in managing indoor air quality. The kit includes best practices, guidelines, sample policies, and management plans at no cost to school districts (USEPA 2012a).

The use of *pesticides* in schools is not currently regulated by the federal government. Pesticides are used to manage rodents, insects, and other pests. A number of states, however, have passed laws that restrict or limit their use in schools. Some states have prescribed the use of alternate methods such as using only nontoxic forms of chemical pesticides. The Environmental Protection Agency (EPA) suggests that school districts use an integrated pest-management system (IPM) to reduce the risk to schoolchildren. IPM utilizes preventative strategies such as vegetation control, sealing cracks and crevices, litter control, judicious use of fertilizers, and so on so that pesticides are only used where and when necessary (USEPA 1993).

According to the USEPA, exposure to elevated levels of radon in homes and other buildings poses a possible risk of lung cancer. Radon is a radioactive gas that results in the natural breakdown of uranium in the environment. One can neither smell nor taste radon gas. Good risk management practices would dictate that school districts should initiate their own radon measurement and monitoring programs. The Indoor Radon Abatement Act of 1988 (IRA) required that the USEPA map all of the counties in the United States for radon-potential level.

Underground storage tanks (USTs) which contain "regulated substances" such as petroleum and hazardous substances are subject to regulation. By May 8, 1986, all owners of USTs were required to notify the appropriate state agency of the age, size, type, location, and use of operating USTs and USTs taken out of operation after January 1, 1974. By 1998 all USTs existing before 1988 had to meet certain spill- and overflow-prevention requirements. Petroleum USTs installed after 1988 must be installed by qualified contractors who follow industry codes with regard to excavation, setting, assembly, backfilling, and grading.

In addition, spill- and overflow-, corrosion- and leak-detection technologies must be installed. School districts that decide to discontinue use of an UST must notify the regulatory agency, investigate the soils around the tank, and remove or properly seal the tank in-ground. School districts are financially responsible for damages resulting in leaking tanks. Damages can include both cleanup costs and compensation for personal injury.

Energy Conservation

Energy conservation and/or reduction can be achieved through one of three strategies. They are: (1) capital projects that replace inefficient systems with efficient ones, (2) the management of utility resources through energy-purchasing solutions, and (3) reductions achieved through implementing energy-conservation measures. The first step in achieving energy savings is to set a goal and complete an energy audit. Table 6.3 shows a typical energy-conservation design.

Capital improvements to save energy are often also sustainable solutions. In 2009, the Oregon Department of Energy indicated that the American Recovery and Reinvestment Act would pay for twenty-two renewable public-school energy projects. The projects included pellet boilers, wood chip boilers, biomass, solar, and geothermal (Oregon Department of Energy 2009).

Managing energy resources is a strategy that usually involves the use of a consultant to determine how the school or school district uses energy resources. By auditing natural gas and electricity bills, consultants are able to determine if the school or district is on the appropriate rate structure and/or are being overcharged for its energy use.

Many districts can reduce energy and save money simply by implementing conservation measures and behaviors. Table 6.4 shows an example of some typical HVAC-conversation measures.

Another approach is to use the EPA Energy Star program for K–12 school districts. Energy Star provides a toolkit to assist school districts in assessing and managing energy resources. They also have a recognition program for schools and/or school districts that recognizes them for their commitment to energy management and best practices (USEPA 2012b).

Green Cleaning

Green cleaning is a strategy that "promotes healthy and sustainable approaches to protect health without harming the environment" (American School and University 2012). The Green Cleaning Award sponsored by

Table 6.3. Example of an Energy Conservation Design

Goal		*Planning*	
20% energy reduction per year	\$250K—\$300K cost reduction	Benchmark	Energy Audit

Table 6.4. Typical HVAC Conservation Measures

Temperature Guidelines	*Establish Occupied Times*	*Temperature Timelines*	*Building Scheduling*
70 degrees for heat	Occupied time is considered 6 a.m.–4 p.m. on school days	Maintain temperature during occupied time	During unoccupied time, events will be restricted to a limited number of heating cooling zones
74 degrees for cooling	All other times are unoccupied	For unoccupied time—no A/C and heat set to 60 degrees	

American School & University, The Green Cleaning Network, and Healthy Schools Campaign outlines five areas for green cleaning: products, equipment and supplies, procedures, use of green paper and plastic products, and shared responsibility. There are many green cleaning standards that a public school or school system can adopt. There are numerous organizations that have developed green cleaning standards. Table 6.6 lists some of the common standards. A common question that arises with green cleaning products is whether they cost more than conventional products. The research seems to indicate that the cost is either neutral or, in some cases lower (Connecticut Foundation on Environmentally Safe Schools 2008).

Allocating Custodial and Maintenance Staff

The key to allocating to custodial and maintenance staff is (1) establishing the expectations for cleanliness for each area, (2) determining how often

Table 6.5. Examples of Electric-Conservation Measures

Lights Out	*Unplug and Turn Off!*	*Natural Light as Much as Possible*	*Treat It Like Your Own Home*
Turn lights off and/or dim as much as possible.	Turn off computer labs and copy machines at the end of the day.	Use natural lighting in gymnasiums and classrooms as much as possible.	Be smart—if something feels like it is wasting energy, it probably is!
	Turn off vending and kitchen equipment for the summer.		

Table 6.6. Example List of Green Cleaning Standards

- Concentrate is nontoxic to humans
- Concentrate does not contain carcinogens or reproductive toxins
- Concentrate is not corrosive to skin or eyes
- Concentrate is not a skin sensitizer
- Concentrate is not combustible
- Use solutions that do not contribute to smog formation or poor indoor air quality
- All individual ingredients are readily biodegradable
- Products contain no phosphates
- Products' primary packaging is recyclable

each area will need to be cleaned to meet the established expectations, and (3) benchmarking staffing levels against local, regional, or national data. It is important to note that each building is different based on the grade level served, student enrollment, size and age of the facility, floor coverings, HVAC systems, plumbing, electrical systems, classrooms, roofs, kitchens, technology, outside facilities, parking lots, and acreage.

There are numerous methods for benchmarking custodial and maintenance services but ultimately the school district will not only have to determine the number of staff members it needs but their duties. Generally, custodial duties relate to the daily cleaning and upkeep of school facilities as well as their management and supervision. Maintenance duties relate to prevention, repair, and renovation of facilities. Grounds duties relate to the upkeep of the outside facilities including fields, athletic facilities, lighting, and parking lots. Table 6.7 shows a sample of custodial as well as grounds and maintenance career paths.

Cleaning standards relate to the frequency each area is cleaned, what is cleaned, and how it is cleaned (appearance). Table 6.8 shows an example of each category.

The appropriate number of staff members is dependent on the benchmarking chosen by the school district. As previously noted, there are many variables that determine how much space a custodian can clean on a shift

Table. 6.7. Custodial/Grounds/Maintenance Career Path

Locker Room Monitor	Level 1	Level II			
Custodian	Level I	Level II	Level III		
Grounds		Level II	Level III		
Maintenance			Level III	Level IV	Level V

Table 6.8. Example of Cleaning Standards

Frequency	*Standard*
Three times a day	Dust mop hallways and gym
Twice a day	Clean restrooms –Clean all toilets, urinals, and lavatory fittings and partitions with disinfectant –Clean walls around fixtures –Refill toilet paper and towels –Check and lock windows –Empty wastebaskets (clean with disinfectant if necessary) Clean drinking fountains –Spray all surfaces top and bottom with disinfectant, wipe with sponge –Polish chrome fittings with dry cloth Clean all entrances
Daily	Unlock and lock building Empty pencil sharpeners and wastebaskets Vacuum classrooms Wipe down streaks and smudges on woodwork tiles and windows Clean and store equipment properly Check lights, replace bulbs as necessary Check thermostat and report issues to maintenance Refill paper and soap in restrooms
Weekly	Clean restroom fixtures Clean whiteboards

(CFT—cleanable square feet). Floor coverings, type of space (classrooms, washrooms, gyms, hallways, etc.), frequency of cleaning, and interruptions from meeting setups are all examples of variables that can affect custodial workload. The best benchmarks for staffing are other similar schools locally. Schools located locally will have the same weather conditions, and most likely similar wage rates, staffing ratios, and union contracts, if they exist.

Using the information from Table 6.9, a school district might establish the following formula for their high schools: Total Square Feet divided by 21,950 = Custodial FTE (full-time equivalent employee). Consideration might also be given to provide a factor for student density since some may argue the higher the density, the more cleaning will be required. That factor, based on the data in Table 6.9, might provide an additional FTE for each 10 percent in density over the benchmarking average of 165. Using this formula, if a high school had a pupil density between 181.5 and 198, it would receive one additional FTE in custodial staffing.

Table 6.9. Example of Benchmarking Custodial Staffing

High School	*Square Feet*	*Student Enrollment*	*Custodial Staff FTE*	*Square Feet per FTE*	*Density—Sq. Ft. per Pupil*
A	320,000	1,775	16.8	19,000	180
B	425,000	2,500	19.3	22,000	170
C	375,000	2,150	16.3	23,000	174
D	300,000	1,800	15.0	20,000	167
E	450,000	3,100	19.1	23,500	145
Average	374,000	2,265	17.3	21,950	165

In some cases, such studies have been completed on a state-wide basis. Arkansas, for example, recommends that the staffing level for custodial personnel should be eighteen thousand to twenty thousand square feet or 2,250 to 2,500 square feet per hour (State of Arkansas 2009). The same report suggests grounds personnel should be staffed based on one employee per eighteen to twenty acres and that maintenance personnel should be staffed on the basis of one employee per eighty thousand to ninety thousand square feet. Of course these are only guidelines. (The Florida Office of Educational Facilities utilizes a slightly different standard that includes both a factor for CSF and a modifier depending on the type of school).

There are still other methods of calculating staffing needs. There are formulas that consider not only building space but the number of teachers, pupils, rooms cleaned, and square footage of the building. Still other formulas utilize a workload formula. In a workload formula, the space that is to be cleaned is assigned a factor (cleaning rate per hour). By determining the type of space to be cleaned, the total number of cleaning hours can be calculated. Table 6.10 shows an example of this method.

The same strategies would also apply to staffing grounds and maintenance staffs. The difference, obviously, is the work that is being completed. For grounds personnel the primary variables would be the acreage of property, size of athletic fields and outbuildings, and type of school (elementary, middle, high school).

For maintenance personnel staffing the variables would be the types of HVAC systems, size of the school, extent to which maintenance services are outsourced, age of the building, and support services required. In private industry, the typical maintenance staffing formula is based on the total replacement cost of equipment, systems, and buildings. School districts are more

Table 6.10. Example of Workload Task Staffing

Custodial Task	*Estimated Square Feet per Hour*
Cleaning of all permanent buildings at a facility (including classrooms, administrative assembly areas, etc.)	2,400
Toilets, showers, lockers	1,400
Portable classrooms	2,000
Outside areas (e.g., sidewalks, courtyards, etc.)	7,500

Total number of hours required for each task divided by 8 equals the total daily workforce required.

inclined to use a formula based on the square feet to be maintained plus a factor for support services (i.e., clerical support to process work orders, for example).

Facilities Management and Supervision

Maintenance management systems (MMS) are an important tool in monitoring facilities. Technology can be used to determine staffing, monitor work orders, track preventive maintenance on equipment, monitor energy usage, and provide a basis for staff evaluation. They can also identify problems with specific equipment that can be used for budgeting building improvements and capital replacements. Furthermore, MMS can identify and track professional development and mandatory training for staff.

A key component of facilities management is insuring that there is sufficient supervisory and support staff to monitor staff, utility usage, supplies, and compliance issues. The appearance standards adopted by a school or school district should be monitored on a routine basis to ensure consistency. Teaching and other school staff should be involved in providing feedback as to whether custodial and maintenance standards are being met.

Most schools schedule the bulk of their custodial staff to work after the close of the school day. Supervision of after-hours shifts by a foreman or head/lead custodian is important. After-hours shifts have to be able to adapt to employee absences as well as set-ups for extra/cocurricular activities and events such as athletic contests, performances, and so on. One strategy for reducing energy costs and maximizing the use of custodial staff is to try to limit school activities to specific days of the week and/or specific areas of the building.

SUMMARY

Significant resources need to be invested in the nation's public school facilities. The schools built for the "baby boomers" are now over fifty years old and in many cases lack the basic tenets that would be built into new schools today such as sustainable energy systems, flexible instructional space, daylighting, air conditioning, safety and security, and so forth. In the immediate future there will be both a need for school closings and new schools being built primarily due to demographic changes occurring in the United States. In either case, a sizeable investment will have to be made to existing schools.

There is a growing body of research that suggests that school facilities can have an effect on student achievement as well as behaviors. Teacher retention, morale, and absenteeism can also be affected by the quality of school facilities. As more evidence is produced to support the link between the quality of facilities and student achievement, the question of the adequacy and equity of facilities for all public-school children will need to be addressed. For the most part, the questions of adequacy and equity of school facilities has never been factored into the equation. At some juncture, researchers will have to determine if the quality of facilities is higher in wealthy districts than in poor ones.

Short- and long-term facility planning is an important piece of a district's overall financial plan. Review of demographics, instructional strategies, safety and security issues, building inventories and capacities are all important in determining future facility needs. Having staff and professional staff such as architects provide annual feedback on the condition of buildings and facilities will lead to better planning. Addressing operations and maintenance items such as building infrastructure can save money by preventing more costly repairs. Any new or renovated facilities should be looked at as an opportunity to improve the learning space for students, staff, and the community.

The management of school facilities has changed significantly. School systems must now address a myriad of environmental laws as well as best practices such as green cleaning and purchasing. With the cost of energy becoming a major part of most school budgets, they have had to look for ways to implement energy conservation measures. The key to having a well-run custodial and maintenance department is to insure adequate staffing, clearly delineate job responsibilities and standards, and evaluate the results of operation. To be cost effective, custodial and maintenance operations should be benchmarked based on the school characteristics and local, regional, and national standards.

CASE STUDY

"Creating an Active Learning Environment"

The Board of Education of Everest Public School System has determined that it will need a new elementary-school building to house approximately four hundred students in prekindergarten through fifth grade in the next few years. After an exhaustive search, you have been selected to become the principal of the new school. The superintendent has asked you to visit new schools that have created an active learning environment for students through facility design. You have also been charged with researching "best practices" with regard to space utilization, flexibility, technology, and design philosophies. Based on your investigation:

- Who would you involve in the design of the new building?
- What would the school look like to a student? How would students be served by the design?
- How would the learning environment be designed?
- What technology would be incorporated into the design?
- How would instruction be enhanced by the design?
- How would teacher collaboration be enhanced by the design?
- What design elements would you include to the future flexibility of the learning space?

EXERCISES AND DISCUSSION QUESTIONS

1. From your own experience as a parent, teacher, or student, what environmental factors most affect your learning and why? Is there any research that would support your perceptions?
2. How can a building principal insure they are operating a cost-effective custodial/maintenance program?
3. Take a walk through a public-school building. Is it clean? What is the general appearance of hallways and classrooms, restrooms? What grade would you give the custodial staff?

4. Interview a facilities director, head or lead custodian. What are their biggest challenges? How do they evaluate the cleanliness of the school or buildings they supervise? How do they allocate custodial staff?
5. Obtain a copy of a school-district facilities master plan. What does the report say about renovating facilities? Will the district need to build new facilities? How much will it cost to implement the plan? How does the district plan on paying for the plan?
6. Develop a list of key features a principal should ensure are included in a new school building.
7. What parts of an operations and maintenance budget should be included in a site-based management approach to budgeting?
8. Investigate the Energy Star program sponsored by the US Department of Energy and Environmental Protection Agency. How would you implement the program in a school building? What would be the main obstacles to its implementation? How would you involve students, staff, and community?

REFERENCES

American Association of School Administrators. (2008). *AASA survey finds rising fuel, energy costs stressing school budgets*. July 29. www.aasa.org/uploadedFiles/Publications/_files/FINALEnergySurvey.pdf.

American School & University. (2012). *Green cleaning award for schools and universities.* July 7. asumag.com/green_cleaning_award/#ixzz1zytWj3l2.

Andrews, J., and Neuroth, R. (1988). *Environmentally related health hazards in the schools* (ED 300292). October. Detroit, MI: Association of School Business Officials.

Black, S. (2007). Achievement by design. *American School Board Journal* 194 (10): 39.

California Energy Commission. (2003). *Summary of daylighting in schools: Reanalysis report*. www.energy.ca.gov/2003publications/CEC-500-2003-082/CEC-500-2003-082-A-04.PDF.

Carnegie Foundation for the Advancement of Teaching. *An Imperiled Generation: Saving Urban Schools*. Princeton, NJ: Author. ED 293940.

Corcoran, Thomas B., White, J. Lynne.Walker, Lisa J. (1988) Working in urban schools /Washington, D.C. : Institute for Educational Leadership,

Casserly, M., Lachlan-Hache, J., and Naik, M. (2011). *Facility needs and costs in America's great city schools.* Council of the Great City Schools: Washington, DC. www.cgcs.org/cms/lib/DC00001581/Centricity/Domain/4/Facilities_Report.pdf.

Cauchon, D. (1999). When removing asbestos makes no sense. *USA Today.* February 11.

Clark County School District. (2012). *Clark County fast facts.* ccsd.net/district/news/publications/pdf/CCSDFastFactsColor.pdf.

Connecticut Foundation on Environmentally Safe Schools. (2008). *Green cleaning in schools is cost effective.* October. www.safehealthyct.org/documents/Green_Cleaning_Cost_Effective__2_.doc.

Corcoran, T., Walker, L., and White, J. (1988). *Working in urban schools.* Washington, DC: Institute for Educational Leadership.

Daniels v. School Board of Brevard County [985 F.Supp.] 1458 (FL. 1997)

Earthman, G., Cash, C., and Van Berkum, D. (1995). Student achievement and behavior and school building condition. *Journal of School Business Management* 8 (3): 26–37.

Edwards, M. (1992). *Building conditions, parental involvement and student achievement in the D.C. public school system.* Unpublished master's degree thesis. Georgetown University, Washington, DC (ED 264 285).

Filardo, M., Bernstien, J., and Eisenbrey, R. (2011). Will Obama embrace FAST (Fix America's Schools Today)? *Schools Matter.* August 19. www.schoolsmatter.info/2011/08/will-obamaduncan-embrace-fast-fix.html.

Hines, E. (1996). *Building condition and student achievement and behavior.* Unpublished.

Horng, E. (2009). Teacher tradeoffs: Disentangling teachers' preferences for working conditions and student demographics. *American Educational Research Journal* 46 (3): 690–717.

Hubbard, J. (2010). Schools must improve athletic facilities. *Wilkes Journal-Patriot.* December 17. www.journalpatriot.com/news/article_42c23348-0a11-11e0-923a-0017a4a78c22.html.

Lowe, J. (1990). *The interface between educational facilities and learning climate.* Unpublished.

Masterson, T. (2011). Mold closes 1 NJ school, puts others on alert. *NBC10 Philadelphia.* September 12. www.nbcphiladelphia.com/news/local/Mold-Closes-1-NJ-School-Puts-2-Others-on-Alert-129658678.html.

McGuffey, C. (1982). Facilities. In H. J. Walbery (Ed.), *Improving educational standards and productivity* (pp. 237–281). Berkeley, CA: McCutchan.

National Center for Education Statistics. (2011). *Enrollment trends.* US Department of Education. nces.ed.gov/fastfacts/display.asp?id=65.+

——. (2007a). *Indicators of school crime and safety.* nces.ed.gov/programs/crimeindicators/crimeindicators2007/.

——. (2007b). *Public school principals report on their school facilities: Fall 2005* (NCES 2007-007). nces.ed.gov/fastfacts/display.asp?id=94.

Oregon Department of Energy. (2009). *Renewable energy projects to receive recovery act funding.* www.oregon.gov/energy/Recovery/Pages/news/0944SEPARRA.aspx.

Picus, L., Marion, S., Calvo, N., and Glenn, W. (2005). Understanding the relationship between student achievement and the quality of educational facilities: Evidence from Wyoming. *Peabody Journal of Education (0161956X)* 80 (3): 71–95. doi:10.1207/s15327930pje8003_5

Rydeen, J. (2009). Test case. *American School & University* 81 (13): 146.

Sandora, T., Shih, M., and Goldmann, D. (2008). Reducing absenteeism from gastrointestinal and respiratory illness in elementary school students: A randomized, controlled trial of an infection-control intervention. *Pediatrics* 121:1555–62.

Shaughnessy, R., Shaughnessy, U., Nevalainen, A., and Moschandreas, D. (2006). A preliminary study on the association between ventilation rates in classrooms and student performance. *Indoor Air* 16 (6): 465–68.

Sieber, W., Stayner, L., et al. (1996). The National Institute for Occupational Safety and Health indoor environmental evaluation experience. Part 3: Associations between environmental factors and self-reported health conditions. *Journal of Occupational and Environmental Hygiene* 11 (12): 1387–92.

Sieber, W., Petersen, M., et al. (2002). HVAC characteristics and occupant health. *ASHRAE Journal* (September): 49–52.

State of Arkansas, Division of Academic Facilities and Transportation. (2009). *Public school facilities, maintenance, repair and renovation manual (custodial and maintenance manual).* arkansasfacilities.arkansas.gov/documents/Manuals/Custodial%20and%20Maintenance/Final%20Manual.pdf.

Tanner, C. (2009). Effects of school design on student outcomes. *Journal of Educational Administration* 47 (3): 376–94.

Tanner, C., and Lackney, J. (2006). The physical environment and student achievement in elementary schools. In C. K. Tanner and J. A. Lackney (Eds.), *Educational facilities planning: Leadership, architecture, and management* (pp. 266–94). Boston, MA: Pearson Education.

The 21st Century School Fund. (2011). PK–12 Public school facility infrastructure fact sheet. *Building Educational Success Together (BEST).* February. www.21csf.org/csf-home/Documents/FactSheetPK12PublicSchoolFacilityInfrastructure.pdf.

Trump, K. (2009). Columbine's 10th anniversary finds lessons learned. *District Administration.* April. www.schoolsecurity.org/trends/Columbine%2010th%20Anniversary%20Lessons%20DA%20article.pdf.

Uline, C., and Tschannen-Moran, M. (2008). The walls speak: The interplay of quality facilities, school climate, and student achievement. *Journal of Educational Administration* 46 (1): 55–73.

U.S. Environmental Protection Agency. (1993). *Pest control in school environment: adopting integrated pest management.* EPA 735-F-93-012 Retrieved from http://www.epa.gov/pesticides/ipm/brochure/

——. (2012a). *Creating healthy indoor environments in schools.* www.epa.gov/iaq/schools/.

——. Energy Star Program. (2012b). *Energy Star for k–12 school districts.* www.energystar.gov/index.cfm?c=k12_schools.bus_schoolsk12.

7

Auxiliary Services: Food, Safety, Security, and Transportation

OBJECTIVES

At the conclusion of this chapter you will be able to:

1. Understand the role that auxiliary services fulfill within a school system (ELCC 3.1, 3.2, 3.3, ISLLC 3).
2. Identify the major components of the National School Lunch Program (ELCC 3.3, ISLLC 3).
3. Understand the legislative history of federally subsidized meals and the various programs offered by the federal government (ELCC 6.1, ISLLC 6).
4. Understand the importance of a crisis-management plan (ELCC 3.3, ISLLC 3).
5. Articulate the federal laws regarding government transporting students (ELCC 6.1, ISLLC 6).
6. Understand the advantages of district-owned and contracted transportation services (ELCC 3.1, 3.2, 3.3, ISLLC 3).
7. Understand the safety issues regarding transporting students and the equipment on which they ride (ELCC 3.3, ISLLC 3).

MAJOR AUXILIARY SERVICES

Food service, safety, security, and transportation services are all auxiliary services that provide an important role in school operations. The purpose of providing these services is to support the instructional environment. Ensuring that students can get to and from school, eat a nutritious meal, and are in a safe and secure learning environment are fundamental services. There are both federal and state laws that regulate the operation of these services. Furthermore, the manner in which these services are provided can differ based on specific state laws regarding the outsourcing of auxiliary operations such as food service and transportation.

The trend toward decentralizing budgeting decisions means that building as well as district administrators must be cognizant of the rules and regulations that apply to these services. Other factors, such as resources, geography, facilities, and demographics can also impact how these services are provided. A school district in an urban area may have completely different issues from a rural district when it comes to providing transportation services. A district with a high incidence of low-income students will have different issues from one with mostly high-income students when it comes to food-service operations. A school building without a kitchen will be challenged to provide a hot meal to students on a daily basis.

FOOD SERVICE

President Truman signed the National School Lunch Act into law in 1946, which established the National School Lunch Program (NSLP). The act was created to provide to provide subsidized meals to qualified students at little or no cost. As originally designed, the program served as a means to not only provide food to public-school children but as a means to support farm surpluses (United States Department of Agriculture, Food and Nutrition Service 2007). The Child Nutrition Act of 1966 established the School Breakfast Program (SBP). The SBP provides free breakfasts to children in public and nonprofit private schools and residential child-care institutions. The act also authorized the Special Milk Program (SMP) that provides low-cost or free milk to children in qualifying schools and institutions that do not participate in the NSLP. In 1968, a three-year pilot was created to provide assistance in supplying meals to children when school was not in session.

After another three-year extension in 1975, the program became permanent as part of the Child and Adult Care Food Service Program (CACFP). In 1998 NSLP was expanded to include cash disbursements for certain snacks for after-school and enrichment programs. Both the NSLP and SBP programs were reauthorized in 2004 incorporating changes to make it easier for qualifying children to enroll. The Healthy, Hunger-Free Kids Act (HHFKA) was signed into law in December 2010 (National Conference of State Legislatures 2011). The key components of the law are as follows:

1. Provides for an increase in lunch- and breakfast-reimbursement rates.
2. Increases the authority of the Secretary of Agriculture over these programs.
3. Expands access.
4. Allows certain communities with a high incidence of low-income students to directly certify for school meals without the usual family applications.
5. Facilitates the expansion of after-school meal programs.

According to the *New York Times* (Dillon 2011), the NSLP provides about thirty-two million lunches of which twenty-one million are free or at a reduced price. In 2010, the cost of the program was estimated to be $10.8 billion. Eligibility guidelines for the NSLP, NBP, SMP, and Summer Food Service Program SFSP are required to be issued annually. The eligibility for free and reduced meals is based on federal poverty guidelines. The threshold for free meals is calculated at 130 percent of the federal poverty guideline and reduced-price meals are calculated at 185 percent. For the 2012–2013 school year, for example, the federal poverty guideline for a family of four is an annual household income of $23,050 for the contiguous forty-eight states. Based on this number, a child in a household of four would qualify for free meals at an annual income of $29,965 and reduced-price meals at an annual income of $42,643 (US Department of Agriculture, Food and Nutrition Service 2012). Income is calculated before taxes, insurance payments, charitable contributions, and bonds.

The most significant error on applications relates to household income. According to The Office of Research, Nutrition and Analysis, "80 percent of students with any reporting error on their applications had misreported income information. One-half of these errors were differences in gross income amounts for a specific person from a specific source, often secondary income sources from non-primary household members" (US Department of Agriculture 2007).

The reimbursement rates for 2012–2013 in the contiguous states ranges between $2.86 and $3.09 per meal based on the percentage of students participating in the free meal program, $2.46 to $2.69 for the reduced-price meal program, and between $0.27 to $0.41 for students who pay for their meals (National School Lunch, Special Milk, and School Breakfast Programs, 2012).

Under the HHFKA of 2010, beginning no earlier than October 2012 an additional reimbursement of six cents per lunch is available for school districts that are in compliance with the new meal requirements. The key changes to the meal requirements for breakfast and lunch for grades K–12 are outlined in Table 7.1.

The new meal pattern is targeted at not only increasing the nutritional value of meals but also addressing the growing concern regarding childhood obesity. It is estimated that more than one-third of all children and adoles-

Table 7.1. New Meal Patterns for NSLP and SBP

Program	*Requirement*
National School Lunch Program (NSLP)	– Daily serving of fruits and vegetables plus a weekly requirement for dark green, red/orange, beans/pea (legumes), starchy, and "other" vegetables – Increased quantity of combined fruits and vegetables – Weekly meat/meat-alternate ranges plus a daily requirement – At least half of the grains offered during the school week must be whole-grain-rich during the first year
School Breakfast Program (SBP)	– After the minimum grains requirement is met, a meat/meat-alternate may be offered – At least half of the grains offered during the school week must be whole-grain-rich in the second year of rule implementation – The quantity of fruit is increased in the third year of implementation
Applies to both the NSLP and SBP	– One food-based menu planning approach – Fruits and vegetables are two separate food components with a daily fruit requirement – Students must select at least one-half cup of the fruits or the vegetables component as part of the reimbursable meal under offer versus serve – Weekly ranges plus a daily minimum requirement for grains – All grains offered during the school week must be whole-grain-rich starting the third year of implementation – All milk must be fat-free (unflavored or flavored) – Minimum and maximum levels of calories for meals – Targets for sodium reductions – A limit on trans-fats – A limit on saturated fat only (not on total fat)

Source: US Department of Agriculture, Food and Nutrition Service, Nutrition Standards for School Meals. 7 CFR Parts 210 and 220 (2012).

cents in the United States were overweight or obese in 2008 (Ogden et al. 2010).

SAFETY AND SECURITY

For many parents, the safety and security of their children is a primary concern. Providing a safe and secure environment in which instruction can occur is also a primary concern of school administrators. A good risk-management program provides both a safe environment free from danger and risk and a secure one in which children feel safe. The American Association of School Administrators (AASA) recommends a balanced approached that combines three elements: awareness, balance, and control.

"Awareness" addresses the need to update policies and share them with students, staff, and parents. It also involves knowing the warning signs of threats to people and facilities. "Balance" involves using various approaches to reducing risk and keeping all stakeholders informed. "Control" speaks to the issue of securing the learning environment, whether through facilities measures or the use of safety officers and other professionals (AASA 2012).

Safety and security starts with providing safe routes for children to get to school. The National Center for Safe Routes to School (2010) is a good source for addressing how to make walking and riding a bike to school as safe as possible for school-age children. Safety and security also involves the physical campus. This includes insuring that the physical structure of the building is free from hazards as well as controlling who gets in and out of the building. Daily inspections by teachers, administrators, and custodial/maintenance staffs can provide a level of assurance and feedback regarding safety issues.

The design of school buildings can also be a factor. Many new buildings are now designed with entry points to control entry into the school. Together with strategically located cameras, these access points provide a deterrent to unauthorized entry and would-be attackers. Communications systems can save lives in times of emergencies. As a preventive measure, schools have incorporated computerized access-control systems that do a quick background check to screen visitors.

As noted in the 2001 report of the Columbine Review Commission (State of Colorado, 2001), there is a fine line between layers of security and maintaining an atmosphere conducive to learning. So that raises the question, "What safety and security strategies are being used in public schools?" The

US Department of Education, National Center for Education Statistics asked public-school principals about their use of safety and security measures in the 2009–2010 school year. Table 7.2 is a summary of those results.

School climates play a major role in deterring school violence. This involves all staff. Examples of violent behavior in schools include bullying, fighting, weapon use, electronic aggression, and gang violence. "Half of all violence against teenagers occurs in school buildings, on school property, or on the street in the vicinity of the school (Larrivee 2005). In 2009, it was estimated that 7.7 percent of all students, 5.5 percent of females and 9.6 percent of males, had been victims of one of these behaviors in the previous twelve months (CDC 2009). In an *Indicators of School Crime and Safety: 2011* report, there were thirty-three deaths associated with schools for grades K–12 in fiscal year 2010. In fact, during this time frame, 85 percent of the schools reporting indicated one or more incidents of theft, crime, or violence (US Department of Education 2012).

The situation is even worse in the nations' urban schools. At the beginning of the 2005–2006 school year, Robeson High School in the Englewood neighborhood of Chicago reported twenty-seven violent incidents (Donovan and Sweeney 2006). In 2012, parents asked for additional protection for their children, saying gangs in their neighborhood were targeting their children who attended a new charter school in the area (Huff Post Chicago 2012). According to data released by Mayor Michael Bloomberg's office, New York public schools saw a 21 percent increase in major crime from July through October from 2005 to 2006 (Gootman 2007).

The *Commissioner's Annual Report to the Education Committees* of the Senate and General Assembly on Violence, Vandalism and Substance Abuse in New Jersey Public Schools reported that for the three years ending June 30, 2011, the incidents involving firearms increased by 25.1 percent. Fortunately, there are various models for addressing violence, drug, and crime prevention that can be adapted for use in schools. For example, the Blueprints project at the University of Colorado's Center for the Study of the Prevention of Violence identifies eleven model programs that meet rigorous criteria for effectiveness. Project SAVE (Safe Schools against Violence in Education) was signed into law in New York in 2000.

A strategy of the legislation was to substitute in-school suspension for all but the most serious offenses as opposed to suspending the students.

Table 7.2. Public Schools Safety and Security Measures

Percentage of public schools that used selected safety and security measures, by school level: 2009–2010

		School Level[1]			
Selected safety and security measures	*Total*	*Primary*	*Middle*	*High Schl*	*Combined*
Controlled access during school hours					
Buildings (e.g. locked or monitored doors)	91.7	93.8	94.4	85.9	80.6
Grounds (e.g. locked or monitored gates)	46.0	50.8	41.9	42.8	25.4
Required to wear badges or picture IDs					
Students	6.9	2.4	11.9	19.0	6.2!
Faculty and staff	62.9	67.6	62.8	58.3	35.9
Metal detector checks on students					
Random checks[2]	5.2	1.9	9.4	12.0	6.9!
Required to pass through daily	1.4	‡	1.5!	4.8	3.8!
Sweeps and technology					
Random dog sniffs to check for drugs[2]	22.9	4.0	43.3	60.1	47.5
Random sweeps for contraband[2,3]	12.1	3.6	20.1	28.7	25.6
Electronic notification system for school-wide emergency	63.1	61.1	70.9	66.6	52.8
Structured, anonymous threat reporting system	35.9	30.1	47.7	45.6	33.2
Use of security cameras to monitor school[2]	61.1	50.6	73.4	84.3	67.2
Limited access to social networking websites from school computers	93.4	92.4	96.0	94.6	92.9
Prohibited use of cell phones and text messaging devices	90.9	92.6	97.1	80.2	83.2
Required students to wear uniforms	18.9	21.5	19.33	9.7	15.1

!Interpret data with caution.

‡Reporting standards not met.

[1]Primary schools are defined as schools in which the lowest grade is not higher than grade 3 and the highest grade is not higher than grade 8. Middle schools are defined as schools in which the lowest grade is not lower than grade 4 and the highest grade is not higher than grade 9. High schools are defined as schools in which the lowest grade is not lower than grade 9. Combined schools include all other combinations of grades, including K–12 schools.

[2]One or more checks, sweeps, or cameras.

[3]For example, drugs, or weapons. Does not include dog sniffs.

Note: Responses were provided by the principal or the person most knowledgeable about crime and safety issues at the school. Respondents were instructed to respond only for those times that were during normal school hours or when school activities or events were in session, unless the survey specified otherwise.

Source: U.S. Department of Education, National Center for Education Statistics. (2012). *Indicators of School Crime and Safety: 2011* (NCES 2012-002), Table 20.2.

STRYVE (Striving to Reduce Youth Violence Everywhere) is a national program with the goal of reducing youth violence through awareness, utilization of evidenced prevention programs, and educating communities on how to reduce violence (Center for Disease Control and Prevention 2011). Teacher Melissa Kelly suggests that teachers can reduce violence in schools by taking charge of their classroom, eliminating prejudicial comments in their classrooms, listening for signs of problems, encouraging such programs as peer mentoring and mediation, learning the danger signs that an act may occur, discussing the issue with students, encouraging students to discuss the issue, teaching conflict resolution, encouraging parent involvement, and participating in school-wide programs (Kelly 2012).

All of these programs reflect the need for schools to have a comprehensive approach. Some school districts are utilizing school-based health centers to implement programs designed to reduce school violence. The Safe Schools Ambassadors (SSA) program teaches various groups communication and intervention skills to prevent violence and bullying (Community Matters 2009).

As a result of the Lauire Dann shootings in Winnetka, Illinois, Columbine in Colorado, and other headline-grabbing school incidents, not only did safety and security in public schools become a national issue but so did the need for schools to have comprehensive crisis-management plans (CMP) on file. CMP templates are available from a wide variety of sources including state boards of education, the Department of Homeland Security, and consultants in the field. Regardless of the plan, it is important to routinely train staff on their responsibilities should a crisis occur.

Furthermore, plans should be coordinated with other local agencies such as police and fire departments. A comprehensive discussion of school facility safety and security issues can be found in the Department of Homeland Security's *Primer to Design Safe School Projects in Case of Terrorist Attacks and School Shootings* published by FEMA in 2012. Generally, to make schools safer and provide a more secure environment they should include (McLester 2011):

- Securing entry into the building
- Eliminating dead spaces
- Creating natural surveillance with clear sightlines
- Utilizing cameras where appropriate

- Securing assets with lighting, smoke detectors, and so on
- Identifying specific security concerns for existing buildings

A comprehensive security program can have a significant financial impact on a school or school district. The Cleveland public schools approved spending 3.3 million for metal detectors (Wagner 2007). A review of research by Hankin, Hertz, and Simmon (2010) on the impact of metal detectors on school violence is mixed. While some studies would support their use, others suggest students might feel less secure. According to statistics compiled by the New York Civil Liberties Union (2009), security is big business. At the start of the 2008–2009 school year, New York City:

- Had 5,055 school safety agents and 191 armed police officers;
- Had a budget for police and security equipment for schools that was $221 million; and
- Used permanent metal detectors to screen at least 99,000 students each day.

Activities, athletic events, and other large group gatherings provide another challenge. For these types of activities, schools should ensure that they have adequate staffing and supervision, planned for the appropriate security strategies, and planned for emergencies. For these types of events, schools may choose to augment their own staff with trained security or local law-enforcement officers. All personnel should be briefed as to the possible security problems for the event, the strategies for deescalating any altercation or problem, and the procedures that will be used in case of an emergency.

TRANSPORTATION

Transporting schoolchildren to and from school has become the norm for most school districts. Busing has been utilized to desegregate schools as well as insure that the students with disabilities have access to an appropriate public education. Safety issues have also evolved over the years and continue to be a focus of concern. It is estimated that there are 480,000 school buses in the United States that transport twenty-six million students to and from school (TheBusCenter.com 2012).

According to the US Department of Transportation, National Highway Traffic Safety Administration (2011), 1,245 motor vehicle crashes from 2000 to 2009 were classified as school transportation related. On average, about twenty-four fatalities occur each year involving school-age occupants and pedestrians. Even so, based on death rates per one hundred thousand passenger miles driven, school buses are the safest means of transporting children to and from school (The School Bus Information Council 2012).

There are a number of issues that impact local school districts with regard to transporting students. They are:

- Who gets transported
- How services are provided
- Route planning
- Safety and risk management
- Bus driver selection and training
- Equipment selection and alternatives

Most states have guidelines as to who is and is not entitled to free public transportation to and from school. There are usually four factors that relate to eligibility. They are distance from school, whether or not there are traffic hazards for students who would otherwise walk, whether or not the student qualifies for special-education services and is required to be transported as part of his/her individualized education plan (IEP), and whether or not parochial-school students are required by state law to be transported. States vary in requirements to transport students.

Some leave it to the discretion of each school district while others provide specific requirements. For example, New Jersey requires that:

> All public elementary school students (grades K–8) who live more than two miles from their school and all public secondary school students (grades 9-12) who live more than two-and-a-half miles from their school are entitled to transportation. Whenever a school district is required to provide transportation to students attending regular public school programs, students attending nonpublic schools who meet those distance requirements may also be entitled to transportation services. In addition, any student classified with special needs who either meets these distance requirements or for whom transportation is required in the student's *Individual Education Plan* must be transported. (State of New Jersey Department of Education 2006)

In addition to transporting students to and from school, schools may also provide shuttle services between schools, and transportation for athletic, field, and activity trips.

There are at least three methods of providing transportation services: public transportation where available, district provided busing, and contractor-provided busing. Additionally, in some areas of the country school districts may choose to use one or more of these approaches to solve their transportation needs. There are advantages and disadvantages to each of these approaches. Not all localities have public transportation and even if they do, it may not be a convenient means of getting students to and from school. Outsourcing and district-run transportation systems also have their own advantages and disadvantages. Table 7.3 shows the advantages of outsourcing versus district provided transportation services:

Route planning involves not only making sure all students can get to and from school, but that they do so in the most efficient manner. "Efficient" refers not only to the cost of providing the service but the time students spend on the bus. The starting and ending times of the school day can have a significant impact on the cost of providing transportation. A district with three

Table 7.3. Advantages of District Owned and Contracted Transportation Services

Type of Service	*Advantages*
Contracted Services	• Contain & reduce costs of operating a bus fleet. • Replace an aging bus fleet. • Improve & lower cost of maintenance & repair. • Improve driver training & safety. • Meet challenges in specialized transportation services such as handicapped transportation. • Keep up with new state and US DOT operating regulations. • Reduce liability and customer service issues with parents and community members. • Meet complex routing requirements.
District Owned	• Have greater flexibility. • Have direct control of employees. • Control day-to-day issues and operations. • Control personnel selection as well as the level of training. • Reduce operational costs. • Have buses available 24/7 to the district for other activities, field trips, and events. • Some states reimburse district owned operations at a higher rate.

elementary schools, one middle school, and one high school might require twenty-two buses if it prefers to start all the schools at 8:00 a.m. If, however, it was willing to stagger the starting times of the schools by forty-five minutes it might be able to accomplish the same task with fewer buses. By doing multiple routes with the same bus, the district might only need eleven buses. Each bus would do two routes in the morning and two routes in the afternoon. The resulting costs savings could be significant.

Maximizing the number of riders on each route also affects efficiency. The fewer the students on a route, the more it costs. In some cases, however, low ridership per bus cannot be avoided due to traffic and the geographical layout of the district. A route that takes an hour and a half to complete to fill the bus will probably be unacceptable to most parents and students. Ohio publishes efficiency targets for ridership annually by school district (Ohio Department of Education 2012).

Many school districts either utilize computerized routing solutions that they have purchased or contract for the service. Computerized systems have the advantage of route optimization using *global tracking systems* (GPS). These systems utilize route information, student loads, usage levels, school start and end times, and vehicle capacities to assist districts in achieving the most efficient and safe routing solution. Route planning also involves a public relations component. Parents are always satisfied when a bus stop is in front of their home where they can visually see their children embark and disembark from the bus. When stops are several blocks away, parents become concerned with not only how far the actual bus stop is from their residence but the safety of the route their child will take to get to and from the stop.

Some districts now use GPS to track buses as well as when children get on and off the buses. Good communications to address parental and community concerns is vital for a successful transportation program. Ultimately, however, there is no such thing as a perfectly safe bus stop. There are just too many variables. The responsibility of the school district is to insure it has done the best it can do at picking a safe stop location, properly trained its school-bus drivers, and educated student riders and parents. According to the National Center for Safe Routes to School (2010), stops should be chosen that:

- Minimize the need for students to cross a road from the stop to the bus and eliminate multilane road crossings unless all traffic is controlled by the presence of a school-bus-stop arm and flashing lights;

- Offer adequate lighting such as near a street light or other light source whenever possible;
- Have sufficient space for students and parents to wait;
- Have had the surrounding environment evaluated for distractions that may affect safety and driver awareness;
- Provide protection from weather but do not impede visibility;
- Have had its location evaluated relative to intersections and mid-block (generally, corner stops are recommended since drivers are more use to stopping at corners than mid-block); and
- Will not result in behavior problems based on the number of students assigned to the stop.

Bus-driver recruitment and selection is the first step in designing a safe pupil-transportation program. Candidates should be subject to a thorough preemployment screening and interviewing process. This would include a background check, driving record check, medical examination, and drug testing. The requirements to be a driver vary by state as to the reasons for revocation of their licensure to drive a school bus. Professional development and training of drivers is also important.

Training programs should include student behavior management, discipline, dealing with irate parents, emergency procedures, bus-inspection procedures, safety procedures, and first aid and security issues. As noted by Poland (2010):

> Drivers must focus attention on the highly complex task of driving the bus while at the same time monitoring and managing the behaviors of 40 or more students who are visible only through a rear-view mirror. This is coupled with the fact that most of the training bus drivers receive is focused on mechanical and safety issues. While these are important training areas, more needs to be done to educate bus drivers in the important areas of effective discipline management, and administrators must begin to look at the school bus driver as an even more important partner in the safety process.

The Illinois State Board of Education, for example, has a comprehensive school-bus-driver-training curriculum that was designed by a statewide committee. It covers not only driver conduct, but also liability, pre- and posttrip preparation, daily inspections, school-bus operations, student management, accidents, emergencies and disasters, school-bus evacuation, and first aid

(Illinois State Board of Education 2009). Training is equally important for faculty and staff who drive students to and from events in *nonconforming vehicles* such as vans. School districts should be just as diligent in insuring faculty and staffs have safe driving records, are properly licensed, and have received appropriate training.

In 2009 the National Highway Traffic Safety Administration (NHTSA) issued a number of rules for new school buses. They included several key provisions. The first was that new school buses must be equipped with twenty-four-inch-high seat backs. The second was that the seat bottom cushions on new buses must be self-latching. A third provision was that buses weighing ten thousand pounds or less must have lap-shoulder belts. All of these new standards were implemented to provide additional safety and protection for children riding school buses (McMahon 2011). Since 1974, it has been illegal for a dealer to sell a nonconforming fifteen-passenger van for school-related transportation.

These types of vehicles were typically used for school-related activities and athletic trips. A new fifteen-passenger van to be used for school purposes must be certified as meeting Federal Motor Vehicle Safety Standards (FMVSS) for school buses. Vans with a capacity of more than ten passengers must meet the safety standards applicable to school buses. In addition to the FMVSS for school buses and vans, each state also issues its own standards with regard to any vehicle that transports students (National Highway Traffic Safety Administration 2012).

A final consideration in the purchase/lease of school buses is their effect on the environment. Alternate-fuel school buses have become a norm in many school districts. Alternate fuels include biodiesel, natural gas, and propane. According to *School Bus Fleet* 2,500 school buses used propane and three thousand used natural gas in 2008. In 2006, eleven states participated in a test of hybrid school buses (EnergyRefuge.com 2006).

SUMMARY

Auxiliary services support the core mission of schools and school districts. Proper functioning of these services removes distractions from the learning environment and allows children and staff to concentrate on learning and instruction. Food, transportation, and safety and security services are the three primary auxiliary services that school administrators must supervise on a daily basis.

In 1946, the NSLP was signed into law. Since that time the law has been amended and expanded. Today, the federal government operates free or subsidized meal programs for breakfast, lunch, after-school activities, and during the summer recess. In December 2010 the HHFKA was signed into law. The HHFKA provides for an increase in the reimbursement rate for breakfast and lunch as well as expands the program for after-school meals. Additionally, it allows certain communities of high-incidence, low-income children to qualify as a school instead of the usual individual application process. In order to obtain the additional reimbursement for meals under HHKFA, districts have to adopt the new nutrition standards.

Good risk management is the responsibility of all staff. A good risk-management program provides both a safe environment free from danger and risk but a secure one in which children feel safe. The AASA recommends a balanced approached that combines three elements: awareness, balance, and control. According to a survey done by the US Department of Education, National Center for Education Statistics in the 2009–2010 school year, school principals indicated that the three most common safety measures they utilize are controlling access to the school, limiting use of social networking sites during the school day, and limiting the use of cell phones and text messaging during the school day.

A little over half of the students in US public schools ride the bus each day to attend school. Most states have guidelines as to who is eligible for free public transportation. There are usually four factors that relate to eligibility. They are distance from school, whether or not there are traffic hazards for students who would otherwise walk, whether or not the student qualifies for special-education services and is required to be transported as part of his/her IEP, and whether or not parochial-school students are required by state law to be transported.

Depending on the state, school districts can utilize their own transportation departments, public transportation, and/or contracted services to transport students to and from school. The keys to operating a safe program are route placement and planning, driver selection and education, and equipment selection. As energy costs rise, more school districts are starting to use propane and natural-gas-fueled as well as hybrid buses.

CASE STUDY

Sun Valley High School is going to host its first state championship football game. Three days before the game, you receive a phone call informing you that Sun Valley students will be assaulted after the game. Word leaks out to the community of the threat and some parents are concerned about whether or the game should be played. As principal, what steps would you take to address the situation? Use the three elements of awareness, balance, and control in your answer.

EXERCISES AND DISCUSSION QUESTIONS

1. Research the legal requirements for transporting students to and from school in your state. Is transporting schoolchildren required of all districts? Is there a "distance threshold" over which students must be transported? Are there provisions in the state's school code to transport students whose walking routes would be considered "hazardous"?
2. What are the major components of the NSLP?
3. Look up the parameters for safe walking routes to schools from the National Center for Safe Routes to School. Pick a location from which to walk to school and evaluate it according to the center's criteria.
4. What responsibilities do a district administrator; building administrator, and teacher have in insuring a safe and secure environment for students?
5. Interview a school principal regarding the safety and security issues in his or her building. How does his/her assessment differ from the items listed in Table 7.2?
6. Investigate what your school district has done to improve nutrition within its school lunch program.
7. Obtain a copy of your district's emergency crisis plan. What are the responsibilities of school principals and teachers?

REFERENCES

American Association of School Administrators. (2012). *ABC's of school safety.* https://aasa.org/content.aspx?id=7354.

BusCenter.com, The. (2012). Go green by riding yellow. www.thebuscenter.com/post.php?cn=59.

Centers for Disease Control and Prevention. (2011). STRYVE: Striving to reduce youth violence everywhere. www.cdc.gov/violenceprevention/STRYVE/index.htm.

Centers for Disease Control and Prevention, Youth Risk Behavior Surveillance System (YRBSS). (2009). National youth risk behavior survey overview. www.cdc.gov/healthyyouth/yrbs/pdf/us_overview_yrbs.pdf.

Community Matters. (2009). Safe school ambassadors (SSA). www.community-matters.org/safe-school-ambassadors/.

Department of Homeland Security. (2012). Primer to design safe school projects in case of terrorist attacks and school shootings (FEMA-428.BIPS-07). www.dhs.gov/xlibrary/assets/st/bips07_428_schools.pdf.

Dillion, S. (2011). Lines grow long for free school meals, thanks to the economy. *New York Times*, November 29. www.nytimes.com/2011/11/30/education/surge-in-free-school-lunches-reflects-economic-crisis.html?_r=1&pagewanted=all.

Donovan, L., and Sweeney, A. (2006). Englewood kids in the crossfire. *Chicago Sun-Times*, March 19. www.suntimes.com/output/news/cst-nws-shoot19.html.

EnergyRefuge.com. (2006). Hybrid school buses. www.energyrefuge.com/archives/hybrid_school_bus.htm.

Federal Education Policy History. National School Lunch Act, 1946 (P.L. 79-396; 60 Stat. 230). federaleducationpolicy.wordpress.com/2011/02/19/1946-national-school-lunch-act/.

Federal Register (2012). *National School Lunch, Special Milk, and School Breakfast Programs, National average payments/maximum reimbursement rates* (77 FR 43232). July 24. https://www.federalregister.gov/articles/2012/07/24/2012-18039/national-school-lunch-special-milk-and-school-breakfast-programs-national-average-paymentsmaximum#page-43234.

Fourteenth National Congress on School Transportation. (2005). *National school transportation specifications and procedures 2005*, rev. ed. May. Warrensburg, MO: Central Missouri State University.

Ginsberg C., Loffredo L. (1993). Violence-related attitudes and behaviors of high school students—New York City, 1992. *Journal of Student Health* 63 (10): 438–39.

Gootman, E. (2007). New York school crime up 21 percent in first third of fiscal year. *New York Times*, February 15. www.nytimes.com/2007/02/15/nyregion/15manage.html.

Gunderson, G. (2012). The national school lunch program background and development. www.fns.usda.gov/cnd/Lunch/AboutLunch/ProgramHistory_4.htm.

Hankin, A., Hertz, M., and Simon, T. (2011). Impacts of metal detector use in schools: Insights from 15 years of research. *Journal of School Health* 81 (2): 100–6.

Healthy, Hunger-Free Kids Act of 2010, P.L. 11-296.

Huff Post Chicago. (2012). Urban prep academy parents demand student protection amid gang violence. www.huffingtonpost.com/2011/09/23/urban-academy-www.huffingtonpost.com/2011/09/23/urban-prep-academy-/parent_n_977686.html.

Illinois State Board of Education. (2009). *Illinois school bus driver training curriculum*. www.isbe.state.il.us/funding/pdf/busdriver_trainmanual.pdf.

Kelly, M. (2012). 10 ways teachers can help prevent school violence. 712educators.about.com/od/schoolviolence/tp/prevent_school_violence.htm.

Larrivee, B. (2005). *Authentic classroom management: Creating a learning community and building reflective practice*. New York: Pearson.

McLester, S. (2011). Designing safe facilities. *District Administration* 47 (8): 71–78.

McMahon, T. (2011). New standards for school bus seat belts. *SchoolBus Fleet*, July 12. www.schoolbusfleet.com/Channel/School-Bus-Safety/Articles/2011/07/New-Standards-for-School-Bus-Seat-Belts.aspx.

National Center for Safe Routes to School. (2010). *Selecting school bus stop locations: A guide for school transportation professionals*. guide.saferoutesinfo.org/school_bus_locations/pdf/SelectingSchoolBusStopLocations.pdf.

National Conference of State Legislatures. (2011). Healthy Hunger-Free Kids Act of 2010 (P.L. 11-296) summary. www.ncsl.org/issues-research/human-services/healthy-hunger-free-kids-act-of-2010-summary.aspx.

National Highway Traffic Safety Administration. (2012). Use of non-conforming vehicles for school transportation. www.nhtsa.gov/people/injury/buses/pub/noncom.hmp.html.

New Jersey Department of Education. (2011). *Commissioner's annual report to the education committees of the senate and general assembly on violence, vandalism and substance abuse in new jersey public schools*. www.state.nj.us/education/schools/vandv/0911/vandv.pdf.

New York Civil Liberties Union. (2009) *A look at New York City school safety.* http://www.nyclu.org/files/a_look_at_new_york_city_school_safety.pdf

Ogden C., Carroll M., Curtin L., Lamb M., and Flegal, K. (2010). Prevalence of high body mass index in US children and adolescents, 2007–2008. *Journal of the American Medical Association* 303 (3): 242–49.

Ohio Department of Education. (2012). *Efficiency targets for bus transportation.* www.ode.state.oh.us/GD/Templates/Pages/ODE/ODEDetail.aspx?page=3&TopicRelationID=1643&ContentID=26936&Content=118395.

Poland, S. (2010). Bus driver training. *District Administration*, July 1. www.districtadministration.com/article/bus-driver-training.

Richard B. Russell National School Lunch Act, 42 U.S.C. 1753, 1757, 1759a, 1766a.

Roher, K. (2008). Alternate fuel on the rise. *SchoolBus Fleet.* www.schoolbusfleet.com/Channel/Green-School-Bus/Articles/2008/06/Alternative-Fuel-Use-On-the-Rise.aspx.

Rossi, R. (2006). High schools to beef up security. *Chicago Sun-Times*, April 17. www.suntimes.com/output/news/cst-nws-security17.html.

School Bus Information Council, The. (2012). School bus facts._sbi.elitedecision.com/index.php?option=com_content&task=view&id=12&Itemid=27.

State of Colorado, The. (2001). The report of the Governor Bill Owens' Columbine Review Commission. May.

State of New Jersey Department of Education. (2006). Frequently asked questions of the office of student transportation. www.state.nj.us/education/genfo/faq/faq_transportation.htm.

University of Colorado Boulder, Center for the Study and Prevention of Violence, Institute of Behavioral Science. (2012). Blueprints for violence prevention model programs. www.colorado.edu/cspv/blueprints/modelprograms.html

US Department of Agriculture, Food and Nutrition Services, Office of Research, Nutrition and Analysis. (2007). NSLP/SBP access, participation, eligibility, and certifications study—Erroneous payments in the NSLP and SBP, vol. 1: Study findings, by Michael Ponza, et al. Project Officer: John R. Endahl. Alexandria, VA.

US Department of Education, National Center for Education Statistics. (2012). *Indicators of School Crime and Safety: 2011* (NCES 2012-002). nces.ed.gov/fastfacts/display.asp?id=49.

US Department of Transportation, National Highway Traffic Safety Administration. (2011). Traffic safety facts 2009 Data: School transportation-related crashes. www-nrd.nhtsa.dot.gov/Pubs/811396.pdf.

Wagner, M. (2007). Metal detectors approved for Cleveland schools, will cost $3.3 million. *The Plain Dealer*, October 19. blog.cleveland.com/metro/2007/10/metal_detectors_approved_for_c.html>.

Epilogue

The intention of this book is to offer insights, strategies, and practices regarding effective school-resource management. There are many challenges facing school educators and our ability to manage limited resources is crucial for school success and student outcomes. The purpose of this epilogue is to summarize key points from the book and some of the major educational challenges that must be addressed if we are to be successful in the future.

The financing of education has gone through a number of changes and we need to pay close attention to *equity*, *equality*, and *adequacy* and the inclusion of more and more students obtaining access to quality public education. While school finance academics were perfecting foundation-level programs, society was challenging the notion of equality. As our states financially struggle, there is a greater dependence upon the federal government.

As discussed in this book, the problem is that federal funds are not "free." Their provision is contingent on a myriad of rules, regulations, and standards. *No Child Left Behind* and *Race to the Top* are just a couple examples of the federal government influencing state educational goals and consequently how schools spend money.

As of fall 2012, thirty-three states had been given waivers from No Child Left Behind. States continue to fail to meet testing targets. In 2011, 48 percent of America's public schools had failed to meet No Child Left Behind testing standards. And in California, 66 percent of the public schools had failed to meet the standards. Across the nation, schools continue to struggle to meet state and federal standards and meeting these standards will become more challenging with less funding. Requests for waivers and alternative testing programs will undoubtedly continue.

As of fall 2012, federal legislators continue to debate educational funding. Secretary of Education Arnie Duncan commented that "services would have to be slashed for more than 1.8 million disadvantaged students and thousands of teachers and aides would lose jobs when the automatic budget cuts kick in" (Gonzales 2012). However, Congressman Richard Shelby stated that "our nation cannot continue to spend money we don't have" (Gonzales 2012). The US economy continues to struggle and there is uncertainty among many people, especially regarding unemployment, jobs, a balanced budget and federal, capital gains, and corporate tax rates. All these factors impact the funding of our education system.

There continues to be a need for better collaboration among federal legislators. Congressman Tom Harkin said that "we all must come together with good will to hammer out a balanced agreement that will not only prevent sequestration, but reduce our deficit and protect America's families" (Gonzales 2012). Meanwhile educators face the challenge of uncertainty and "doing more with less." Undoubtedly educators need to be creative in managing their fiscal resources.

Some of the *consequences of limited funding* include: definitions of adequacy and variation in funding among school districts, and the overreliance on local property taxes and resultant funding inequalities. This financial situation is compounded with the ever-changing, diverse student populations and educational-resource needs; need for improved instructional approaches and relevant curriculum materials; and the role and responsibilities of staff, parents, and taxpayers in the educational and financial process.

School districts also need to use adequate and *appropriate accounting.* As stated before, unlike businesses, which are concerned with the results of operations to make profits, schools are more concerned with accounting for revenues and expenditures and services they provide. Funds need to be allocated to reflect the goals, objectives, and outcomes desired by the school district.

Moreover, with the current trend toward using student outcomes as an accountability measure, there is an inherent progression toward tracking costs by site level, disaggregated group, and/or even by student, and reporting systems may need to be adapted to account for the resultant increased fiscal accountability.

Not only are there financial issues, but administrators are faced with a myriad of *human resource and organizational challenges.* Administrators need to be equipped to recruit talented human resources to meet the educational demands of the school system. Therefore, the primary goal of human resources planning is to forecast the future needs of an organization and to ensure that all resources are obtained; anticipate changes in staffing; understand and stay current with federal laws, state laws, and local district policies; and work with school community to match future needs and current organizational resources with future resources.

Given the progressing financial constraints, *compensation of employees* will continue to be an issue. Compensation represents about 80 percent or more of a school district's total budget. Educators and the board will need to carefully examine all the factors that motivate employees for good performance other than only relying upon compensation. They will also need to rely upon other creative compensation structures such as pay for performance, skills-based, knowledge-based, gain-sharing, and merit plans that can be successfully utilized.

Proposing creative and different *compensation structures* will undoubtedly create increased conflict among the board, teachers, and unions. This will demand increased challenges in the collective-bargaining process and call for all parties to work collaboratively to reach agreement. The collective-bargaining process will need to be approached by all parties with good-faith intentions, with the students' education as a foremost goal given the constraints of financial resources.

The *operations of the school* are highly dependent upon adequate safety and security, transportation, custodial care, facility maintenance, and meaningful auxiliary programs. All these programs require support staff, teachers, facilities, technologies, supplies, and equipment. Administrators and the board will need to continue to be resilient and creative in managing and acquiring these resources in the most financially efficient manner. This will necessitate innovative purchasing programs, responsible contracting, technological advances, and cost-benefit determinations.

In summary, future school-resources administrators will fundamentally need to learn how to do *more with less.* They will need to be skilled in process mapping and organizational-improvement strategies to maximize resources and improve current operations. This approach consists of identifying obstacles (wastes, bottlenecks, redundancies, delays, conflicts, inadequate technology, and budget systems) that hinder efficiency among human resources and financial management.

Educators will need to employ viable actions (value-added solutions) to address obstacles, and provide accountability for fiscal stability and optimize financial practices. Lastly, administrators will need to assist all stakeholders in understanding the ever-important paradigm of efficient *fiscal stewardship* to maximize the limited resources for the education of students and meet the future demands of our community, government agencies, society, and workforce.

REFERENCE

Gonzalez, A. (2012). Education secretary urges balanced budget cuts. *Associated Press*, July 25.

Appendix: School Resource Websites

Association of School Business Officials International (ASBOI), www.asbointl.org

Center for Safe Schools, www.safeschools.info/emergency-management

Department of Labor Summary of Major Laws, www.dol.gov/opa/aboutdol/law

Education Commission of the States, www.ecs.org

Employee Rights, https://www.nlrb.gov/rights-we-protect/employee-rights

Employer/Union Rights and Obligations, https://www.nlrb.gov/rights-we-protect/employerunion-rights-obligations

Equal Employment Opportunity Commission Laws and Statutes, www.eeoc.gov/laws/statutes/index.cfm

Federation of Tax Administrators, www.taxadmin.org/fta/rate/tax_stru.html

Governmental Account Board, www.gasb.org/

Government Finance Officers Association (GFOA), gfoa.org

Great Schools by Design, www.archfoundation.org/category/featured-programs/great-schools-by-design/

National Center for Educational Statistics (NCES), nces.ed.gov

National Clearinghouse for Educational Facilities, www.ncef.org

National Conference of State Legislatures (NCSL), www.ncsl.org

No Child Left Behind, www.ed.gov/nclb/

Prohibited Employment Policies/Practices, www.eeoc.gov/laws/practices/index.cfm

Statutes that Ensure Nondiscrimination in Employment, Search: Equal Employment Opportunity Commission (EEOC)

The Taft-Hartley Act employer–employee conduct, Search: National Labor Relations Board (NLRB)

US Department of Agriculture, Food, and Nutrition Service, National School Lunch Program, www.fns.usda.gov/cnd/Lunch/AboutLunch/ProgramHistory_4.htm

U S Department of Education, www.ed.gov

US Department of Labor Occupation Safety and Health Administration (OSHA), www.osha.gov/

US Environmental Protection Agency, Healthy School Environments (EPA), www.epa.gov/schools/

Index

About the Authors

Craig A. Schilling is an associate professor of educational leadership at Concordia University Chicago, River Forest, Illinois. He has been a public-school administrator, systems analyst, and CEO. He received his BS degree in sociology from the University of Maryland, MS in human services from Boston University, and EdD in educational administration from Northern Illinois University. He has consulted from numerous school districts and has spoken and presented at over one hundred workshops and training seminars throughout the United States, Canada, and the Caribbean. He has served as an expert witness in school finance cases. Craig has served as the president of the Illinois Association of School Business Officials (IASBO), on the Board of Directors of the Association of School Business Officials International, and on the Illinois Financial Accounting Committee. In 1999 the Association of School Business Officials awarded him an Eagle Service Award for contributions to the profession of school business management.

Daniel R. Tomal is a professor of educational leadership at Concordia University Chicago, River Forest, Illinois. He has been a public high-school teacher, administrator, corporate vice president, and professor. He received his BS and MAE degrees in education from Ball State University and a PhD in educational administration and supervision from Bowling Green State University. He has consulted for numerous schools and has testified before the US Congress. While a professor at Purdue University North Central he was voted the Outstanding Teacher. Dan has authored ten books and over one hundred articles and research studies. He has made guest appearances on numerous radio and television shows such as: CBS *This Morning*, NBC *Cover to Cover*, *Les Brown*, *Joan Rivers*, *Tom Snyder*, CBN *700 Club*, and ABC *News*, *WYLL Chicago Talks*. He is author of the books *Action Research for Educators*, a CHOICE Outstanding Academic Title, and *Challenging Students to Learn*, both by Rowman & Littlefield.

Lightning Source UK Ltd.
Milton Keynes UK
UKHW021141260620
365433UK00018B/264

9 781475 802528